BOBST

ELMER HOLMES BOBST

BOBST

*The
Autobiography
of a
Pharmaceutical Pioneer*

David McKay Company, Inc.
New York

The passage beginning on page 143 is from:
Morris Fishbein, M.D.; An Autobiography, by Morris Fishbein, Copyright
© 1969 by Morris Fishbein. Reprinted by permission of Doubleday
& Company, Inc.

To my beautiful wife, Dodo.

Nearly eleven years have flown by since God sent you to me and you became my wife of the most glorious years, filled with inexhaustible love, tenderness, and kindly care. You have been all and even more than anyone could justly expect from his helpmate. Your beauty of body and soul have been my greatest stimulation and pride.

Kipling wrote: "Oh, East is East, and West is West, and never the twain shall meet." If he had met, loved, and married a girl of wonderful looks and brains like Mamdouha As-Sayyid, he would never have written these lines.

May God bless and keep you always.
Elmer

● *Foreword*

● Elmer Bobst's autobiography is an important contribution to the record of American achievement. It reveals the struggles and accomplishments of a man endowed with a remarkable combination of keen intelligence, exceptional energy, commanding personality, strong character, and powerful determination to succeed. These qualities have enabled Mr. Bobst not only to become a pioneer in the development of the modern pharmaceutical industry but also to be a national leader in voluntary public service and enlightened philanthropy. Mr. Bobst has made history. Therefore his autobiography has significance for us all.

This autobiography has special significance for those who are interested in education. The name of Elmer Holmes Bobst is becoming part of the daily experience of thousands of students, professors, visitors, and neighbors of New York University, where one of the great library buildings of the world honors him and his generosity. His autobiography will enable those who know his name so well also to know something of his personality and life.

Mr. Bobst has made a major philanthropic contribution to a library because he knows the value of libraries in his own self-education. Self-education, which requires access to good libraries, is the heart of the educational process. Through his generosity, Elmer Bobst has given future generations of students the opportunity to pursue the self-development he was able to accomplish. This autobiography will help them and countless others to understand and draw inspiration from his achievements and vision.

James M. Hester, President
New York University

● *Chapter One*

● Not far from Hagerstown, Maryland, there is a small country village nestled so securely amid the soft green foothills of the Blue Ridge Mountains that the rising urban tide of eastern America has not engulfed it. It is called Clear Springs, and aside from time's inevitable changes — paved streets, electricity, a few new buildings — it was much the same when I visited it last as it was on December 16, 1884, when I drew my first breath in the Lutheran parsonage there.

The rich countryside around it, the farms, and the sloping fields where fat cattle grazed, still looked the same to me as they did when, as a small child, I watched the intermittent procession of covered Conastoga wagons, awkwardly loaded with the possessions of Americans still seeking new frontiers, jouncing along the old National Highway, a two-lane dirt road that passed through Clear Springs. Even my father, the Reverend Isaac Walton Bobst, dead now almost half a century, would find the land still warmly familiar. If he could walk those Maryland hills today, I have no doubt that he would come upon the same lanes along which he marched first with the 128th Pennsylvania Infantry that summer in 1862 on his way south to Antietem. It was to be his first battlefield experience, the bloodiest one-day engagement of the Civil War.

I still have his first letter to my grandmother, in which he described, with the blunt naiveté of an uneducated fifteen-year-old Pennsylvania Dutchman, that dreadful clash of American against American — his first "blooding" in the national catastrophe that was to wrench away three years of his life, first as one of Burnside's infantrymen and later as a trooper with Sheridan's cavalry. It also swept him unmercifully into two of the most wretched hellholes of our history: the dreaded Libby prison of Richmond, and infamous Andersonville in Georgia. Many years later, after he had become by his own determined energies a learned and eloquent clergyman, my father passed along to me his remembrances of those traumatic years. They remain almost as vivid in my memory as they did in his, so that I feel at times that my life spans not only my own eighty-six years, but the years of my father as well.

The letter from Antietem, written to his mother the day after the awful battle, is worn now from more than a century of handling, and its yellowed edges are as fragile as an Egyptian papyrus, but the words are clear, and one can still sense the pressure of the large, firm hand that wrote them.

We hirt the musket roar all night long in the morning aboud 6 o clock we formed a line of battle, and then we ware aboud two 100 yarts from the battle and there we did stand in the woots wated for the orders and wile we ware standing thare the bomps siselt over our hats . . . but we not scared we ware gay and happy yet. and so we got orders to march forwards and so we wend into the woods doupple wick and came in a ploud feelt and they firedt on us like devils and the corn fild but forward we went and wen we came in front of the corn fild we fired out and the 46th redg in frond of ours we gave them jersy and drove them out the corn fild. our Col was shot as soon as we came out the woods and our lewtdt wonded and so in to the corn filt we wend and Capt Andrews took oud his sord and holard come on boys and then wen he sait that he was shot and so we went oud the corn fild into the ploud feeld and the boolets fow werry fast. and then we went out and our Capt went out a fellow was shoot right a site of me. we ware aboud 2 ours in the fight and then our majer took us out down to the hosbittle our orderly was wondet. if only (you) hat seen the battle fielt after the battle was over. thare ware 30 kilt and 80 wonded in our redg. you must send me paper and invellops and postege stams if you want anny more letters . . . if i can't anser ride aways i always anser as soon as i can.

From his wartime recollections, as much as from a knowledge of the five destructive wars America has fought in my own lifetime, I think I take my abhorrence of settling the problems of the world on the battlefield. My father's experiences are a part of me, ineradicable elements of my mind, my personality and my philosophy. So are my mother's. In fact, I am so much a product of my father's strengths, my mother's gentle sweetness, and their mutual love of the beauties of art and nature, that I must describe their origins and their lives in order to explain my own.

At the time of Isaac Bobst's birth in 1847, it must have seemed doubtful that he, or his brother and two sisters, would survive childhood; surely it was inconceivable that he would rise above the bitter hardships of his youth to become a cultured man and a minister. Although the very name Bobst, derived from the Swiss-German *Probst,* suggests a strong family link to the church (a *probst* was the lay financial manager of a parish), Isaac's prospects of receiving any education, much less an advanced one in theology and the humanities, were so slim as to be invisible. He was born into poverty at the lowest ebb of the fortunes of a Rhineland family that had settled in Berks County, Pennsylvania, in 1732. His first American ancestor, one of three brothers who received land grants from William Penn, had prospered in the undeveloped English colony, as had most of his descendants. But my grandfather David Bobst had come upon hard times before Isaac, his first child was born. There remained nothing of the family properties except a drafty shack in a field outside of Kutztown. There Isaac and his younger brother and sisters grew up, after a fashion. They often went to bed hungry, and on winter mornings they would awaken to shake from their coverlets the dusting of snow that blew in through the cracks in the house.

Looking back upon his childhood, my father agreed with the observation of Lord Dunsany (in *The Golden Doom*) that "the play of a child is more important than the throne of a king"; but such joy was rarely his. Child labor, almost inconceivable to-day, was common then. In order to help support the family, Isaac began full-time work at the age of six, stripping tobacco. This tedious process of removing the tough veins from the pliable tobacco leaves was a kind of cottage industry that cigar-makers parcelled out to poor women and children. My father, barely out of his infancy, earned sixty cents a week toward the support of the family and at the same time developed the qualities of patience and determination that were to sustain him throughout his life.

With the family's very survival at stake, there was little time for school. Isaac attended only two terms of a one-room wooden schoolhouse where reading and writing were taught, not in English but in Pennsylvania Dutch. By his eleventh birthday, he had acquired the skill of an excellent cigar-maker and found a job in Kutztown, rolling cigars with the fine, Pennsylvania finishing leaves used as the final wrapping over cruder tobacco leaves from the South. When David Bobst died at fifty, Isaac was thirteen and working as an expert cigar-maker in a factory in Reading, Pennsylvania. From that time on he was the sole support of his family. By his own account and the descriptions of other relatives, he was extraordinarily mature, physically and emotionally, even as a young boy. He had grown to his full stature, a strong and stocky six feet, by the time he was fourteen, and his steady blue eyes, firm chin, and sober Nordic features under tightly curled light-brown hair gave him the appearance of an eighteen-year-old. Thus he wasn't questioned closely about his age that summer day in 1862 when the drum and bugle corps of the Army recruiters came marching down the street where he worked in Reading.

The war had begun. President Lincoln had called for 300,000 volunteers to save the Union. The excitement and drama of such a cause were too much for the not-quite-fifteen-year-old boy to withstand (an attraction that I understand, for the same intensely emotional appeal to militant colors stirred my own blood at the same age). As he heard the sound of the bugles and drums, Isaac carefully folded his apron, arranged his tools neatly on his workbench, and hurried out of the tobacco factory to sign up. He told the recruiter that he was seventeen years old. Within forty days he was under fire at Antietam.

After the bloody encounter, Isaac's unit of the Army of the Potamac fell back into bivouac near Washington. One day, he told me, all of the units there were called into parade formation for inspection and review.

"I stood in the first rank," he said. "We were called to attention. Then the President of the United States, Abraham Lincoln, rode slowly in front of us on a black horse. He was gangly looking, so tall that the stirrups did not quite fit his long legs. He wore a high silk hat, and his coattails flopped behind him. To the rear was a small Shetland pony, bearing Tad, his son."

As winter approached, bivouac ended. Isaac's unit joined Burnside's army of 90,000 in its vain attempt to seize St. Mary's Heights at Fredericksburg on a biting December day. He came through that battle unharmed, but his next encounter was a fateful one. He was captured in the battle of Chancellorsville, when Stonewall Jackson brilliantly enveloped a part of the Union Army. It was Jackson's last tactical masterstroke. As Isaac and his fellow prisoners were being herded from the battlefield, they saw a wounded rebel officer being carried hurriedly to the rear. He was General Stonewall Jackson, fatally injured.

Isaac was sent directly from Chancellorsville to Libby prison in Richmond. Fortunately his stay there was brief. Twenty days after entering the dismal place he was released in a prisoner exchange. When a Southern guard congratulated him on getting out of the war, he said prophetically, "I'll be back." But his memories of captivity were not all grim. He liked, later, to tell the story of a stolid Pennsylvania Dutchman captured by a rebel who fiercely threatened him. "Do you know what we do to Yankee prisoners? First we cut their throats, and then we put a bullet in the middle of their foreheads."

"Well," the Dutchman shrugged, "whatever is the rule."

As a repatriated prisoner of war, Isaac was honorably released from the Union Army following the exchange. He did not stay out of action long. After eight months of cigar-making back in Reading, he learned that he could receive the unimaginable sum of $350 if he enlisted as the substitute for a man who did not want to serve. He signed up in the Pennsylvania Reserve Cavalry and gave the bonus to his mother to tide the family over until he returned. The sum, plus his Army pay, which he sent home, was more than he could have earned on his meager wage as a cigar-maker.

Miraculously, he survived thirteen cavalry battles, including two of Sheridan's celebrated raids in the Shenandoah Valley (Richmond and Charlottesville), without serious injury. On one of the raids he recalled being startled by the sight of a surprisingly young Union General at the head of a mounted unit. "Who is the officer with the long, blond hair?" he asked one of his own officers. "That's General George Custer," he was told.

Not long after that, while returning from the second Shenandoah raid in June, 1864, he was again captured by rebel troops, this time at a place called Whitehouse Landing. And once again he was clapped into Libby prison. Bad as it was, it would have been well for him to have stayed there, but with Grant's forces encroaching on Richmond, the Confederates moved the prisoners to the deep South: Andersonville, Georgia.

When I read MacKinlay Kantor's great novel, *Andersonville,* it was as if the vivid mental pictures of the prison first drawn for me by my father had been freshly illuminated. The author's carefully researched descriptions of the prison and its inhumane conditions were so familiar to me from my father's accounts that I felt as if I could have written the book myself.

It is perhaps unnecessary to review the grisly history of that Southern prison camp, but as an illustration of man's inhumanity to man far closer to home than Buchenwald, Siberia, Algeria or Vietnam, it serves still as a reminder to me that our basic instincts are not unique to any one nation or people; there is a lamentable universal equality to human cruelty.

At Andersonville, according to my father, there was little food, no shelter, and less compassion for the prisoners. They were massed by the thousands inside an open stockade of high logs, overseen at frequent intervals by high sentry platforms manned by riflemen. Biting cold winter rains turned the red clay prison ground into a gluey quagmire on which the prisoners had to band together to create whatever form of primitive shelter they could devise. Most of them, like my father and his companions, hollowed out caves in the sticky clay.

"The winter was exceptionally cold," my father said, "very often below freezing, which is not uncommon in Georgia. Six or eight of us would huddle spoon-fashion, for warmth, inside our crude cave. Now and again, someone would give the command to turn, and we would shift to the other side like a stack of spoons flopping over. But sometimes, one wouldn't turn, because he was dead."

The food rations were abysmally poor. On alternate days, each man was given a pint of wormy, uncooked beans, or a container of corn meal which consisted mostly of ground corn cobs. The prisoners pooled their uncooked rations and boiled them into gruel in makeshift cooking vessels over open fires. My father ate his portion with a broken iron spoon. In order to gather wood for the cooking fires, the men had to volunteer to carry out the dead; after dropping the bodies of their comrades outside the prison stockade, they were permitted to gather a few twigs.

In one part of the prison compound there was a foul-smelling marsh which was used as an open prison latrine. Most of the men suffered from dysentery, so the marsh was in constant use. Its most accessible portion quickly became its most foul, and the prisoners were tempted to drag themselves to another part of the marsh for relief. But the prison guards drew an imaginary "deadline" across the marsh, confining the prisoners to its foulest section. Any man who crossed the "deadline" was summarily shot, and instead of facing punishment, the guard who shot him was rewarded with a two-week furlough. My father remembered watching as one fourteen-year-old drummer boy, already emaciated from dysentery, dragged himself toward the "deadline." He had not even reached it when a guard killed him with a single shot.

Just before Christmas, word passed that three prisoners had tunnelled under the log stockade and escaped into the pine woods outside. Troops of prison guards, led by bloodhounds, searched for them in vain. The escapees got away clean. But their success so enraged Captain Henry Wirz, the notorious Andersonville commander who was executed for his crimes after the war, that he cut off all rations for three days, including Christmas. Instead of offering prayers for peace on Christmas Day, he drove into the prisonyard on a heavily-guarded, mule-hauled wagon, stood arrogantly above the starving, apathetic men, and berated them.

Not long before the war ended, Isaac was again included in a prisoner exchange. He had been in the Andersonville stockade for six months. He was covered with lice. His athletic six-foot frame had withered to a skeletal eighty pounds. His shirt was in tatters and his trousers, held together at the waist by a twig, had shredded off above the knees. He had lost the first joints of three toes on each foot to frostbite. But he was lucky. Of all the prisoners who were held at Andersonville, many for less time than Isaac, 17,000 died.

In the chaos that accompanied the approaching end of the war, the return of the prisoners was ironically painful and slow. Isaac made part of the journey north in a crowded cattle car in which two of his comrades literally went mad because they could not believe that they were free. Others, near death when they were released, died on the way home. After the rail trip, Isaac limped the rest of the way north on crippled feet, shrinking within his tattered clothes as defeated, angry Southerners jeered at him. At last he reached Wilmington, North Carolina, and a military hospital. From there, he was moved to Annapolis, where he began to recuperate. Shortly, my grandmother got this letter from him:

Naval Sochool Heosbidal
Anabolis

March 14th
Dear Mother
    *I will ones again write at fiew lines to you. I led you know
that I arriod here at the hosbidal yesterday from Wilmonton. I was*

*wery sick bud I imbroveing werry fast and god such a good adputite.
I cand get enough to eat. I shall come home in les than 10 days.*

*Write as soon as you resiod this letter. So no more at present
from your Dear Son.*

All he had left when the rags were taken from him at the
hospital was the broken iron spoon with which he had eaten his
prison gruel. It remains my most treasured possession today.

Harper's Ferry already was a celebrated place when Isaac
first saw it, as a soldier, during the war. It was the scene of
the famous raid on the federal armory by John Brown, whose
body not long thereafter was to begin "moulderin' in the grave,"
as the mournful song had it. Brown was tried and sentenced
to hang for his zealousness, and among the distinguished resi-
dents of Harper's Ferry who journeyed to nearby Charlestown
to witness the execution was a man named George Holmes.
Holmes was a descendant of one of the nation's most noted families, namesake of the first American George Holmes who founded
both the northern branch, from which Oliver Wendell Holmes
sprang, and the southern branch, which produced my mother.

George Holmes of Harper's Ferry was a pragmatic man who
had become comfortably well-off as a builder by the time the
Civil War began. As a true Southerner, descended from the
Holmes of Virginia, he was torn between his heritage and his
common sense. He favored the Union cause, for the futures of
both North and South lay in unity, not separation. But Confederate troops occupied the hills overlooking Harper's Ferry and
might at any moment visit retribution not only upon his property,
but upon him as a Union-loving Southerner. Wisely, he departed
and for a time waited out the Southern threat in Kansas City,
returning only when it seemed clear that the fought-over town
was safe. However, his return to Harper's Ferry was premature.
Not long after his daughter Alice was born in 1863, the family
had to take shelter in the cellar of their brick house while the
roar of cannon and musket sounded outside.

The family happily survived the war with no greater loss
than the destruction of some of the buildings George Holmes
had erected. In the postwar years he prospered again, and Alice

advanced joyfully into her adolescence, well blessed with the education and the graces of a young southern lady. By the age of
fifteen she had completed her basic schooling and had finished
one year at the seminary. She was an accomplished pianist, played
the organ, taught a Bible class at the Methodist church, led the
church choir, and sang beautifully in both soprano and alto. She
was slender, well-formed, and tireless, and her sweeping brunette
hair framed a beautiful, delicate face.

Like many of the Swiss and Germans of the Pennsylvania
Dutch country, Isaac Bobst was a churchgoing Lutheran whose
faith was a natural corollary of his life and surroundings; that
is, as a young man who had become the sole support of a father-
less family, he worked too hard to have the time or energy for
mischief, and he went to church on Sundays. A wry, but probably
accurate portrait of the early American Lutherans was drawn by
the Reverend H. M. Muhlenberg, first patriarch of the church
in colonial Pennsylvania. "Behold," he instructed five young missionaries in 1752, "I send you forth as sheep in the midst of wolves;
be ye therefore wise as serpents and harmless as doves." Doubtless
it was good advice, for while the Pennsylvania religionists — Lutherans, Quakers, Moravians, Dunkards, and others — were men
of faith, they were stubbornly independent pioneers who did not
lightly change their ways. Yet, if they decided upon a new course,
they followed it with fierce determination.

Isaac, quite naturally, resumed his trade as a cigar-maker
after he regained his health at the end of the Civil War. Soldiering
and cigar-making were all that he knew. Possessed of a natural
desire to improve his income and to excel at his trade, he moved
from Reading to a better job in a small cigar factory in Pottsville.
His employer there was a devout Lutheran who took a liking
to Isaac and invited him to go along during the summer of his
twentieth year to a two-week religious revival nearby. The experience suffused him with a new ambition. In describing it to me
later, my father said that there was no particular moment of
drama, no transfiguring event like Saul of Tarsus' vision on the
road to Damascus. After hearing two weeks of preaching, he simply became determined to gain an education so he could preach

the gospel himself. Apparently no one took him seriously at first. He was twenty years old, the sole support of his mother and three youngsters, and he had to work twelve-hour days, six days a week, just to make ends meet. Not incidentally, as his letters show, he was semiliterate, a product of impoverishment who had attended school only a few months of his life. Yet suddenly he was determined to acquire a sufficiently sound primary and secondary education so that, within a few years, he could enter the Lutheran Seminary at Gettysburg. Even his mother scoffed at the notion.

Undeterred, he moved his small family back to Kutztown where he enrolled in an "eclectic" course at the State Normal School and began an incredible work-study schedule that was to continue for years. He arose before dawn and began work in a cigar factory at 5 A.M. At 10 A.M. he folded his apron and went to school, where he studied English and Latin grammar simultaneously, and took on a double load of history, mathematics, and other courses. From afternoon until evening he resumed cigar-making, then he studied in the light of a kerosene lamp until late at night. In four years he passed his exams, entered the Seminary at Gettysburg, and resumed the same monastic routine. At one point, the exhausting schedule became too much for him and he had to drop out of school, but he returned a year later, still determined to become an ordained clergyman.

Another Lutheran minister, named the Reverend Mr. Kroll, whom I met many years later, recalled marvelling at my father's devotion to his learning both at Kutztown and Gettysburg. "I would see him constantly in the library, pouring over Scott, Addison, DeFoe, Boswell's Life of Johnson — he was indefatigable," he said. It was during this same period that he became so enamoured of Isaac Walton that he took Walton as his middle name.

In 1879, at age thirty-two, Isaac graduated and was ordained. His first charge as a preacher was Harper's Ferry, the small town that he had first seen in battle under General Niles during the Civil War. His own church bore reminders of the fight. The marks were patched over, but one could still make out the holes where a rebel cannon ball passed through the walls of the sanc-

One of the author's most treasured family mementos: the broken, silver-coated iron spoon used by his father, Isaac Bobst, during his second confinement in a Confederate prisoner-of-war camp.

tuary. (If he had known, there was a far more gruesome reminder of the war hidden away in a long-sealed closet in the cellar of the church. Just a few years ago the closet was discovered and opened, revealing the fully-clothed bones of a Union soldier who apparently had crawled there and died of his wounds during the battle.)

It was natural, when Isaac arrived in Harper's Ferry, that one of the most prominent families of the town would invite him to stay with them until he found suitable lodgings. In fact, for a clergyman whose salary was less than $300 a year, such hospitality was heaven-sent. Thus, the Reverend Mr. Bobst was delighted when the builder, George Holmes, welcomed him to his home. I am not sure how soon he noticed Holmes' lovely daughter, Alice, but it could not have been long before he fell totally and irrevocably in love with her. Nor was it long before the emotion was returned.

On Memorial Day, 1934, my mother had occasion to return to Harper's Ferry and, while sitting by the graves of her parents, to recall her feelings about the young minister.

"In memory," she wrote that day, "I turn back the spinning wheel of time, some fifty years or more. I see now, on this cliff, overlooking the Potomac river, and again the Shenandoah, a vivacious young girl, barely fifteen.

"Shall I say good looking? At least attractive, and well developed. With her a fine-looking young man, with a mop of bronze curls; more mature, in fact almost seventeen years her senior. He is reading to her, *The Vicar of Wakefield*. A mere subterfuge, I think, for he really is wooing and winning the young girl. She is by no means aware of his intentions, and wonders why he should ask her to accompany him on these jaunts, when there are so many young ladies more suitable to his age. However, he gained his point and succeeded in getting this young girl to respond to his love.

"In a short time, she became his girl-wife."

She was seventeen when they were married, sixteen months after their first meeting; and while her formal education stopped at that point, it continued informally under the tutelage of her minister-husband. He read to her from Plutarch's *Lives*, from Shakespeare, Lamb, and Goldsmith and eagerly brought Dickens and Mark Twain to her whenever their new works appeared. From her, he acquired an appreciation of fine painting, a heritage of the art loving French Huguenots from whom her mother was descended, and together they cultivated their love of nature, of flowers, of the natural wonders of the universe, so abundant around Harper's Ferry.

The young couple soon took a big step to the West, a journey of several days in a railroad car to Lancaster, Illinois, on the

Wabash River. My father had been called to its small Lutheran Church, and there, in the worst possible surroundings, my brother Harry was born. (My sister was born in Harper's Ferry.) Although admired and respected as a clergyman, and even pleased with his calling and his life, my father was as poor as the mice in his church. His salary was about $300 a year, well under the poverty line even in those days. And the physical surroundings in the Wabash river valley were so unhealthy that he feared for his family. Both Isaac and Alice contracted malaria soon after arriving in the mosquito-infested river valley, and it was obvious that if they remained, the children would suffer, too. Happily, he was soon called to return to the East to serve the Lutheran Church of the Reformation of the General Synod at Clear Springs, Maryland; his salary: $350 a year, plus parsonage. And there, nine days before Christmas in 1884, I was born. My mother was twenty-one years old and had given birth to three children, spaced a little more than a year apart, since her marriage at seventeen.

Not many years ago, after buying the Bromo Seltzer Company of Baltimore for my own Warner-Lambert Pharmaceutical Company, I slipped behind the wheel of my car and made a sentimental pilgrimage to Clear Springs. It was like opening a long-shut spillway in the dam of my memory as I approached the small town, nestled in hills that were still crowned, as in my childhood, with patchy shrouds of translucent blue mist. Although I was only six years old when I left Clear Springs, I had no trouble locating the parsonage, for I had traversed the town and its surrounding hills so many times on foot, and it had not changed much. I remembered as if it were yesterday skipping to the crystal clear spring for which the town was named. My first daily household chore, at the age of about five, was to retrieve a large tin bucket of water, and while I swung the pail with youthful abandon on the way to the spring, it was a heavy burden on the way home. But I actually enjoyed the effort and took delight in the visible hardening it produced in the muscles of my arms and shoulders.

On the day of my last visit I got out of my car and walked

across a small lawn to the front of the old parsonage, long since sold to a private owner. Next door was the Episcopal churchyard, whose alien ground my father sometimes strolled when preparing for his sermons in the Lutheran church not far away. There was an elderly lady working in a garden beside the house.

"What do you want?" she asked me, rather sharply.

"I'd like to look inside your house," I said.

"It's not for sale. We have no interest in giving up our home."

"Well," I ventured, "I'm here only because I would like to see the room in which I was born."

"You were born here? What is your name?"

"My name is Bobst."

"Don't tell me you're the son of the Reverend Bobst who preached here many years ago?"

"Yes, I am."

"Oh, that's wonderful." She ran to the back garden and called out to an even older lady, who walked vigorously toward me.

"You're Elmer Bobst, I can see that," the second lady said. "Do you remember the grocery store where your father and mother shopped? That was my husband's store. I remember your mother and father."

Together they took me through the little house, three rooms downstairs and three above, and I could almost see my family there. I remembered my father, already growing stout by the time of my first awareness, but still straight and tall, taking an occasional bite from a small plug of molasses-saturated tobacco as he read or jotted notes for his sermons. My mother said that one day in that house he roundly condemned the tobacco habit which, despite his former trade as a cigar-maker and his own taste for the chewing variety, he recognized as unhealthy. In that moment of reformist determination he took the tobacco plug from his pocket and hurled it out the window toward the Episcopal churchyard. The next day, mother said, she watched him strolling around the churchyard with his head down, deep in thought to other observers, but to her knowing eyes he obviously

was searching for that plug of tobacco. Later he quit the habit
for good.

In the dining room of the house lay my first memory. I
recalled sitting in a high chair at the table, only two years old,
watching with delight as my father re-baptized my brother Harry,
gently laying drops of water on his head. Why it was necessary
to baptize him a second time after presumably baptizing him once
before as an infant, I never learned.

Upstairs, the bedroom where Harry and I slept brought back
a vivid memory that was both tender and unpleasant. Across the
way, in the familiar Episcopal churchyard, was an apple tree,
and I remembered how eagerly I waited for the fruit to appear
each year. When I was five I wolfed down an early, green apple.
Not surprisingly, I soon had a stomachache. But it was no passing
discomfort. Soon my stomach swelled so grotesquely that, lying
on my back, I could not see over it. I became feverish and my
father called the doctor. I didn't know it then, and wouldn't have
know what it was even if they had told me, but he diagnosed
peritonitis. Coincidentally, my mother was then bedridden, perilously ill with typhoid fever. As I lay under my blankets, shivering
and grimacing with the pain in my abdomen, the doctor and
my father entered my bedroom. Between them they held my
mother, who despite her own grave illness encouraged me with
sweet words of endearment and a wan smile; her tenderness gave
me strength. She told me later that they thought I was dying.

I remembered, too, the great surge of pride that I felt not
long after that when I was allowed to wear my first pair of pants.
They were short pants, but they represented a great step towards
adult masculinity, because in those days it was the custom for
small boys such as me to wear skirt-like short kilts. My mother
later marked the occasion for me with a sentimental poem by
Folger McKinsey that I still treasure. It is called Mother's Boy.

> *Where has he gone to, Mother's boy,*
> *Little plaid dresses and curls of joy?*
> *Who is this gentleman, haughty in glance,*
> *Walking around in a new pair of pants?*

The author at age seven, nestled between his father's knees and holding his mother's hand. Brother Harry is at the left, in front of sister Catherine (Kathie).

Where has he vanished, the little Sir Smile
That Mother once folded in gentle beguile?
Who is the stranger that comes in his place?
The very same eyes and the very same face,
But, oh, the lost Babyhood! Come back if you can
from the stream that is drifting you onward to man!

In the margin of the poem she had written, "This is the way I felt when you donned your first pair of pants." But I had felt only great pride, and relief to see the skirts put away forever. So many years ago.

As the two aging ladies and I stepped out on the high porch of the old frame parsonage, I asked if they remembered a well-to-do family named Snyder that had lived in a substantial brick house across the street. Not only did they remember, but they insisted that we walk across to the old Snyder house. There, blind and crippled with arthritis, I found Viola Snyder, sitting in a chair in the center of the living room, gazing into nothing.

"You're Elmer," she said. "I remember you. Such a little boy."

And I remembered her, too, as a cheerful, vivacious, teen-aged girl, playing with her brothers. Now the two elderly ladies across the street took care of her, preparing her food and medicine and watching with despair as she tried to make ends meet on a small pension. We talked of happier times until it began to grow dark. Then I left, after pressing money for food and medicine upon her and insisting that the three ladies accept an additional sum from me for presents. I had not thought to bring gifts to them, and I should have.

As I drove away, I recalled my last memory of Clear Springs: climbing into a stage coach with my father, mother, brother, and sister early one May morning in 1890, to journey to the train depot at Harrisburg. We started at dawn, and it took us all day by stagecoach and train to reach our new home in Lititz, Pennsylvania, 135 miles away.

● *Chapter Two*

● In the German and Swiss farm houses of Lancaster County, Pennsylvania, one used to find intricately painted household slogans such as "What Is Home Without a Mother?" hanging as proud focal points on parlor walls. Such a painting was called a *fractur,* and often it would be as rich in color and design as the title page of an illuminated manuscript in a medieval monastery. A classic one, richly inscribed in German, was *Die Sieben Regeln Der Weisheit,* or The Seven Rules of Wisdom. The rules were:

> Do not do all you can do for that is officious.
> Do not question all you do not know for that is unwise.
> Do not believe all you hear for that is to be credulous.
> Do not give all you possess for that is prodigal.
> Do not tell all you know for that is foolish.
> Do not sit in judgment on all that comes before you
>   for that is presumptuous.
> Do not desire everything under the sun for that is absurd.

It was a healthy mixture of the wisdom of Solomon and Benjamin Franklin, both of whom were justly revered in Lititz. The small town was — and still is — a living embodiment of those seven rules, a reflection of the solidly grounded, unprepossessing, thrifty, honest, unhurried Pennsylvania Dutch. And it was thus that we found it that evening in 1890 after a day of jouncing across the countryside in stagecoach and railway cars. We must have presented an unusual sight to the town's mostly Moravian inhabitants as we left the old train depot at Lititz Springs Park and turned up Broad Street: a somberly dressed preacher, his stylishly attractive, almost child-like wife, and three small children, all loaded down with handbags and bundles. The street was lined with elegantly simple prerevolutionary buildings and houses of limestone and frame construction; some of them still showed traces of their original log walls behind newer veneers of planking. From the porches and from behind windows I could see the people peering out to size up the new pastor of St. Paul's Lutheran Church and his family. They must have liked what they saw, for we were welcomed warmly by all whom we met, even though the Lutherans were a distinct minority in the town.

Lititz was founded as a Moravian community by Count Nikolaus Ludwig von Zinzendorf, who revived a moribund central European Protestant sect called the Unity of Brethren in the early 1700s and launched missionaries to the New World. He renamed the church after a province of the old Austro-Hungarian empire, Moravia, which is now the central part of Czechoslovakia. After establishing communities in Savannah, Georgia, and Winston Salem, North Carolina, von Zinzendorf and his co-religionists moved to Pennsylvania, where they founded Bethlehem and Nazareth. Finally, in the 1740s, they planned and began to build Lititz. From the beginning they insisted that each structure erected in the new town be "well built," a bit of foresight on their part that I wish was more often emulated by builders today. Because of solid foundations and durable materials, including great quantities of limestone quarried from the iron-rich hills around Lancaster County, dozens of the original prerevolutionary buildings still stand, and the town remains much the same in appearance as it was when I was a child.

At that time, the Moravian church still owned much of Lititz, including one of its several general stores and, for a short period, its only distillery. There was nothing overbearing about the Moravian view of life, however, and even though most of Lititz's 4,000 inhabitants were Brethren, they made no attempt to impose their doctrine upon the rest of us or to run the small town as a theocracy. Christianity, to them, was a question of personal service and the Golden Rule, not dogma. They were quite content to live in harmony with anyone, whatever his faith. Thus, it was probably unworthy of an outsider like me to express my pride when I noticed, for the first time, that St. Paul's Lutheran Church had a much taller steeple and a louder bell than the Moravian church. We topped them there, but I was a little chagrined that the Moravians had the most prestigious educational institution in town: Linden Hall Seminary, where my sister Kate studied music on a scholarship. Today, I believe, it is the oldest operating girls' seminary in the United States.

The new parsonage, which was to be home to us for the rest of my childhood, was a small frame building set directly off the cobbled sidewalk of Orange Street, just a few blocks from the town square, and a block away from St. Paul's Church. Behind the parsonage there was a chicken house, a woodshed, and a small vegetable garden which my father tended with our help. There was a far larger garden in back of the church, a half-acre that we devoted exclusively to growing potatoes. From our earliest days, Harry and I did the lion's share of the work there. Our father would guide the plow for us as we pulled it, but it was our responsibility to plant the potatoes, to pick the bugs from the leaves of the plants, and to harvest the crop, which we stored in a large trough in the cellar of the house.

For some reason — a natural difference in temperaments, I suppose — I liked to work and volunteered for it, whereas Harry usually waited to be told what to do. As a result I tended to become more and more like my father when he was a boy, far too busy to get into trouble. I looked for odd jobs all over Lititz and generally found them, and I took great delight in watching my father's proud smile when I gave him the nickels and dimes that I earned. When there was nothing else to do I went to the backyard and worked in the vegetable garden, piling mounds of dirt around the celery stalks to bleach and tenderize them before they were harvested at the first frost, or digging the frost-proof six-foot-by-four-foot trench in which we stored fresh cabbage through the winter, or picking the ripe products of our two fine peach trees and our blackberry and raspberry bushes for Mother to put up as preserves. When cherries were in season I would go out into the country and bargain with the farmers to climb their trees and pick the fruit, providing I could keep one half of it. Then I would bring home a peck or more of cherries for Mother to can.

When one looks back over as many decades of life as mine, he is bound to find a bewildering number of incongruities, elements of the past that simply do not fit the present, but I often wonder at the changing attitudes of both young people and adults toward the kind of spontaneity in work that I enjoyed as a boy in the 1890s. Few would bother today to volunteer for such activities unless they had to, yet in my early days it was simply inconceivable to me that any day, other than the Sabbath, should slip by without my doing some kind of a job. I don't think it had anything at all to do with the so-called work ethic; at least I never thought of it in such a pompous way. I simply liked to work. It was fun. It was a means of getting around the town and meeting people, of learning things that I didn't know. It made me feel good, not with false pride, but with the pride of accomplishment. The harder I worked, the stronger my muscles became, and I liked that, too. And to my delight, I found that I could earn money at it.

I used to whitewash fences for twenty-five cents, and learned how to increase my profit by slaking my own barrels of lime for whitewash. For a time I tended heifers and horses for a neighbor who sold them to farmers around the county. I would often walk eighteen or twenty miles, herding the livestock along behind his wagon as he made his sales calls. He gave me fifty cents a day for that, and I felt overpaid, particularly when he permitted me the luxury of riding home on his wagon. I shoveled snow every winter. I dunged out livery stables and mucked out cow barns. The latter was the only job to which my mother ever objected. Cow manure left such a wretched, lingering odor that she hated to let me in the house when I got home.

But my favorite job was my first regular one as an independent entrepreneur. I was seven years old when I decided, entirely on my own, to help the town baker increase his sales. His name was Bowman, and he was a member of my father's church. I think my proposition startled him.

"Mr. Bowman," I said, "may I carry a basket of buns and cakes from house to house and sell them for you?"

"You're pretty young for that, Elmer," he smiled.

"But I'm strong," I said, and I flexed my muscles.

I suppose he thought he was indulging a child's brief whim when he let me strap a basket of buns and sugar cakes across my shoulders and set off to play salesman, but I kept that concession for years. As I got older and stronger, I could carry more goods and range more widely. By the time I was in high school I carried sixty-five or more pounds of baked goods at a time and covered the whole town. My profits were not large — six or eight cents a day after school snd sixty-five cents or so on Saturday — but sometimes a special occasion would grant me a windfall. One of these events I will never forget.

Buffalo Bill Cody's Wild West Show was coming to Lancaster, which we thought of then as the big city, about nine miles south of Lititz. Like every other boy in town, I idolized Buffalo Bill and wanted to see his show. But I could not afford to pay the price of admission. My father's salary as a Lutheran minister was then only $750 a year, and every penny, including the pennies I earned at my various jobs, counted. So I went to Mr. Bowman and proposed that I take a basket of buns to the Wild West Show and try to sell them there. He was skeptical, but he agreed to let me try it. My hope was that I could sell enough of the bakery goods to spectators as they arrived at the show to pay for my own admission. To my surprise, the ticket collector waved me through without paying; with the basket of buns strapped across my shoulder I was obviously a vendor, not a paying spectator. So I not only got to see Buffalo Bill, sitting splendidly on an elaborate western saddle, his long white hair falling over a tooled leather jacket, but I made a profit on the buns as well.

The largest sum I ever made at one time in those years was during a week off from high school — teacher's week, they called

The Bobst family around 1901. The author is at the right, standing behind his mother. Standing also are his brother Harry and sister Katie. Sister Mildred is by her father's side and sister Dorothy by her mother's.

it. Mr. Bowman, with his constantly fired baking ovens, needed a large store of split wood, and I agreed to replenish it for him. He indicated some felled green trees, and I began to work on them: two saw cuts on each log and then four splits with a sledge-hammer and wedge. At the end of the week I had turned out seven cords. Mr. Bowman paid me two silver dollars and a half dollar for the week's hard labor. My father was almost down to his last nickel at the time, and I will never forget the pride I felt at the little jingling when he put the three coins in his pocket.

He never asked me to work, nor did he ask me for the money that I earned from my work. I did it because I enjoyed it, and I gave him the money as a matter of course. I knew even from my earliest years that the family needed it. By the time I reached my teens I realized also that someday my parents would be old and that I would have to at least help to support them. No one told me that. I simply assumed that future responsibility as part of the nature of things, and it motivated me to work all the harder.

My brother Harry did not have the same temperament, and ocassionally time grew heavy on his hands. One day, for lack of anything better to do, he joined a group of older boys in Lititz Springs Park, a lovely green sward surrounding a crystal clear stream that flows from three natural springs in a huge limestone outcropping near the center of Lititz. It was once an Indian camp-ground, and we used to find tomahawks and arrowheads there. Somehow, Harry and the other boys got carried away in their exuberance and damaged the play equipment in the park. I learned about the incident almost immediately afterwards. When I heard that a complaint had been filed with the town constable I was distraught, not just for Harry, but for my father. I knew that it would embarrass him deeply if one of his sons was publicly cited, perhaps even arrested, for misbehavior.

Without even pausing to consider the problem, I went to see the constable, a man named Holtzhouse who also ran the local livery stable. It was there, I suppose, that I first learned of the power of economic suasion.

"Please don't do anything to my brother," I pleaded. "It will hurt my father if you do."

"Well, Elmer," he said, "those were pretty bad boys Harry was mixed up with."

"I know they were, Mr. Holtzhouse, but Harry is a good boy. It won't happen again. I'm sure of it."

The constable lifted his eyebrows skeptically and frowned.

"Please," I repeated. "You know we hire a team from you every Sunday to take my father to Kissel Hill and Neffsville." My father preached at two country churches as well as at St. Paul's. "I know you won't do anything that will indirectly hurt my father."

I had no intention of threatening Mr. Holtzhouse with an economic boycott of his livery stable, but that final argument was the clincher. He let Harry off with a quiet scolding, and Father never learned of the incident. Mr. Holtzhouse and I kept our secret when on Sundays I would go to the livery stable, harness one of his horses to a buggy, and drive my father to one or both of his country sermons.

Kissel Hill was about a mile and a half from Lititz and Neffsville was four miles away. Every week after preaching at St. Paul's, Father would preach another, different sermon at one or both of the other churches. He spoke extemporaneously, from cryptic notes. Often he would deliver the rural sermons in Pennsylvania Dutch. I sat through all of them, entranced both by what he said and by the way he said it. He had a natural histrionic ability and a sense of stagecraft that added great force to his words. His voice might rise to a high pitch, then descend suddenly to a low and ominous rumble, shifting again to calm, soothing, and always articulate exposition. He used arm, hand, and facial expressions as eloquently as he used his voice, so that all were an integral part of his communication. And on special occasions such as religious revival meetings when the preaching was purely evangelistic, he would integrate a softly singing choir as a dramatic background to his sermons.

When I wasn't working, I spent a great deal of time in my father's company. He was demonstrative in his love for his children, and he liked to have us with him, even when he made his pastoral calls on the old and the sick. I idolized him and stayed by his side as much as I could. My favorite time with him was in the evening, when we walked together to the post office to pick up the mail and the daily paper. On the way home we frequently stopped off at an establishment that was peculiar to a small town in those times: a shop that combined the crafts of furniture manufacture, coffin making, and undertaking. The proprietor was a short, heavyset, bearded Dutchman named Enck, who was something of a raconteur.

In the center of the shop's front room, directly off the street, Enck kept a potbellied stove which squatted over a boxed hearth of shavings from his coffins and furniture. Chairs surrounded the stove, and it became a gathering place for many Lititz men who would drop in, listen to Enck and the latest news of the town, and spit tobacco juice into the shavings. Even though many of the men were not his parishioners, my father liked to stop at Enck's place in the evening just to say hello. I don't know whether this frequent exposure to adult company helped to mature me, but I do know that I learned more than a few lessons from it.

One evening when we stopped to stand by Enck's hot stove there were three or four loungers sitting in the chairs, chatting and blessing the wood chips with their tobacco juice. One of them was a man named Graver, who appeared to have had a few drinks before he sat down. He had a reputation as a heavy drinker, and my father worried about him. He had often chided Graver for his habit, and this night was no exception.

"Brother Graver," Father said, "remember that there is a snake in every glass of liquor that you drink."

"I haven't seen a snake yet, Reverend Bobst," Graver laughed.

"Sooner or later it will bite you," my father said.

Not long after that, Graver was seized with an attack of delirium tremens. Whether he was after snakes or some other hideous hallucination I don't know, but he grabbed a knife in his distress and stabbed himself in the abdomen. He was rushed to the hospital, and a doctor sewed him up. As soon as he was left alone, however, Graver tore open the wound and literally disembowelled himself. The snake had bitten him, fatally. I remembered that example always, and although I never adopted my father's strict prohibitionist views, I have treated alcohol with the respect and moderation that Brother Graver lacked. It is a marvelous social lubricant if used wisely, but the human body, like a complex machine, will run away with itself if it is overlubricated and will burn out.

On the evenings that I could not go with my father, I waited patiently by the front window of the house, so anxious was I to see him when he came home. I also got a visual dividend for waiting by the window. As darkness approached, Mr. Ochs, the lamplighter, would come briskly down the street with his professional paraphernalia strapped to his back. He would pause in front of our house, carefully lift the globe from the coal oil street lamp outside, and wipe it clean. Then he would refill the bowl of the lamp with kerosene. I was awed by that careful process, and a special kind of warmth spread through me when Mr. Ochs ignited the wick. His illuminating efforts were far more interesting to a little boy than the routine click of an electric switch.

Many of the conditions of life that are considered primitive today had their own special compensations, not the least of which was that we did not then consider them primitive at all. Take our heating system, for example. It consisted of two coal stoves on the first floor, one of them in the dining room and the other in the parlor. Tending them may have been a sooty nuisance at times — one of my chores, in fact, was to sift through the coal ashes when I emptied them in order to salvage unburned lumps for a second use — but there were benefits, too. One of them was the ventilation system. In order to get some heat from the stove-warmed rooms to the rest of the house, there were grilled registers that opened from the parlor and dining room ceilings into the rooms upstairs.

The heat register in our bedroom sometimes gave Harry and me an after-hours perspective on the adult world. There was a regular ritual to our bedtime and we literally followed it religiously. Every night each of us children would light his kerosene lamp in the kitchen, pick up his Bible, kiss Mother and Father, and go upstairs to bed. There we would say our prayers, read for a time from our Bibles — oh, how the begots and the begats of the Old Testament bored me — and go to sleep between blankets on springless, slatted beds. But often our special ear on the adult world — the heat register in the floor — would tell us that there was something worth observing down in the parlor. It was never anything more exciting than a meeting of the church council or some other group connected with St. Paul's, but it fascinated us to listen from our hidden vantage point.

One night, as I was listening in on a church council meeting, my father was urgently called away to attend to a sick parishioner. After he had gone, a church councilman named Gabel was emboldened to say something that he apparently did not have the courage to say in my father's presence.

"Brothers," he ventured to his fellow council members, "I think the Reverend Bobst is reaching an age where perhaps we should begin thinking of a younger man in the pulpit."

My father was about forty-eight years old at the time and, as he demonstrated, had not yet reached his prime as a preacher — he had another generation of active and successful ministry ahead of him — but Gabel apparently did not care for him.

The other council members did not agree with the lone dissident, but I worried about his remark and decided to tell my father, even though it meant revealing that I had been eavesdropping through the heat register. When he got home, my father listened gravely as I repeated Brother Gabel's remarks, and thanked me. I was delighted that he didn't reprimand me for listening.

The next morning Brother Gabel pulled up outside our house with his horse drawn milkwagon, as he did every day, to deliver our milk.

"I think I'll have a word with Brother Gabel," my father said. He stepped out onto the sidewalk and I followed him.

"*Good* morning, Brother Gabel," Father said.

"Good morning, Reverend Bobst."

"Brother Gabel, I am one of Shakespeare's pure, blunt men. And I understand that last night you gave us some more of your officiousness. I want to warn you to discontinue. *Good* morning, Brother Gabel."

So far as I know there were no further efforts to unseat my father from his pastoral chair in St. Paul's, although he did move on some years later to larger churches in Trenton and Philadelphia.

My father was, as he told Brother Gabel, a blunt man. I remember a sermon in which he told how, during the Revolutionary War, one of Washington's officers quartered his troops and his horses in a part of the Lititz Moravian church. The townspeople, he said, thought it was terrible for horses and manure to defile such a holy place. Then he thundered to the startled congregation:

"I am prepared to tell you that many of my congregation are bringing their dung into our church — their dung of selfishness, of unrighteousness, or improper living. See to it that you have a proper respect for the church of God and all its teachings."

If, while walking down the street, he heard someone using profanity on the other side, he would walk across and admonish the person to curb his tongue. But privately he was a gentle man, fond of quiet, scholarly pursuits, who for recreation liked nothing better than to take my mother for long walks in the countryside, looking for wild flowers.

Both of my parents adored flowers, particularly carnations, and when they were blooming Mother had them tastefully arranged in every room in the house. She liked to say that "the two most beautiful things in the world are babies and flowers." She was an immaculate housekeeper. Although she had grown up in modest wealth, she cheerfully adapted to the parsimonious life of a preacher's wife and, with his ever-willing help, became a superb household manager and cook. But no matter her husband's occupation or small income, she never lost her fashionable style or her taste for careful grooming. None of us ever saw her in the morning wearing housecoat or kimono, as other women met the day, or with her hair down. She was always stylishly dressed, and her long hair was carefully combed into a bun at the back of her head when she came downstairs. Somehow she managed to dress attractively on an infinitesimally small budget, sewing all of her own and Katie's dresses, and most of the male attire as well. When my two youngest sisters, Mildred and Dorothy, were born in 1896 and 1898, she made all of their clothes, too. I still marvel at how calmly and smoothly she managed her responsibilities: the care of five active children and a busy husband in a house that had no modern conveniences (the most modern was the wooden washing machine that Harry and I pumped for her by hand) and the full-time pastoral obligations of a clergyman's wife. Yet she glowed with her love for all of it and for all of us. There was never a person in the world who disliked my mother or was ever offended by her, for everything that she did was touched by kindness and love.

Both Mother and Father were acutely conscious of preventive medicine and nutrition, which put them at least twenty-five years ahead of their time. At Father's direction, for example, Mother prepared one diet for us in the wintertime, when cold weather and vigorous activity demanded a high intake of calories, and another lighter diet in the summer, when there were no icy winds to drain our energy. Although vitamins were unknown, Father saw that we had enough ascorbic acid, thiamin, and iron in our diets to protect us from the diseases of deficiency.

Perhaps their health consciousness was a legacy from his months in Andersonville and Libby prisons and their early life together in the malaria-ridden river valley of Lancaster, Illinois. They guarded us especially against the ravaging diseases which killed thousands of children every year. I shall never forget the diptheria epidemic that struck Lititz in 1895. In a few weeks time, more than thirty little children died, and there was scarcely a day that Father was not officiating at the funeral of one of the victims. He willingly went into their houses to comfort the bereaved families. But when he came home, he hung his Prince Albert coat on the clothes line outside in order to safeguard us against possible infection, and he kept his hands in his pockets until he had washed them.

The short Prince Albert was his daily uniform, fitted snugly around his broad shoulders and his increasingly portly mid-section. On Sundays he wore a swallowtail coat in the pulpit, unlike most Lutheran ministers, who liked to don formal ecclesiastical vestments. "I tried to preach in a long gown once," he explained to me, "and I tripped and almost fell down. I said, 'I'll never wear one of those miserable things again,' and I never will."

We children had to dress appropriately, too. Mother never let us run barefoot in the summertime, lest it reflect on our father. At noon on Saturdays our play — or, more often in my case, work — had to stop, and we came in for our baths, which were administered in a galvanized tub on the floor of the summer kitchen, a small outer room, off the regular kitchen, that contained a cistern for rain water. After our baths, Harry and I were dressed up in suits and stiff white collars, Katie and, later, the younger sisters, in fresh long dresses. We remained thoroughly respectable looking until we went to bed on Sunday night. On Sunday afternoon after I had driven Father to Kissel Hill and Neffsville, we could walk along the railroad tracks which cut through the center of town, or relax in Lititz park, watching the live trout in the cold spring-fed stream. But when the church bell rang for evening prayer meeting, we abandoned the park on the run and hurried to St. Paul's.

Life was not all work and prayer, however. Far from it. I went on fishing trips in clear mountain springs that fairly burst with trout. I hiked with my friends around the Lancaster countryside, marveling at the old hex signs, elaborately painted geometric figures on the barns that were said to protect the livestock from evil spells; and we marveled, too, at the variety of swallow holes near the gable peaks of the same barns. It was said that a barn without swallows was no barn at all, and the farmers enticed the graceful birds with entryways of all shapes: stars, crescents, crosses, diamonds, circles, or whatever the rural imagination could conceive. We ranged as far as our legs would carry us.

One day not long after the beginning of the Spanish-American War in 1898 a group of us walked from Lititz to Mount Gretna, near Lebanon, where the Army was running a recruit depot. As each of the rawboned new recruits, mostly Pennsylvania Dutchmen, went in to the Army stockade, a crowd of hangers-on would shout, "Fresh fish, fresh fish." There was a blind youth with a tin cup singing mournful songs to cheer the recruits along, too. One of his songs, I remember, was a pathetic thing about the battleship Maine called "In the Harbor of Havana, Far Away." Another one of his songs stuck like treacle. "Just take the news to Mother," he sang, "and tell her that I love her . . . Just say goodbye for me, for I'm not coming home . . . Just think there'll be no other, that can take the place of Mother."

The scene was calculated to inflame the emotions of a fourteen-year-old boy. When I got home I went immediately to my father and pleaded with him to let me join. "General Gobell is up there," I said. "You served under him in the Civil War. I'm big enough and strong enough. Please get me into the Army as an aide or an orderly or something." Fortunately, he laughed off my keen desire and sent me back out to play.

It was true, though, that I was big enough to be a soldier, as he had been almost four decades before. Like my father, I reached my full growth early. I was six feet tall by the time I was fourteen and I had such a heavy mop of wavy brown hair that my schoolmates called me "Curly." Much of the work I had done even before my teens was hard, unskilled labor, such as cutting and bailing hay and shucking corn in the summers, so my chest and shoulders were every bit as broad and muscled as those of a grown man. I could lift 200 pounds at fifteen, and I could broad jump twenty feet. I loved to run and usually jogged or trotted whenever I went on foot. My grandfather George Holmes, a robust man, taught me to high jump by laying my body out flat and rolling over the bar, and I could clear six feet with ease. With such a fortunate endowment, I was naturally attracted to sports and played games year-round. In the spring and summer I played first base with a semiprofessional sandlot baseball team. In the fall I played in the backfield of the town football team, and in the winter I ran, wrestled, and boxed.

Every winter there was a special cross-country footrace called "Fox and Hounds" that occupied a place as prominent as the

Olympics in the minds of the people of Lititz. It was the kind of sports event that you look forward to eagerly, then wonder, after you are halfway through with it, whatever possessed you to undertake such an ordeal.

About an hour before the race was to begin, several of the town's best athletes would lay out a devious trail of paper strips, through the woods, over hill and dale and past insufferable obstacles. The course was twenty miles from start to finish, and many of the runners never finished it. When I was fifteen I entered the race with my best friend, a tall, sturdy, dark blond named Mahlon Yoder. He was three years older than I — valedictorian that year of my sister Kate's high school graduating class — and had every expectation of beating at least me, if not everyone else. At the starting gun we loped off together. The temperature was near zero and although both of us felt the cold air cutting like shards of glass into our lungs, neither of us would slow his pace nor let the other get away from him. When we passed a large warehouse, most of the runners broke off to duck inside and appropriate pieces of burlap for warmth, but Yoder and I ran on. We refused to give one another an inch. I think both of us were running on sheer willpower and not much else as we neared the last obstacle, close to the finish line. It was a six-foot stone wall, broken only by a narrow gap that looked barely big enough to pass a slender boy through. Mahlon ran straight for it, so instead of crowding him I gathered what little reserve I had left and vaulted the fence, jumping as my grandfather had taught me. Looking back as I dashed first toward the finish, I saw Mahlon, laughing breathlessly and irretrievably stuck in the gap in the wall.

The Pennsylvania winters seemed more bitter then than they do now, mainly because central heating was almost unheard of, and snow removal equipment consisted only of strong arms and shovels. I remember one evening returning home from a job of clearing snow, my shovel on my shoulder. I was walking along the hard crust of a snowbank when suddenly it gave way and I dropped eight feet to the bottom. For a moment I thought I would suffocate, buried alive in the high drift, until I realized that I still held my shovel in my hands, and I dug my way out. We looked forward to the snow, though, and loved it.

There was a long steep hill running down from the house of my high school sweetheart, a lovely girl named Erla Buch who, incidentally, is still living in Lititz as I write this. It sloped off into Lititz Springs Park, and not long after the first snowfall, the hill would be as smooth as blue-glazed glass from the pressure of sled runners and crude toboggans on which we coasted down its 300-yard length. At the bottom of the run there was usually an open fire where we could toast ourselves before trudging up the slippery hill again, towing our sleds behind us.

My sled had an interesting history, although it was a decade or more after I got it that its original owner became notorious. My father bought it for me, secondhand, at an auction of left-behind articles conducted by the Beck Boys' Preparatory School in Lititz. It was marked as having originally belonged to a former student named Harry K. Thaw. Father paid twenty-five cents for it. The name meant nothing to me until 1906, when Harry Thaw murdered the famous architect Stanford White over the love of a girl named Evelyn Nesbitt who, strangely, became the source of mild embarrassment to me many years later. I took my wife and some rather distinguished guests to a nightclub that was owned by Miss Nesbitt. In the course of the evening she came to our table, a somewhat faded relic of the once beautiful girl who had aroused such murderous passion in Harry Thaw. As she was introduced around the table, she paused at my place and said, "Why, Elmer! I've known Elmer for years!" I don't think my wife was ever quite convinced that I had never laid eyes on the woman before in my life. The closest connection I had ever had with her was when I coasted happily downhill on her future lover's twenty-five-cent sled with my girlfriend, Erla Buch.

Erla was the prettiest girl in Lititz. Although she was one year older than I was, we were tied as only adolescents can be by the strong bonds of pure first love. It never occurred to either of us that once we saw the world outside of Lititz we might feel differently. Our horizons were limited to each other. Had they not been, I might have followed more closely in my father's foot-steps. He had often told me that the most noble professions were the ministry and medicine, obviously hoping that I would enter one or the other. In my earnestness to please him and my mother, I decided rather early in my high school years to become a Lu-theran minister. Erla, noting how little my father earned from his charge at St. Paul's, wasn't exactly thrilled by the prospect of becoming a minister's wife, but I persevered through the last year of high school. I liked to make public speeches and even enjoyed sermonizing when the occasion was right. In my class graduation speech that year I talked on "Life is What We Make It," and delivered more than a few lines that would have served me well in a Sunday morning pulpit. Among them, one which, incidentally, I still firmly believe, went: "No, let us not criticize the success attained by others but arise from our positions in the mire and dark and let the whole of manhood play its part."

Quite clearly, I was destined to wear the cloth. But I didn't reckon on several factors, including Erla's persuasiveness. I also had no idea how I would manage to work my way through two years of college in order to qualify for admission to a Lutheran theological seminary. That summer after graduation, however, the latter problem seemed to resolve itself.

Although I had a full-time summer job in a silk mill in Lan-caster — leaving Lititz by trolley at 6 A.M. and returning home at 7 P.M. — I used my free time for preseason workouts with the town football team. At that time, small town football was played by community against community, rather than by high schools, and we had awkward players in their twenties on the team. Late in the summer we scheduled a game against the formidable and well-coached team of Franklin and Marshall Academy in Lancas-ter. Our team was a pickup collection, a group of young men who simply liked to play football and played well against other similar teams, but we were no match for a well-drilled college team and we knew it. We met them for fun and practice.

I played fullback, both offensive and defensive, and I was all over the field, running with the ball, tackling and defending, but it was hopeless. Moreover, I didn't help matters much when

The 1901 graduating class of Lititz High School. The author is second from the right in the top row. His brother Harry is fourth from the left in the top row. Seated, third from the left, is Erla Buch, the author's girlfriend at the time and the "prettiest girl in town."

I had a brief altercation on the field with one of the F & M boys. They beat us 27 to 0.

After the game I was both surprised and frightened when someone told me that Dr. Thaddeus Helm, the headmaster of Franklin and Marshall, wanted to see me. I thought I was in trouble for fighting with one of his boys. I dressed quickly and appeared in his office.

"Do you like to play football?" he asked with no reference to the fight.

"Very much," I said with relief.

"And I hear you play baseball."

"Yes, I play first base."

"Well, we've got education and school learning here," he said, "but we believe in athletics, too. We like athletes. I want you to join us."

Dr. Helm caught me completely by surprise. He offered me an almost full athletic scholarship — only twenty-five dollars a year tuition. So I left the silk mill and enrolled in the fall of 1901. Even with the nominal tuition, however, money remained a problem, and I knew that it was a terrible drain on my father's slender resources to keep me there. My first impulse was to cram enough courses into a single year to accomplish two year's work so that I could enter the Lutheran Seminary at Gettysburg, where I would have church support. I took Latin and Greek simultaneously and doubled up on my other courses. But by Christmas time, I had begun to question what I was doing. Then, abruptly, I decided to change my course in life. I have always acted promptly once my mind is made up.

Erla's attitude was one factor. She said that she simply would never consider marrying a minister. That was not the main reason for my change, however. Deep inside I knew that I did not really want to become a minister. In the years previous, I had often volunteered to help the family doctor. I held his horse for him when I was small, and later accompanied him on housecalls; for a time I worked in his office, washing his equipment and bottles so that I could be near the mysteries of medicine and try to learn something about them. I wasn't positive that I wanted to become a doctor, but medicine, frankly, appealed to me more than the ministry. And there was an even more pressing reason. I knew that school represented a great strain on my father's bare finances. And I could see that the day would come when Mother and Father would have to rely on me for their support. I could never manage that as a minister.

Thus ended my ecclesiastical career, and I shall never forget the night that I sat up with my father until 2:30 A.M. explaining my decision and asking his permission to go to Philadelphia to find a particular kind of a job. He was disappointed, but his unhappiness over my decision would have been complete had I not proposed the alternative of the second most noble profession, medicine. Obviously I couldn't afford to go to college and medical school on my own. However, at that time there was a way to work your way through medical school without all of the college preliminaries and without paying tuition. That was by becoming the hospital pharmacist of a medical college. All of the schools permitted their house pharmacists to take free courses in medicine if they wished.

My brother Harry already was working as a clerk in a Philadelphia drugstore, hoping to become a pharmacist, and I resolved to join him, get my certificate as a pharmacist as soon as I could, and somehow worm my way into a medical school pharmacy and a free education. My father reluctantly approved, and the next day we wrote to Harry, asking him to place an advertisement offering my services as an apprentice in any Philadelphia drugstore that would have me.

On February 21, 1902, I went to Mr. Souders, the blacksmith, and borrowed his wheelbarrow. Then I loaded my heavy wooden trunk, decorated with flowered wallpaper, onto the barrow and wheeled it to the trolley station. Erla and my mother and father and three sisters laughed at the sight of me pushing the heavy wheelbarrow, but I didn't mind at all. By getting the trunk to the station myself, I saved the twenty-five cents hauling fee, and there was plenty of time to return Mr. Souders' barrow before departure time. Finally, my father handed me a five-dollar bill, and my mother gave me a box lunch. The trolley fare to Lancaster was fifteen cents, the train fare to Philadelphia, $3.61. I said goodbye to Erla and my family and swung aboard the trolley. As I paid my fare, a local boy named Warren Buch, no relation to Erla, said, "You know, Curly, when you break a five-dollar bill, it goes pretty fast."

"You're telling me," I said. It was the first time in my life that I had ever even briefly held a five-dollar bill in my hand. And it was to be quite a while before I got another one.

● *Chapter Three*

● When her son, the novelist-to-be, was still a small child in the late 1820s, the mother of Anthony Trollope visited America and recorded her observations in a journal later published under the title, *Domestic Manners of the Americans*. She spent some of her three-year tour of the young nation in Philadelphia, and she didn't like it much. One day she visited a park by the Philadelphia State House. While the leafy retreat won her heart, the busy Philadelphians didn't. "Here there was an excellent crop of clover," she wrote, "but as the trees are numerous, and highly beautiful, and several commodious seats are placed beneath their shade, it is, in spite of the long grass, a very agreeable retreat from heat and dust. It was rarely, however, that I saw any of these seats occupied; the Americans have either no leisure or no inclination for those moments of *délassment* that all other people, I believe, indulge in. Even their drams, so universally taken by rich and poor, are swallowed standing, and, excepting at church, they never have the air of leisure or repose."

I found the people unchanged when I arrived that February night in 1902. The Broad Street railroad station was awash with activity, and the lamps of hurrying carriages bobbled wildly out on the streets. Even Harry seemed preoccupied with the hustle of the big city when he met me at the station. I wanted to approach my new surroundings in an orderly manner so that I could savor them. And first on my list of priorities was the water-front. As an inland boy from a country town, I had never been to a port city before, and I had always dreamed of standing beside the tall-masted schooners that I had seen pictured beside crowded city wharves.

"Harry," I announced with confident anticipation, "I want you to take me down to see the ships."

"I can't take you down to the river tonight," he frowned.

"Why not?" I was crushed.

"Because it's evening, and it's snowing. You can go down there another time."

Reluctantly, I fell into the spirit of things and let Harry put me on a horse-drawn trolley that took me to the combination home and drugstore of my new employer, Dr. Bennett N. Bethel, at 632 North 18th Street. There, without much ado, I was shown to a small, unheated room at the end of a long hall. It contained a cot that was perhaps long enough for a small ten-year-old, a straight chair, a washstand with metal pitcher and bowl, and a straw mat on the floor. The gas jet that dimly lit the room was stuffed with cotton in order to conserve fuel. There was an indoor, family bathroom, but I was told that I could not use it. I would have to go outside to the privy in the backyard. Dr. Bethel also told me not to worry about normal meal times. I was not to be permitted to eat with members of the family but would eat alone in the dining room only after they had finished. My life was to be as bleak as Dr. Bethel could make it.

For this, I had left a loving household in a beautiful small town where even the most disagreeable people were cordial most of the time. I stretched disconsolately on the cot, adding the chair to the end of it so that I would have someplace to rest my lower legs, and longed for Lititz. As I contemplated going out to the snowy backyard, I remembered how often at night my father, out of love, had gone to the pump in back of our house, drawn icy cold water, and brought each of us a glassful in bed. When the servings were scarce at our table, he saw that each of us had filled his plate before he served his own. If he had enough money to buy delicacies, such as a few bananas, he first gave Mother one, then divided the rest between us children, happier to observe our enjoyment than to taste the fruit himself.

Dr. Bethel clearly was not going to become a father figure to me. He made no effort to be, as it turned out. To him I was nothing more than an inexpensive apprentice clerk, hired to work from 7 A.M. to 10:30 P.M., with every other Sunday afternoon and evening off, in exchange for room, board, and three dollars a week. "Board" meant a single slice of meat or a fishcake, the latter served three times a week. There is not a labor leader alive who can tell me anything that I do not know from personal experience about the exploitation of labor: I was so regularly underpaid and overworked during my early years, in fact, that my whole business philosophy was altered by it — for the good — and when I reached a position where I could do something about decent working conditions and generous employee benefits in the pharmaceutical industry, I did.

Dr. Bethel was a dour, often grouchy man who told me at the start that no matter how hard I studied and practiced, it would take me years to learn enough about pharmacy to pass the state licensing examinations, and that it probably would be two years before I would even be able to fill a prescription. With little else to do between menial chores in the drugstore, I plunged into the *Pharmacopeia, Gray's Quiz Compendium,* and works on therapeutics that I borrowed from libraries. Fortunately, my study habits were good, and I had learned, from my father, to take pleasure from reading even tedious technical material. Father early exposed me to his own library of the English classics — Shakespeare, Addison, Goldsmith, DeQuincy, Scott, Charles Lamb — and such American authors as Cooper and Mark Twain. I think the first time that I realized that reading could be fun as well as enlightening was, when quite young, I read Charles Lamb's essay, *A Dissertation Upon Roast Pig*, and laughed uproariously at the image of primitive man burning down the barn again and again in order to recreate that first accidental pork roast.

The *Pharmacopeia* was no match for Lamb's elegant wit, but I found myself entranced by its formulae and anxious to connect the compounds I was studying to their therapeutic effects. Within a few months I was filling prescriptions with Bethel's grumbling consent. It was then that I had my first innocent contact with narcotics.

At the time that I began working as a druggist, opium and its derivative alkaloids were thought to be beneficial for many ailments. It was known that heavy doses of opium when smoked or eaten might become addictive and certainly were hypnotic — witness Coleridge's wispy vision of *Xanadu* in an opium-induced dream — but there was little understanding of the menacing nature of the new chemical forms of morphine. Heroin, for example, was hailed as a near miraculous wonder drug when Merck refined it from opium-based morphine in Darmstadt, Germany, and there was another, dionine. Physicians, unaware that they were dispensing the most dangerous narcotic drug in history, prescribed it to relieve coughing. Until the early 1920s, when the free importation of opium and other narcotics was outlawed, and its medicinal uses strictly controlled, you could buy opium and its derivatives at the corner drugstore without so much as a prescription. Few of us understood what a dreadfully destructive medicinal bomb we were holding in our hands.

One of my first duties was to prepare Dr. Bethel's narcotics. I also had to make a batch of catarrhal powders, mixing boric acid, menthol, sugar of milk, and cocaine in a large stone mortar. Most tedious of all, however, was the weekly gallon of laudanum, which was a tincture of opium that was used widely as an all-around remedy in the United States for more than a century. At the time, I knew far less than most druggists or physicians, who knew little enough about its effects, or I would have resented having to produce it. Many people innocently became addicted to the stuff. It was laudanum, for example, and later morphine, that led playwright Eugene O'Neill's mother into her lifelong drug addiction, setting such a tragic background to his famous work.

The mixing process was laborious. First I took a rounded ball of Turkish opium, cut it into small pieces, and ground it with bird gravel into a near powder. Then I poured a solvent of alcohol and distilled water over it for maceration. After a period of time this maceration of opium, alcohol, and water was filtered in a large, cylindrical glass filter, which meant that all of the active alkaloids of opium in the filtered powder, such as morphine and codeine, had been exhausted. The result was called laudanum, but just what its true chemical strength was, no pharmacist was exactly sure. The process was so crude that we could not tell what were the real percentages of morphine, codeine, and the twenty-odd other minor alkaloids of opium, because the strength of the original substance varied so.

I shudder today when I think of the abandon with which, in our ignorance, we dispensed the stuff. We knew, of course, that the opiates contained a narcotic kick, and no reputable pharmacist would sell them to children. But any grownup who came into the store could buy laudanum, at the rate of two ounces for a quarter. And some adults obviously were damaging themselves with copious quantities of laudanum.

I remember one of our customers who bought a gallon of laudanum every other week. He was an Episcopal clergyman, which shocked me. Had I been in charge of the store, I think I would have refused to fill such a large order on a regular basis, but Dr. Bethel never permitted me to wait on the good, gray-haired reverend, nor would he tell me how much the gentleman paid for his bi-weekly bulk purchase. My only satisfaction came in a veiled needling of my boss whenever the clergyman came into the drugstore. I would see him through the peep hole of the prescription counter and announce, in a stage whisper, "Here comes Mr. DeQuincey." I don't know if Bethel was literate enough to recognize the allusion to Thomas DeQuincey's *Confessions of an English Opium Eater*.

Another of our regular laudanum customers was a washerwoman who came into the store daily for two ounces of the fiery liquid. Often she belted down a half ounce of it "neat" right at the counter. Then, presumably in a happier frame of mind, she would go off to toil over a washtub all day.

Aside from my work, my apprenticeship with Dr. Bethel was uneventful, if for no other reason than that he allowed me little time for anything outside of the store. My pleasures were simple ones. After work, late at night, I would often run the fifteen blocks to the drugstore where my brother Harry worked to visit with him for a little while. For a time the policemen on the beat regularly stopped me, thinking I was a thief in flight, but they soon recognized me and waved as I jogged down the street. I also began to explore Philadelphia, which I came to love deeply. On my Sunday afternoons off I would sometimes go down to Front Street and to Wildey Street, the waterfront, and soak in what I had so sorely missed on my first night in Philadelphia. For a little while I would browse with wonder along Richmond Street, which paralleled Wildey, goggling at ship chandlers' show windows filled with brass pulleys, red and green lanterns, chocks, cleats, and coils of rope. Then I would sit on a sycamore-shaded bench in Penn Treaty Park, at the foot of Columbia Avenue, and watch the big schooners as their crews hoisted canvas on the arms of tall masts and prepared to set sail. It was a wondrous sight, far more majestic and romantic than the antiseptic loading and take-off of a modern jet plane or the sailing of a thousand-foot passenger liner.

Or, sometimes, I took the advice of old Tom Daly, who was called the poet laureate of Philadelphia. "Whenever it's Saturday and all my work is through," he wrote, "I take a walk on Chestnut Street to see what news is new." In my case, however, the couplet was applicable only every other Sunday afternoon.

By the end of the year I had learned a great deal, but I was more than fed up with crusty Dr. Bethel. Quietly, I advertised for another apprentice position and within a few weeks I was hired by a crippled druggist R. J. Burton, who had, a store at 1306 Girard Avenue, near Broad Street, a much more refined neighborhood than 18th Street. When I gave my notice to Dr. Bethel he stared at me with utter distaste and growled:

"If you take my advice, Bobst, you'll give up the drug business for good. You're better equipped to be a truck driver than a pharmacist or a physician."

I didn't see Bethel again until fifteen years later when, for old time's sake, I drove to his shop in a fancy new Hudson Super-

Six that I had just bought. He stared at the glittering car and then looked at me with faint recognition.

"Oh, yes," he nodded, "I see you have become a chauffeur."

Dr. Burton, my new employer, had locomotor ataxia and was forced to spend most of his workdays sitting in a chair in the back of the shop. Consequently, I practically ran the store, in return for which he paid me $7.50 a week. The increased salary was not the boon that it seemed, however. I had to pay for my own room and buy my meals at fifteen cents or a quarter apiece. But after such customers as the round-collared "Mr. DeQuincey" and the addicted washerwoman, Burton's clientele was a happy change for me. The neighborhood was a good one, and some of the customers were famous.

One of my favorites was Oscar Hammerstein, the impressario who built the Philadelphia Opera House and fathered a prolific and creative son who brought such excellence and joy to the New York musical stage. Mr. Hammerstein came into the store daily, wearing a high silk hat, and bought a deluxe twenty-five-cent cigar (ordinary cigars still sold at two-for-a-nickel then). He insisted that only I could wait on him.

Another customer whom I liked especially was a nearsighted school teacher, a middle-aged spinster named Anna Jarvis. She was totally devoted to her mother, who was ill. Consequently Miss Jarvis came into the store frequently to have her mother's prescriptions filled. When I had mixed the prescription, she invariably would say, "Elmer, fix me up a fifteen-cent box of ice cream for Mother." Her mother died in May, 1906, long after she had tasted the last of my medicines and ice cream. On the first anniversary of her death, Miss Jarvis arranged for memorial services in the Methodist church which she attended in Philadelphia and in their old hometown church in Grafton, West Virginia. Afterwards, she went to John Wanamaker, the department store owner and civic leader, and proposed that a special day be marked each year in honor of mothers. Philadelphia responded by formally observing Mother's Day on May 19, 1908. In 1914, Congress made it a national observance. And my father, who by then occupied a pulpit in Philadelphia, became the first clergyman in the city to devote his second May Sunday sermon to mothers.

There was another good customer who came by the store frequently when he was home from college. I had read about his athletic exploits at the University of Pennsylvania, where he was an all-around star, and I enjoyed chatting with him about football and boxing. He was my age, and we had a kind of easy camaraderie which I liked. Years later, when Vincent Impellitteri appointed me to a Mayor's Committee in New York City, I was surprised to find the former star athlete sitting on the committee beside me. By then he had developed Sak's Fifth Avenue and was head of the Gimbel stores.

"Bernard Gimbel," I exclaimed, "I bet you don't remember me."

"I know we've met, and I know it was a long time ago," he replied.

I reminded him of the drugstore on Girard Avenue, and from that day until his last we remained close companions. Before he died, Bernard told the Philadelphia *Enquirer*, "The oldest friend that I have in this world is Elmer Bobst," and of all the friends that I had by then, I could say the same about him.

But my closest friend as a youth was Mahlon Yoder, the runner who got stuck in the fence during the Fox and Hounds cross-country race. After finishing Lititz high school, Mahlon had gone on to Franklin and Marshall Academy and graduated from the two-year course. He had the vague ambition of one day study- ing medicine, but first he took a job as a freight agent for the Reading Railroad. I urged him to abandon the job; it could lead nowhere, certainly not to medical school. Instead, I pleaded with him to come to Philadelphia, get a job in a drug store, and apply for admission to Jefferson Medical College there. By then my own desire to become a doctor was waning, but Mahlon's hard- working father had saved enough money hauling rocks to road contractors to pay his tuition, and I thought he would be a fool not to take advantage of his opportunity. Mahlon agreed to come, and I applied, on his behalf, to a drugstore in Germantown that had advertised for a clerk. I was a brash youngster, never shy

Dr. Mahlon Yoder, the author's closest boyhood companion and life-long friend.

Dr. Herbert K. Cooper, the ortho-dontist who founded the Cleft Pal-te Clinic in Lancaster, Pa. "Her-ie" became a good friend and fre-quent cruise guest of the author.

about thrusting myself forward among adults, and I was determined to see that Mahlon got the Germantown job, so I went
to see his prospective employer. I drew myself up very seriously
and introduced myself with a short speech.

"Doctor" (all pharmacists were called 'doctor' in those days),
"I'm Elmer Bobst. I work in a pharmacy downtown. You have
an application from a very close friend of mine named Mahlon
Yoder. I want to say that I've known him since boyhood, and
he's a fine young man. He comes from Lititz, where he was valedictorian of his high school class. He was Number One in his
class at Franklin and Marshall Academy. I want to recommend
him most highly. You'll find that he will be a very valuable addition to your store."

The pharmacist looked at me across his spectacles.

"You give him a very good recommendation," he said.

"I give him the highest recommendation."

"Well, who recommends you?" he asked dryly.

I stammered my thanks for his time and left the store, somewhat flustered. But Mahlon got the job.

We moved into a rented room together — $1.50 apiece a
week — and with the exception of a few brief periods, we stuck
together for the next four years. I don't know exactly why, but
for some reason we took to calling each other "Ike." Both of
us were naïve country boys, and it took us a while to catch on
to the ways of the big city. One day we passed a fruit store and
our eyes caught on a display of citrus fruit, which to us was a
great delicacy.

"Ike, I never saw oranges as big as that in my life," I said,
pointing to some huge, yellow specimens on the counter.

"Neither have I, Ike," Mahlon said. "Let's get three or four
of them and eat them tonight."

Back in our room, we cut one across the middle and each
took half. As we bit into them, Mahlon looked up startled and
said, "Ike, mine's bitter."

"Mine's bitter, too. Let's open another one."

We went through all four of them before it dawned on us

that perhaps they weren't oranges. Neither of us had ever seen a grapefruit before.

As Mahlon and I began to explore Philadelphia by night, I became restless by day in the confines of Burton's drugstore. It was springtime, and I wanted to get outdoors. As it happened, one of our regular customers, who worked for an express company, heard me musing about the joys of outdoor work. He offered to recommend me to his boss, Mr. Harry Cook, of the United States Express Company. When I went to see him, Mr. Cook offered me a job as a dray wagon driver's helper at forty dollars a month. The prospect was too good to pass up. I joined a barrel-chested Irish driver named Ed Walsh, who took a liking to me and soon recommended me for a wagon of my own. First I was given a one-horse express wagon, which carried relatively light loads, then I graduated to a two-horse van that could carry almost anything. It was a coveted honor to get one of the big ones, but there was a hooker to it. The heavier load meant bulkier trunks, crates, and packages to shoulder on and off the wagon as I made my delivery rounds.

I had to be at the livery stable by 6 A.M. in order to quickly harness one of my horses while a hostler decked out the other one. Then I had to race to back my wagon into the platform of the Baltimore and Ohio Railroad platform. If I lagged, some other driver would grab my place and I would lose a day's work. This competition for position often led to violent quarrels and fistfights, and being young and new I came in for more than my share from older drivers who thought they could easily push a nineteen-year-old boy around. But I handled both my horses and my fists well enough to work six days a week.

One day Mr. Cook, who was a handsome, well-dressed man with leonine gray hair, said, "Bobst, you and I are about the only intelligent people working for this company." He raised my pay to fifty, then sixty dollars a month and gave me the company's best route in Philadelphia. It was the thrill of my life, driving down Chestnut Street, the best delivery area in town, sitting high on the seat of my express van and slapping the reins on my two gray horses, Prince and Duke. But the company was a hard one to work for. We had to buy our own uniforms and pay five dollars for the badges on our hats. If due bills weren't paid, and we couldn't collect them, the money came out of our pay.

The physical training was good, though. I hefted 275-pound barrels of oil and carried heavy trunks from dawn to dusk every day. Today the muscles of my shoulders, chest and arms are still large and strong, and it must be from that experience, because I never did that kind of manual labor again. The worst loads were theatrical trunks and the trunks used for salesmen's samples. Each was almost as big as a telephone booth and invariably weighed more than 200 pounds. Occassionally, however, the big trunks provided me with a bonus. I would arrive at the front door of a house with one and ask, politely, "Where do you wish this trunk?" The answer, usually, would be "second floor" or "third floor."

"My delivery is only to the front porch. I'm not supposed to take this trunk any farther."

"Well, we need it up there. Can't you do it for us?"

"Yes, but second floor will cost you ten cents, third floor will cost fifteen cents."

I was delighted to get the extra money, and sometimes the customer would throw in a piece of cake and a glass of milk, as well.

One hot night near the fourth of July, I came home from the express company exhausted and flopped on my bed. Mahlon was not there. I felt a sensation of prickly heat and lit the gas light to see what was bothering me. The entire room was swarming with bedbugs — on the walls, the floor, even dropping from the ceiling. I quickly bathed, shook out my uniform, got dressed, and hurried from the infested room. Soon I was walking along Vine Street, on the edge of Philadelphia's rough "tenderloin" district, ruminating over my wretched living quarters, when I saw a slight young Pennsylvania Dutch fellow from my rooming house. He had naïvely fallen in with five tough characters who were getting drunk on his money, and he was afraid to try to break away from them.

"Look, kid," I called to him, "I'm going over to Eighth and

Vine to buy some fireworks. Come along with me."

"All right," he said with relief. "Glad to go with you."

As we turned to leave, one of his unwanted companions snarled at me, "You're going to rob him, you son of a bitch."

"You can't call me that," I cried, and flattened him with an uppercut. In my innocence, I thought he would get up and we would have a fair fight, but all five of them jumped on me at once. My timid friend from the rooming house saw his opportunity to get away, and ran. It was the toughest fight I have ever had, with the six of us scrambling, like a small scale mob riot, up and down the sidewalk. I fought with my back to the storefronts and managed to get two of them down, but one of them felled me and kicked me in the face. It cracked my jawbone. I scrambled to my feet again. Fortunately, a saloon keeper who had been watching the fracas ran out of his bar with a club in his hand and chased them away from me. I stopped at an all-night drugstore, bought some arnica — an herbal tincture that is still sometimes used for bathing sprains and bruises — and went to the stable of the express company. There I sat on my wagon all night, bathing my jaw until it was time to harness up for the day's work. I could not chew, and I had lost my cap with the five-dollar badge on it. I was determined to return to the scene of the fight and retrieve my cap that night.

After work I got a short length of broomstick and drove some nails through one end. I had no intention of taking on that gang again without a weapon. Then I went down to the tenderloin to look for them. I found them standing in a drizzling rain under a street light. As I approached, one of them came across to me and cried, "Your fault! Your fault!" I don't know whether he saw the stick up my sleeve, but suddenly he called out to his group, "Foley, come over here." The others ambled over. "Show Doc your tongue," he said, calling me by that name because he knew I had worked in a drugstore. Foley, the first person I had hit the night before, stuck out his tongue. It was stitched clear across where my uppercut had clamped it between his teeth. Because of that feat, they weren't interested in fighting me again. On the contrary, they looked upon me with such surprising respect that they wanted me to become the leader of their gang. I politely refused, retrieved my cap from one of them, who was wearing it, and went home.

Mahlon and I almost never drank hard liquor, but when we had a little money to spare we used to enjoy a few beers in the evening. On Halloween night that year, after Mahlon had entered medical school, we were drinking beer and reminiscing about Lititz. Mahlon began talking about his sweetheart back there, Lillie Baker, and my thoughts turned longingly to Erla Buch.

"Ike," I said, "how much money do you have?"

"A couple of bucks, Ike."

"Then let's hop a freight train and go see Lillie and Erla." Neither of us had ever ridden on a freight train in our lives, but it struck us as the only way to get to Lititz and still have enough money left over to take our girlfriends out when we got there.

We went down to the Pennsylvania Railroad yards and I saw a freight-train brakeman. "I'm a United States Express Company driver. My friend and I want to visit our girlfriends and do not have enough cash to pay for passenger fares. Where's your train going?" I asked him.

"West," he said. We hopped on a bumper between two cars, found a foothold on a narrow plank and put our arms through the brake wheel. The train ran unexpectedly fast for a freight and stirred such an icy wind between the cars that our hands and faces grew numb. After a long interval, it stopped, and the brakeman came along with a lantern.

"Where are you guys really going?" He asked us. We told him where we planned to get off.

"Do you know what you're on?" he asked. "This is the Empire Freight for the west coast. Don't stop in Lancaster. Tell you what, though; it'll slow down a little bit at the tower."

I knew that signal tower about a mile outside Lancaster, close to the silk mill where I had worked. "Ike," I said as we approached it, "there's a pretty high bank of cinders at that tower. We won't have any chance for fancy hopping off this train. We'd better jump just as soon as it slows down." Both of us tumbled all the way to the bottom of the bank of cinders, but happily only scuffed our numbed hands a little bit.

Mahlon was worried about what his father would say when we got to Lititz. I didn't have that problem, because a few months before my father had received a call from a Lutheran church in Trenton, New Jersey, and moved there with Mother and my two youngest sisters, Mildred and Dorothy. Katie by then had married a well-to-do young man named David Bricker and settled down in Lititz, where she spent the rest of her life cultivating her love of music — she played well enough, I think, to have become a concert pianist — and writing poems which occasionally were published in national literary magazines.

When we had walked the nine miles to Mahlon's house and greeted his mother, his father asked us in Pennsylvania German, "How did you get here?"

"Pop, we hopped a freight train," Mahlon replied.

"What kind of freight train holds people?" his father inquired.

"We came between the bumpers," said Mahlon timorously.

"Bei Gott, the next time you come up here, you come on a passenger," his father growled, and no more was said of our hair-raising night on the train.

About noon we went into town and ran into the football team, getting ready to leave for their annual game with Ephrata, a town about five miles east that had become Lititz' chief rival and, so far as I know, still is.

"Elmer! Curly!" one of the players shouted. "You've got to come along. You've got to play. We need you."

"I replied, you have your team, and I have only had a couple of hours sleep in two days." I tried to shrug them off.

"But we need you! Give your uniform to Curly," one of them said to a boy about my size. The next thing I knew, I was on the train to Ephrata, like it or not.

I played fullback and had a chance to make quite a few tackles in the early part of the game. I used to make pretty rough tackles — a big jump, dive, and hit the man as hard as I could.

One of the Ephrata players who was much heavier than I was broke through the line, and I leapt for him. He rose up at the same time, and we collided in midair, then collapsed in a heap with his hip on my right shoulder. I could hear my collarbone crack. There were no trainers or doctors with football teams in those days, but I didn't need anyone to tell me that I was in trouble. I had a greenstick fracture, and the bone was almost protruding through the skin. Two girls in a pony cart drove me to a local doctor, who strapped my collarbone and shoulder with tape. He advised me to see another doctor and have the break taken care of as soon as I got back to Lititz. But when I got back, Mahlon said, "Erla and Lillie are waiting for us." So I went to the barbershop to clean up and have a shave, then stopped off at the doctor's office in a hurry. He told me I ought to go into the hospital to have the break set, and I promised him that I would just as soon as I got back to Philadelphia. I was anxious to see Erla. But our date was miserable, literally so painful that I wished I had never hopped the train to begin with. I don't think Erla enjoyed the evening either. Whether it was that, or the fact that both of our horizons had broadened a great deal since high school days, I don't know, but we never dated again.

I was miserable on the train ride back to Philadelphia. As soon as we arrived, Mahlon took me directly to the Medico-Chirurgical Hospital, and I groaned at the irony of the inscription over the hospital entrance. "Think not the beautiful doings of thy soul shall perish unremembered," it admonished me, "they abide with thee forever."

Inside, an intern found my injury so swollen that he couldn't locate the fracture. He added about thirty yards of tape to my chest and shoulder and sent me home. By the next morning I felt even worse so I went over to Hahnemann Hospital, where I knew a surgeon named Nelson Hammond. He got the hospital's top surgeon and two other doctors to help him. One of them put his knee in the small of my back, and two others grabbed my shoulders, while the fourth pushed the collarbone down, then they taped me up tighter than ever. It was six weeks before I could begin lifting trunks off my express wagon again.

With Trenton so nearby, it was not long before my father had to visit Philadelphia on church business, and he came to see me. I already knew that he was dismayed by my decision to quit work in the pharmacy and take a semiskilled muscle job on an express wagon. He expressed his disappointment more forcefully than ever when he visited me. But even without the motivation of his unhappiness, I was ready to resume my old career. Express hauling was a rough business, and if I had been born in this world for a purpose, I did not think it was to spend my life lifting heavy trunks. Except for my working uniform, however, I had only one suit, and it was badly worn, so I knew that I wouldn't look presentable enough for a drugstore job in one of the better neighborhoods. I settled for Philadelphia's Irish Hell's Kitchen, a rundown neighborhood on Gray's Ferry Road, where a physician druggist named Doctor Matthews maintained a pharmacy in his home. As with my first job in Philadelphia, I lived in, but Dr. Matthews, at least, let me eat with him and his wife. She fixed the stingiest meals I had ever encountered: a small piece of mackerel cut into three pieces, or two eggs scrambled and divided on three plates; Dr. Matthews and I were hungry all the time.

There was no other doctor in that poor neighborhood, so both Doc Matthews and I found ourselves practicing medicine. We revived attempted suicides and failed to revive a few; we tended injured people who came into the pharmacy for help. Once a man staggered into the store with a hatchet blade stuck in his head; we gave emergency first aid and called for help. He survived. Another time, I tried to save a seven-year-old girl whose legs had been severed by the wheels of a trolley car, but she died.

As soon as I had earned enough money for a new suit, I got a better job at Eshelman's Drug Store at 18th and Berks Streets, in a good section of town, and Mahlon and I again took a room together, this time in the home of Ed Walsh, my former wagon mate from the express company.

One day a lovely teen-aged girl with a peach-blush complexion, soft brown hair, and a perfect figure came into the store shedding tears from a cinder in her eye. I picked up a matchstick and a homemade instrument that most druggists kept handy for such emergencies: a small piece of wood with a hole at the end through which I had looped a strand of horse-tail hair. The girl confidently lifted her face to me as I turned back her eyelid with the matchstick and removed the cinder with the horsehair loop. She told me that her name was Ethel Rose. She was sixteen years old.

A few days later, she returned to the store, and I rushed to wait on her. After I had wrapped her few purchases, she asked me where I lived. I told her that I lived downtown with Mahlon Yoder, a twenty-minute trolley ride away. I wished that we could find a room closer to the store.

What a remarkable coincidence, she said. She and her mother lived with her aunt, a Mrs. Moore, who had a beautiful third-floor room for rent on Berks Street, just a half block away. Within a week, Yoder and I had moved into Mrs. Moore's room, far nicer quarters than Ed Walsh's, and far more genteel. It was time for the two of us to settle down after several rather impulsive years. He was working under heavy pressure at the medical school, and I was anxious to get my certificate as a Qualified Assistant Pharmacist, the final step before full certification as a Registered Manager Pharmacist.

I was getting most of my pharmaceutical education in libraries and at Leary's bookstore, one of my favorite haunts at the corner of Ninth and Ludlow. In those days they maintained used-book stalls, tucked under an overhanging shelter that projected from the wall of Leary's between Eighth and Ninth, and I liked to browse there. Among the old volumes, I had found fifteen or so medical books that I consumed in my self-administered education in pharmacy, and from reading them I had gained almost as good a knowledge of medicine as Mahlon had acquired at school. He was so confident of my understanding, in fact, that one day when he couldn't make it to Jefferson, he asked me to stand in for him in his surgery class. I went in Mahlon's place and watched "Black" Jack De Costa, a famous surgeon, remove a thirty-five-pound tumor from a woman. I gave Mahlon a detailed clinical description of it that evening. He said it was as good as if he had been there himself.

With my reading and my work — by now I had been filling prescriptions off and on since mid-1902 — I felt confident enough at age twenty to take the one-day examination for Qualified Assistant, and I passed it without difficulty. This permitted me to fill prescriptions and to take full charge of a drugstore for up to twenty-four hours without supervision, something that I had been doing anyway for months. The Registered Manager's examination, however, was much more difficult, and I wanted as much time as I could have to study for it. While reading the paper at work one day I received a shock. The Pennsylvania Legislature had passed an amendment to the pharmacists licensing law decreeing that after December 31, 1905, that very year, the minimum requirement for Registered Managers would include three years in an accredited college of pharmacy. Unless I could get in under the wire, I had no chance at all. The list for the last open examination was to close on December 1, and applicants had to be twenty-one years old by that time. I moved my birthday back three weeks so that I could get on the list and applied for the last examination.

While waiting in a hallway for the examination to begin, I chatted with a middle-aged druggist who had been in business for a number of years but had failed in his previous attempts to pass the manager's test. He was worried. "If I fail again, I'll have to hire a Registered Manager to· supervise the store," he said, "and my profits aren't big enough for that. I'll be out of business."

During the laboratory phase of the two-day test, we were required to mix a number of prescriptions. I watched my hallway acquaintance out of the corner of my eye as he failed twice to make a proper emulsion of turpentine, which was prescribed but rarely for chronic bronchial conditions. I was overcome with sorrow for the man whose failure would mean the loss of his livelihood. Whether he passed the test, I never learned. I was satisfied enough to be informed a week later that I had scored a high grade and was, from that day forward for the rest of my life, a full-fledged Registered Pharmacist.

Mahlon, meanwhile, had been doing extremely well in medical school and was ready for his final examinations. There was not the slightest doubt that within a few weeks he would be graduated near the top of his class as a Doctor of Medicine, and I was already thinking of a suitable celebration to mark the momentous occasion. He went off to his final surgery examination one morning, bright and cheerful as always. But when he came home in the evening, he looked as if every ounce of his spirit had drained away.

"Ike, I can't take it," he said. "I just can't take it. I don't know what to do."

"Tell me what's wrong. You look terrible."

"I got caught giving some notes to a couple of other guys who weren't doing so well. I wanted to help them out. Now I'm not going to pass because of it. I've got to repeat the whole year to get my degree. It'll cut me down. I'm ruined. My father carried stones on his wagon all his life to pay for this education, and look what I've done. It will kill him. My girl Lillie. I don't know what to do, Ike. I can never go home to Lititz again."

While he was explaining his awful plight, I was thinking.

"Yes, you can go home, Ike," I said. "I've got an idea. You sit tight here, and I'll go up to Lititz and talk to them."

"What can you say? I'll be disgraced. I'll not be able to practice medicine there, even if I do finish school. I'll be disgraced."

"No, you won't. You'll be honored."

"Are you crazy, Ike?"

"No. Listen. I'll see your father and mother first, and I'll see Lillie, and then I'll see all the guys we know. And I'm going to tell them that I've got great news for them. That you won't be back for another two or three weeks, and that you've done so well — that's the truth, isn't it? — that you've decided to take another year, so that you can become an even better doctor, a real star in medicine. You won't have to explain a thing, because I'll circulate that story all over town."

No one doubted my story. On the contrary, they were all

proud of Mahlon, and he did nothing to disillusion them when he got home. It did not bother my conscience in the least to have concocted that disingenuous explanation for his extra year of medical school. He was a superior medical student, and the forbidden act which got him into trouble was one of compassion, not of dishonesty. If he had been forced to live with its terrible consequences, he probably would never have finished medical school. As it was, he graduated without trouble the following year, returned to Lititz, married Lillie, and hung out his shingle. I don't know how many thousands of babies he delivered, but I do know that there are people still living in Lititz today who would be dead had it not been for the skill and devotion of Dr. Mahlon Yoder. He went on to take special courses at the Harvard Medical School in later years, became the Lancaster County coroner and President of the county Medical Society, and he served with distinction on the school board and the county Board of Health.

Mahlon died in December, 1969, at age eighty-eight, and was buried in the Lutheran cemetery in Lititz beside his wife, Lillie. I marked his passing with two main regrets. One was that he had been the last living person with whom I could reminisce over the toughest and best years of my youth — now we would never reminisce again; and the other was that I had not seen him for a few years, and I never had the chance to say, "Goodbye, Ike."

"Sometimes methinks that the precious mental relics of younger days oft become the most delightful pleasures of old age."

*The author's first wife, Ethel, and
his mother, in the late 1930s.*

Chapter Four

● There were two places in Philadelphia that became deeply familiar to me during 1906 and early 1907, one for its intellectual fare and the other for its emotional significance. The latter was Willow Grove, where orchestras and important bands — notably that of John Philip Sousa — gave free concerts. By this time, my brief thrill at administering first aid to my landlady's niece, the lovely young Ethel Rose, had ripened into a full-scale infatuation. I went walking with her at every opportunity and took her by trolley to every concert that was offered in the park. Willow Grove became dear to us both. My feeling for Ethel soon was so obvious, in fact, that her mother, a straight-laced Roman Catholic, with a distinct aversion to Protestants, decided to separate us.

Ethel and her mother had been living with Auntie Moore while Mr. Rose was away working in Jersey City. Quietly, and without saying in so many words that she thought me an unsuitable companion for her daughter, Mrs. Rose rented a small house in another part of Philadelphia and moved. But still Ethel and I managed to see each other, meeting for a bowl of green turtle soup at a lunch counter in the evening, or going to the park concerts on weekends. The more Mrs. Rose resisted our relationship, the more determined I became to continue it, and I am a stubborn fellow.

My intellectual fare was provided by the vast old Mercantile Library on 10th Street. It became my university, and I went there often, with a purpose. Studying for my final examination in pharmacy had reacquainted me with the excitement of learning, and I didn't want to stop there. Moreover, I had begun to form an entirely new ambition, having by now given up any thought of studying medicine. I had no desire to return to a religious career, either, but my new ambition involved the same kind of reformist zeal. The papers every day were filled with stories of the rottenness of the old Matthew Quay and Boise Penrose machines that ran the government with ruthless disregard for honest principles. Izzie Durham, Sonny Jim McNichol of the "Gas House Gang," and the Vare brothers were making fortunes on shady city contracts. I wanted to prepare myself to help clean up the corruption under which the governments both of Philadelphia and of Pennsylvania were sagging.

It seemed to me that the only way a man could acquire enough power to be able to throw the rascals out would be through the legal profession. I decided to study law, without going to college, and pass the bar examination. I had, after all, passed my pharmacy exams without much trouble, so I was emboldened to believe law would present no great obstacle, either. Little did I know.

I have always believed in planning before acting, and my plan was quite straightforward. After passing the bar exam I would become an assistant district attorney and establish a reputation as a prosecutor. Later I would become a defense attorney in private practice and gain more renown. Then, when the opportunity arose, I would enter politics, first as a Republican candidate for district attorney of Philadelphia, then for mayor, and finally for governor of Pennsylvania. It did not strike me as too great an ambition for a 21-year-old druggist, not even when I found out what was involved in just the preliminary bar exam, the prelude to the full-scale professional tests. To pass the preliminary tests, I would need virtually the equivalent of a four-year course in a liberal arts college. Then I would have to gain a clerical job in a law firm, find a preceptor to sponsor me, and study law for the final bar exam.

One of the greatest advantages of youth is confidence based on inexperience: I had so little notion of how difficult it was going to be to cram that much education into my head without the benefit of formal schooling that I went ahead without a qualm. Nothing was impossible. I went down to Leary's used-book stalls and invested about forty dollars in some of the books that I would need. In my spare time I haunted the Mercantile Library, spending hours with my elbows on an oak table and my head bowed over open books. The building was silent as a tomb, dominated by ancient, stained-glass windows that filtered varied beams of sunlight onto the reading tables below. There was a glass-panelled room at the back where chess players sat all day, contemplating their moves, and I used to envy not only their leisure but the fact that it was the only room in the building where one was permitted to smoke, a pernicious habit that I had by then adopted. When I did have a moment to spare there, however, I never joined the smoking chess players; I took my pleasure in looking over the library's famous collection of rare books, an antiquarian's delight. (I became so enamoured of the old volumes and looked forward to a day in the future when I would be able to acquire a fair-size collection of first and limited editions of leading authors, especially American and the English schools.) One of my finest hours was when I received an original copy of *Poor Richard's Almanac,* printed by Benjamin Franklin in 1758, given to me as a present from the Board of Trustees of New York University.

Benjamin Franklin, in my opinion from my early youth, was one of the great, perhaps the greatest, American in history I became a student of his life.

I was careful about plotting my course of study, based upon what I thought I would be asked at the examination. Among other things, I reviewed all of my high school mathematics and independently extended my knowledge through college algebra and geometry; I read and memorized extensive passages of the books of fifteen major English authors, studied political and economic geography, Latin, ancient history, and the histories of England and America.

At first I tried to fit this in with my full-time job at Eshelman's drugstore, but it soon became apparent that the two would not work easily, so in order to gain more flexibility in my schedule, I quit the job and began freelancing as an odd-shift pharmacist in various drugstores that needed relief help. For this I earned $1.50 for ten hours of work, and $3.00 if I worked all day on Sunday. It was not enough to support me through my studies, so I took an additional job, selling sundry rubber goods to Philadelphia drugstores. I carried my books with me to read in spare moments during the day, and studied every night, rarely sleeping more than four hours before it was time to go to work again.

As the date of the exam approached, I found two young men who had been taking night courses at Temple University in preparation for the same preliminary bar test. I arranged with them to review the material we were required to master. Each night at 11, when my duties in whatever drugstore I was working in were ended, I would join them. We rehearsed and grilled one another in the various subjects until 2 or 2:30 A.M. Frequently I would have to report to another pharmacy counter for work or begin my rounds as a rubber goods salesman at 7 A.M. Still, I found time to see Ethel Rose, despite her mother's strong objections. By now Mrs. Rose had flatly forbidden Ethel permission to see me at all. Her Auntie Moore, my landlady, sympathized with our predicament and helped us to get together, although I might add that she almost always was in attendance as our chaperone. Young love was not so free in those days as it is now; but we didn't mind. It was enough to be together.

On July 9, 1907, I reported to City Hall to take the preliminary bar examination, after preparing for the better part of a year. About 150 of us, including my two cramming companions, took seats at small desks in a huge room that was overseen by twenty court tipstaves perched around us on high chairs. The overseers were so determined to forestall any cheating that if a candidate for the exam even wanted to go to the bathroom he had to be accompanied throughout the occasion by a tipstaff. The examination lasted three days, and I can still remember most of its content, sixty-four years later.

First I took up a folded sheet of paper from my desk. It informed me that I had ninety minutes in which to write an essay of at least 1,000 words on "The Course of Study that has Benefited Me the Most." I took English literature, which of course had been my favorite since reading my father's books as a child, and managed to write fast enough to exceed the minimum length in an hour and a half. The mathematics section of the test consisted entirely of algebraic equations, which presented no difficulty, but some other sections of the arduous three-day test were enough to make my head swim. Some of them, I remember, were:

"Name five important Greek philosophers, and explain the method of teaching of each."

"Translate these passages from English into Latin." (There followed several lengthy paragraphs of translation text.)

"Translate into English the given passages from Cicero, Caesar, and Virgil." (Again, several lengthy paragraphs of translation.)

"Identify the authors of each of the given quotations and name the works in which they appeared." (Followed by quoted passages from various authors, some of which were quite obscure.)

"Give in chronological order the rulers of England from the beginning to the present, and state by what intermarriage they ascended the throne."

"What was the Guy Fawkes Gunpowder Plot?"

"What were the Star Chamber Proceedings?"

There was much, much more, some of which I knew and some of which I did not. Ethel met me at City Hall at the end of the third day and we celebrated my final departure from the test room with an ice cream soda. On the trolley, taking her home, I became so nauseated from the emotional tension of the last three days that I had to run to the back platform and throw up. The tension was not to be entirely relieved for some time,

however. The test results, which naturally I was anxious to discover, were not to be announced until September.

Ethel and I, in the meantime, were undergoing an even
deeper anxiety. Her mother's efforts to separate us had served
only to drive us closer together and left me with a stubborn determination to win her away from her family for good. I began
reading extensively about Catholicism, so that I would know what
I was up against, and started diplomatically working on Ethel's
conversion to Prostestantism, for it was inconceivable to me that
I could deny my own father's ministry by becoming a Catholic.
Religious differences such as ours are not so pronounced today
as they were, a significant advance in tolerance and understanding
that all of us must applaud; but at that time, the courtship of
a Protestant and a Catholic was considered scandalous on both
sides. Thus, without the slightest possibility of gaining the advance approval of Ethel's parents or mine, we continued our
courtship in secret. My advantage lay in Ethel's heart: she loved
me more than she loved her mother or the church.

Not long after the preliminary bar examination, she went
with Mrs. Rose to Atlantic City for a short vacation and I followed, meeting her clandestinely on the Steel Pier when her
mother wasn't about. On the eve of my return to Philadelphia
we were strolling along the pier, both almost overcome by the
mixed joy and anguish of frustrated young love, when she turned
her face up to me and said, "I can worship God as a Prostestant."

At that moment we became secretly engaged, and soon we
had made plans to elope. My salary then, while small, was
enough, I thought, to support us. I had given up free-lancing
as soon as I completed the bar exam and took a twenty-one-dollar
a week job as a full-fledged pharmacist in the Rothwell and Cameron drugstore at 15th and South Streets. I had not been working at the job long enough to accumulate any savings, however.
So I went to my employer, Charles Cameron, who was to figure
prominently in my life again many years later, and borrowed
twenty dollars with which to spirit Ethel away to New York.

As my father wrote in his boyish letter from Antietam, "the
bomps (figuratively) siselt over our hats," but we were "gay and

happy yet" when we arrived at Pennsylvania station. We climbed into a two-passenger hansom cab and asked the driver to take us to the Little Church Around the Corner, which was world-renowned for the number of couples married there. The place was as cold as a heatless office; a dozen embarassed couples were sitting in a barren waiting room, where a clerk told us to "sit down and fill out this form."

"This is too commercial for me," I retorted. "I can't do it."

Innocently, we wandered around downtown New York, looking for another church in which to get married, but we couldn't find one. With time running short, we returned to the Little Church Around the Corner, but in doing so, we found even more couples than we encountered before. I repeated. "We'll either have to find another place or come back to New York again on another day." Ethel was as much put off by the place as I was. We got into another hansom cab. In a final attempt to solve our problem I asked the driver, "Do you know this town well?"

"I certainly do," he said.

"Well, can you find me the house of a clergyman?"

"There's a church not far from here," he replied. "I'll take you to it."

He drove us to the Dutch Reformed Church at Fifth Avenue and 29th Street, now the Marble Collegiate Church of my friend, the Reverend Norman Vincent Peale. The minister and his wife had just returned from summer vacation. He obligingly read the marriage service in the parlor of his parsonage while his wife stood up as our witness. As the brief ceremony progressed, I recalled my father, presiding over hundreds of weddings in Clear Springs and Lititz and decorously concealing his hope that the groom would present him with a decent honorarium. Usually it was a dollar, but often not even that. I remembered one groom who gave him only seventy-five cents. Some gave him nothing. When the ceremony ended, I handed the Dutch Reformed minister a five-dollar bill, far more than I could afford. He seemed pleased. The date was August 15, 1907.

When we returned to Philadelphia, we kept our secret from

all but one person, Auntie Moore. She had been so kind and encouraging to us when the rest of Ethel's family were determined to keep us apart that we felt we had to share our momentous news with her. But she told no one, and until Thanksgiving Day neither Ethel's parents nor mine knew that we were married. My apprehension over the reception the news would receive when we did reveal it was exacerbated by the actions of my brother, Harry. Without even knowing what Ethel and I had done, he ran off to New York a week after our wedding and married an Irish Catholic girl whom he met there. She was a lovely, charming girl and my mother and father accepted her, but I knew they were crushed because she remained a steadfast Catholic, and Harry had agreed that their children would be raised in her religion.

For Ethel and me, secret connubial life was hectic but blissful. Auntie Moore, a lively, attractive forty-five-year-old woman who had been twice widowed, happily indulged us our stolen hours together. Only two occasions interrupted our total concentration upon each other during our brief conspiracy of silence. One was on September 17th, when I received formal notice that I had passed the preliminary bar examination, subject only to reexaminations in Latin and English History. My two cramming companions failed. For me it was a tremendous victory, for I feared that I might have failed altogether, too; now, with only two subjects to concentrate on for the reexamination, I had no doubt that I would pass and carry on with my ambitions as a political reformer.

But the second occasion put a sharp brake on the expectations generated by the first. Before Thanksgiving, it became clear to Ethel and me that we could not by any stretch of the imagination keep our marriage a secret much longer.

At Ethel's insistence, Mrs. Rose grudgingly permitted me to join her family for Thanksgiving dinner. After we had eaten, Ethel courageously addressed her mother:

"I want to announce that Elmer and I eloped and were married in New York on August 15th."

Mrs. Rose blanched. "Who married you?"

"A Dutch Reformed clergyman."

"You're not married," said her mother, positively. "How can you be? You're a Catholic. You cannot be married by a Dutch Reformed minister."

"Mother, I'm no longer a Catholic." There was a pause while Mrs. Rose absorbed her second shock. Then Ethel added, "Furthermore, Mother, I'm going to have a baby." It was a grim evening thereafter.

There was a grumbling acquiesence in Ethel's family when we set up housekeeping together, but it had a disquieting undertone, and I soon discovered why. The depth of suspicion and hostility that existed between Catholic and Protestant Americans in those days occasionally led to violence, and that seemed to be what was in store for us. We learned that Ethel's mother, supported by a few of her male friends, planned to kidnap our baby when it was born and have it baptized as a Catholic. Fortunately, the gestation of a child is sufficiently long to allow sometimes for the gestation of common sense. By the time our son, Elmer Walton Bobst, was born on June 3, 1908, I had managed to negotiate with Ethel's mother and father my own "Treaty of the Roses" bringing our two families together in a more agreeable union. Mrs. Rose remained somewhat cool, but Ethel's father put out his hand and said, "Son, all I ask is that you take good care of my girl." He even took to attending my father's church a few years later.

When Ethel became pregnant I saw no reason, at first, to alter our plans for the future. I was ready to proceed with my law studies, and even registered informally to become a clerk-student with the prestigious law firm of Simpson and Brown, both of whose senior partners, Francis Jenk Brown and Alexander Simpson, were to become attorneys general of Pennsylvania. But soon I realized that law, marriage, and fatherhood were for me a poor mix. I was working at Charles Cameron's drugstore from seven-thirty in the morning until eleven at night, and if I was to have even a few minutes a day to spend with Ethel and, later, with our son, I had to give up my studies. I told myself that some day when time permitted I would resume them and become a lawyer, but that day never came. A business career, in which I am still intensely active, intervened.

● *Chapter Five*

● In his tragic play, *Death of a Salesman,* Arthur Miller's requiem for Willy Loman includes these lines: "A salesman is got to dream, boy. It comes with the territory." I suppose that my dreams — my whole taste for business — began on the day when, as a seven-year-old, I first shouldered a basket of Mr. Bowman's bakery goods and started selling them door-to-door. Even then, unlike Willy Loman, I think I realized that a successful salesman has to have far more than a smile and a shoeshine if he wants to excel. He must have the intellectual power to match his mind, as he would his physical strength, against the brain of the man he wants to sell; for the good salesman must convince his customer that he needs something for which he has no desire whatever. There is no trick or skill to selling an article to someone who knows that he needs it; the skill is in selling to someone who doesn't need the product, or at least doesn't know that he needs it. Obviously this requires a pleasant personality and an innate curiosity that focuses on the needs of other people; but a salesman's enthusiasm must not be effervescent or overbearing, lest his potential customer become afraid that he is being put on, or fooled.

I liked to sell, largely for the same reason that I enjoyed it when I was seven years old. I simply enjoyed meeting people and learning something about them. In addition, I think I had

a naturally competitive spirit from my earliest childhood, and selling not only lent me self-confidence, but sharpened my competitive instincts. In a sense, a salesman enters a competitive arena
every time he faces a potential customer; he engages in intellectual
conflict with a persón whom he knows is going to resist him,
and he has to overcome that resistance. The payoff, whether it
is on a nickle-profit item or a $400-million corporate merger, both
of which I have "sold" successfully, comes when the customer
(or competitor) agrees that he is getting as good as he is giving,
that he really needs the product, and buys.

Salesmanship at Cameron's drugstore was a haphazard affair
that generally depended upon the customer knowing what he
needed before he even entered the store. He bought that one
article and left without being urged to think of other needs. As
a result, the stock moved slowly. One particular product called
"Hot Springs Blood Remedy," an iron tonic that did iron deficiency victims at least some good, was vastly overstocked and
moved at the rate of only about a bottle a month. It was a challenge to me. I cornered every customer who came into the store,
struck up a friendly conversation, then pointed out the gravity
of iron deficiency, about which medicine knew little those days.
It was enough to inquire whether the customer felt tired or
"washed out" and to suggest the possible cause. Within three
weeks I had cleared the shelves of "Hot Springs Blood Remedy,"
and customers were coming back for more.

When it came time to reorder, a representative of the Frederick Stearns Company of Detroit, which made the tonic,
showed up at the store. His name was Penrose Jones, and he
was an old-fashioned travelling drummer, the kind of salesman
who was as ubiquitously American as high-buttoned shoes in those
times, but whom I would prefer not to have on my sales staff
today. He had a way of instantly sizing up the personality of
a store manager and adjusting his own character, like a chamele-
on's coloration, to suit the background. If the pharmacist appeared to be a religious person, Penrose would open his sales
spiel with a short prayer. If the customer was a more earthy man,
Penrose would launch into a thigh-slapping dirty joke. He could

drink and play poker, or pray and commiserate with the best of them. I didn't like him, but I found his sales tactics amusing to observe, and he was responsible for my first important sales job. He was so astonished by my extraordinary sales of "Hot Springs Blood Remedy" that he reported it to his home office, which promptly offered me a commissions job as the Stearns salesman for Philadelphia county, lower New Jersey, and west as far as Harrisburg. My product was the Nyal line, a group of pharmaceutical products that included the blood remedy, cures for liver and kidney ailments, a cough remedy, muscle liniment, and some other proprietary products. Proprietaries are the non-prescription pharmaceutical products — including the "patent" remedies of the old days — that are advertised generally to the lay public. There were no "ethicals" — prescription drugs advertised only to the medical and dental professions — in the Nyal line, so I called only on drugstores in my territory, not doctors. The attractive thing about the Nyal remedies was that they were sold on an exclusive franchise arrangement under which one store in a marketing area was guaranteed exclusive rights to their sale and could market them as its own house products.

As a working pharmacist myself, I was in a good sales position when I went out into my territory with the line, and I soon had about twenty-five stores signed up for Nyal franchises. Even with a steady stream or reorders, however, my commissions were small, and my travel expenses, which I had to pay out of my own pocket, made them shrink even more. So I supplemented the sales income by working several nights a week as a pharmacist. Ethel, little Walton, and I struggled through an impoverished summer in two furnished rooms that we rented on North 11th Street for twenty dollars a month.

In retrospect, it was a dismal beginning. We were in the midst of what was called the Teddy Roosevelt Depression of 1907-08, so even the commissions that I earned came in slowly. I had to hustle for reorders, hope that my customers could pay for then when they arrived, and then hope that the company sent my commission promptly after that. To add to the hectic nature of life, Ethel knew nothing about cooking or about babies, so

I had to teach her to prepare meals, something that I had learned from my mother, and to take care of Walton. Fortunately, I had cared for both of my baby sisters — Mildred and Dorothy — after they were born, so Walton did not pose a completely bewildering problem to me. Even so, the first eighteen months of his life were a physical ordeal for all of us. Walton suffered from an intestinal ailment and cried a good deal, which tired Ethel so much during the day that she was exhausted when I came home late at night. Together we would prepare dinner on a three-ring gas burner behind a screen in one corner of our "living" room; then we would wash our laundry in the bathtub of the community lavatory down the hall from our rooms, and finally I would spend half the night walking Walton to relieve his discomfort until he slept. For both Ethel, still a protected child, really, at eighteen, and me, an exhausted twenty-three-year-old, the challenge and ardor that had swept us into marriage had faded into a mutual struggle for survival.

I suppose that the initial passions of many marriages are blunted by the grim realities of privation and the responsibilities of early parenthood. This trauma, in fact, is responsible for the high rate of divorce among couples who marry young, according to most authorities. While it did not have so conclusive an effect upon us, it did undermine the sweet, romantic emotions on which our marriage was based. The circumstances of our life together abruptly changed us from two persons who were wholly absorbed in loving one another, to two persons who still loved each other but were almost wholly absorbed in making ends meet today, then trying to catch a moment's rest for the next day's struggle. Once a marriage has descended thus from its first romantic peak, there seems no way to ascend that high again. From all that I have read and heard from others, that is a common, and regrettable, experience. Although we lived contentedly and often happily together for almost half a century, we never recaptured our initial ardor. It was as if our lives from then on followed parallel but independent pathways, climbing, turning and going onward side by side, but never fully merging as we had dreamed they would when we were married.

Our troubles, actually, were compounded by my success as a Nyal salesman for the Stearns company. Penrose Jones, with his unquenchable drummer's enthusiasm and sales ability, talked me into accepting a "promotion," working under his brother, who ran the New York office. The move was not too bad in a business sense. I found that I could sell just as well in New York as I had in New Jersey and Pennsylvania, although my customers, all hardened, big-city pharmacists, were a tougher breed. But the move was an unqualified personal disaster. Instead of improving our living conditions, it worsened them.

Ethel's father found a room for us in a theatrical boarding house in Jersey City, and I commuted from there to Brooklyn each day. The boarding house was an awful place, half-filled with poor workingmen and half with transient actors, some of whom skipped out without paying their rent, leaving empty theatrical trunks behind. Our room was cramped, with a sagging old double bed and a bassinet for Walton. The paint and wallpaper had been fingermarked by a hundred previous tenants, and the open windows admitted hordes of monstrous mosquitos until I stretched cotton netting over them. There were several ratholes in the baseboards. When I realized what they were, I stuffed broken bottles into the apertures. At night we could hear the rats working to clear the obstacles away.

Ethel's only companion during the days was the woman in the room next door, the wife of a foreman of sandhogs who was working on the first tunnel under the Hudson River to unite the island of Manhattan with the Pennsylvania Railroad, which at the time ended its run in its station in Jersey City. One day her husband, a Scotsman, came in from the job with a sorely infected thumb. I had become fairly expert in treating local wounds and infections. Having him take off his shirt, I found ominous signs of swollen lymphatic glands in his arm pit. To me this was a signal of the possibility of blood poisoning. At that time, a real case of blood poison usually proved to be fatal. I cut away the rotting around the wound. Then I prepared a one-to-two-thousand solution of bichloride of mercury and had him cover the wound with solution-soaked bandages night and day.

He recovered. From then on we at least had two friends in the wretched place upon whom we could rely. But the dirt, dissolution, and dreadful food of the boarding house were more than we could stand. One evening Ethel looked at me woefully and said, "Dearie, I never ate so many fried potatoes in my life." I resolved that it was time to go home to Philadelphia. Only once in my life, when I resigned the presidency of one of the largest pharmaceutical companies in the world, did I take more pleasure in quitting a job than when I left the Stearns company for good.

Back in Philadelphia I resumed working my old south Jersey to Harrisburg territory, this time for the Frederick F. Ingram company, selling perfumes and a fast-moving cosmetic item called Milkweed Cream, which, among other virtues, was supposed to remove freckles. My sales calls were phenomenally successful, but the Roosevelt Depression made most of them pointless; day after day I would find as many as four out of five of my orders cancelled because my customers were delinquent in their accounts or could not meet Ingram's credit requirements. I was barely making expenses. As I made my rounds, I would see long lines of men and women waiting for something to eat at public soup kitchens. They were unemployed and penniless. I knew that if the credit pinch continued, my shrinking commissions might present us with a similar plight. Reluctantly, because I preferred active selling to standing behind a counter, I decided to go back to my work as a pharmacist. But this time I wanted to work in the best drugstore in town.

George B. Evans, who pioneered the all-service drugstore in Philadelphia, was the giant of local druggists at that time. He owned five stores that were probably the most innovative retail drug outlets in the United States. Thirty or forty identical delivery wagons, all bearing the slogan "Get It at Evans," were in constant use, shuttling around the city. All the stores were in good locations, and they had even become social centers of sorts because Evans was the first druggist to combine food service and gift shelves with the regular soda, sundries, and prescription services of his stores. He also was making a small profit on the side from a then unmentionable product called MUM (the epochal advertising creation "B.O." was still many years away), which he bought from two elderly ladies who owned the formula and manufactured the cream in their home.

Evans was a pioneer in other areas, too. The most appealing to me was his enlightened attitude towards his employees. Working hours were from 8 A.M. to 6 P.M. one day, 10 A.M. to 10 P.M. the next, with Sundays off. Not many people would like that kind of work schedule today, but after my experience it seemed the most leisurely business routine imaginable. Evans' zealous pursuit of enlightened business practices presented me with a major obstacle, however. In his commendable efforts to upgrade the profession and help the Philadelphia College of Pharmacy, of which he was a trustee, he refused to hire any prescriptionist who lacked a college diploma.

A little apprehensive, but determined to succeed, I dressed neatly in my best suit and called on George B. Evans at his main store on Chestnut street. He stared at me coldly and said, "Well, what do you want?"

"I've come to you for a position."

"What kind of position?"

"As a prescriptionist."

"What college did you graduate from?"

"I didn't graduate from college, Mr. Evans."

He looked sternly at the doorway, as if wondering who had let me in to waste his time. "I never hire any prescriptionist who is not a college graduate, and I prefer them to be graduates of the Philadelphia College of Pharmacy. Good day."

I had been expecting that response, but I was determined to hold my ground.

"Mr. Evans, I could not afford to go to a college of pharmacy. My father is a clergyman with a very poor salary. I wish I could have gone to the Philadelphia College, but I could not even borrow the money to go there. I had to get second-hand books and library books and study on my own while I apprenticed with other pharmacists. I passed both of my examinations, for Qualified Assistant and for Registered Manager, before I was twenty-one years old."

"That's very interesting, but I have my rules and I stick by them. We have twenty-four prescriptionists in my stores, and every one of them is a graduate of a college of pharmacy. I've never hired one who wasn't."

"Mr. Evans, I know you insist on college graduates," I continued my quiet plea. "But I know that you respect professional skill. I'm willing to work a week for you for nothing if you will give me the chance. If I cannot fill prescriptions as well as or better than your best men, it will cost you nothing."

That startled him. "Wait a minute," he said and called out to Bob Matter, the manager of the store. "Bob, here's a young fellow who wants a job. He did not go to college, but he's a Registered Manager. Claims he can fill prescriptions as well as anyone in your department, and if he can't prove that to you in a week, he'll work for nothing. What do you think?"

Matter looked sympathetically at me and said, "Why not give him a chance?"

"All right. Your name Bobst? Go down there. Bob will report to me. I'll start you at seventeen dollars a week if you work out."

My tryout week passed smoothly; I stood beside several other young pharmacists at a long double prescription table with my own scales, mortar, and small bottles of commonly used chemicals, filling forty or more prescriptions a day. In a sense, the tryout was something of a breeze because I had more experience than the recent college graduates, who had constantly to stop and check references in the *U.S. Pharmacopeia*. Furthermore, it was the first time in my career that I didn't have to pause between prescriptions to write out their labels; a typist did that for us on a bat-winged Oliver typewriter as each preparation was completed. At the end of the week I became the first, and so far as I know the only, self-made pharmacist who ever worked for George B. Evans.

Bob Matter was a literate fellow and an agnostic who liked the works of the iconoclasts Elbert Hubbard and Robert Ingersoll. Knowing that I was the son of a clergyman, he delighted in teasing me by walking up behind the prescription table and announcing in a gloomy voice, "Mr. Bobst, Jerusalem is not yet." Or,

"And will there, some time, be another world?" One day he came up to me and said, "Bobst, here's a book I think you will find worth reading."

I thought he was pulling my leg with an Ethical Society tract, but instead he handed me a book entitled *How to Become Rich*. I can't recall who wrote it or much about what he had to say, because it was mostly nonsense. But one remark — a trite one, to be sure — made a lasting impression because it found me at just the right time. The author wrote that you can have anything that you want in this world, providing that you want it badly enough and that you are willing to work patiently, continually, and hard to get it. It was a cliché, but the virtue of many clichés is that they are true and they present worthy ideas in shorthand form. I was ripe for that worthy idea.

At the time there were a number of things that I wanted: more challenging work, preferably having to do with sales; a chance to progress to an independent, managerial position; and a better life for Ethel and Walton. These dreams would be a long time coming if I stood many years behind a drug counter. One day a fellow pharmacist named Strickler, who took care of the proprietary drug counter and filled few prescriptions, and hence had time for idle talk, began ruminating aloud over the possibilities of future advancement with George B. Evans. I had been advanced at that time from seventeen to twenty-one dollars a week.

"What about you, Bobst?" Strickler enquired. "Are you going to work your way up?"

"How far can you work your way up at Evans?" I asked him.

"Maybe twenty-five dollars a week," he said, "something like that."

"No," I said. "I shall stay here until I find an opportunity to better myself outside."

I already had begun looking for the opportunity. After fifteen months at George B. Evans I knew as well as Strickler did

that the future there was limited to a lifetime behind the counter
at low pay. In the evenings, as I rode home on the trolley, I
had taken to framing letters of application to various pharmaceutical houses, seeking a job as a sales detail man. A detail man
in the pharmaceutical business is a salesman who calls on physicians and professors of medical colleges, explaining the therapeutic values of his company's prescription drugs with the hope that
the doctors will be impressed enough by their effectiveness to
prescribe them for their patients. He was the principal educational link between the pharmaceutical manufacturers and the
medical profession, for despite advertising and articles in medical
publications, many physicians then did not learn of effective new
remedies until the detail men called upon them. Although still
a vital link today, he is not so important as he was when communications were more primitive.

As a salesman I had never called on physicians, but I had
come to know many of them well in the course of my prescription
work, so in my letters I made it clear that my medical contacts
were extensive; although I was careful not to state a bald untruth,
the implication was that I already had some experience as a detail
man.

Since my handwriting is a hurried, almost illegible scrawl,
I had Ethel copy the letters in her firm hand when I got home,
and we would mail them late at night.

One letter, which I took particular care in writing, was addressed to the American branch of a Swiss company, the
Hoffmann-La Roche Chemical Works at 65 Fulton Street in New
York. I knew nothing about the company, but Evans stocked one
of its products, an injectable form of the heart stimulant digitalis,
sold under the trade name of Digalen. I had been impressed
in filling Digalen prescriptions by the tasteful packaging and la-
belling of its red-stoppered, brown bottles. Any company that
took such care with its products, I reasoned, must be a good
one to work for. While many of the letters that I wrote went
unanswered, Hoffmann-La Roche replied promptly.

Mr. E. H. Bobst
2109 N. Camac Street
Philadelphia, Pa.

Dear Sir:

Your application for a position with our house is acknowledged with thanks, and while we are not at this moment in need of extra detail men salesmen we are pleased to place your name on our "waiting" list.

You should give us some idea of the remuneration you would expect.

Awaiting your further advices, we remain,

> *Yours very truly,*

> *H.R. Saunders*
> *Manager, Propaganda Dept.*
> *The Hoffmann-La Roche Chemical Works*

I drafted a reply telling Mr. Saunders that I would expect a salary of thirty-five dollars a week and gave it to Ethel to copy. "Dearie, please, thirty-five dollars is too much," she pleaded. "He will not even answer you. It would be wonderful if you got even twenty-five dollars. Make it twenty-five."

"No, leave it at thirty-five. I have indicated that I am a man of experience, and a figure of twenty-five dollars would be contrary to what I have implied."

On March 15, 1911, Saunders replied that the only "stumbling block" to considering my application favorably was my salary request. I wrote that I would meet the company half way, and he replied by asking me to come to New York, expenses paid, for an interview. On the train to New York I reviewed all of the literature I had been able to procure on digitalis and Digalen, the company's most important ethical drug product. When I arrived at the offices on Fulton Street, I knew the product almost as well as its makers.

I was only slightly put off by the dingy appearance of the establishment and its location in a rundown neighborhood near the fish market. Most pharmaceutical companies then were lo-

cated near waterfronts, and despite the desirability of clean surroundings they usually were just as grubby and haphazard in their
layout as ordinary manufacturing concerns. It was a small establishment, but I expected that, too, because the company's headquarters were in Basle, Switzerland, and most of its products,
already packaged, came from there. Only a few preparations were
bottled at the Fulton Street address.

Saunders already was favorably inclined to hire me on the
basis of my letters, so my interview with him went well. Afterwards, he introduced me to a strikingly handsome, nattily dressed
Prussian named Carl P. Schlicke, and the interview began again.
Schlicke was an imposing figure, the image of what passed before
World War I as a man-about-town. He let me know that he had
served with the German army and that he was a stickler for discipline. He was the general manager of the American office, an
autocrat, but for the most part an affable man. Perhaps he was
impressed by my knowledge of Digalen, or by the fact that I
was not cowed by his imposing presence. At any rate, he hired
me at thirty dollars a week starting April 15, 1911, to detail physicians in the Philadelphia area. The company would pay for car-
fare to make my calls, but all other expenses, including postage
on the daily reports that I was to mail to the New York
office, were to be borne by me.

Hoffmann-La Roche was a relatively young manufacturer
which produced about a dozen specialties, as well as quinine and
opium derivatives including heroin. In addition, they also produced a restricted line of bulk pharmaceutical chemicals such as
the fine alkaloids from plants, atropine, eserine, homatropine,
pilocorpine, and others. My responsibilities were strictly for the
specialty products. Another salesman, named William Pratt, older
and more experienced than I, handled the lucrative bulk pharmaceutical sales in my territory. Although we worked for the same
company, each of us operated from his own home, so we did
not see one another often. He called on drug manufacturers and
wholesalers, and I called on physicians.

Many salesmen in those days (and today, too, for that matter)
were unimaginative men who took the easiest path they could

find, falling into a routine like leaves into a stream and floating with it until the territory dried up. I had enough experience by then to realize the importance of working systematically to expand my contacts and to search out new sources of business for my company. My first act was to obtain a list of all the physicians in the area, carefully noting in each case whether the doctor was a general practitioner, a specialist, or a surgeon. Surgeons were of little interest to a detail man, because they wrote few prescriptions, and specialists were prized because there were so few of them — not many doctors specialized then, although most of them do today.

I also kept a meticulous diary in which I noted personal observations about each of my seven or eight calls a day. I would record the results of the call and add little observations such as the name of the doctor's medical school (from his framed diploma), or the presence of golf clubs or fishing tackle in his hallway, or his remarks about his family or his work. On my return call three to six months later, I could recall the details of a case he had described to me and inquire about its outcome or ask him how he enjoyed the fishing trip that he had been planning when I visited him last. This personal touch paved the way for a number of lasting friendships, and my physician friends taught me a great deal about medicine.

Within a few months, Hoffmann-La Roche sales in relation to the number of physicians in the Philadelphia area were at the top of the company's American list. It was not as prodigious a feat as it sounds, because the company only had eight detail men in the United States, but it was my doing and I was proud of it. I kept Philadelphia on top and finally the company rewarded my efforts with a ten-dollar-a-month raise. Even so, I was still a long way from the independence and financial security that I had dreamed of when I left George B. Evans.

Pratt's salary was not much more than mine, even though he had been with the company longer, had a larger territory that included Baltimore and Washington, and handled bigger and more profitable direct sales. His orders were for bulk quantities of basics such as quinine, strychnine, morphine, heroin, cocaine, atropine, homatropine, and other pharmaceutical chemicals, most of them imported from Basle.

From time to time, when I saw him he would complain of a weakness in his arms, but at first it didn't seem to trouble him too much. One night when we were both in New York on company business, we were having a drink together in an old ale house on John Street. Suddenly his pewter mug fell from his hands and the ale poured over his shoes. Almost in agony, he looked at me and said, "I can't control my hands anymore. I was carving a turkey at home and I knocked it off the table."

"Have you gone to a doctor?" I asked.

"The doctor says I have nervous trouble."

"I think you should see one of my friends," I said. I was well acquainted by then with all of the leading practitioners in Philadelphia. I took him to see Dr. Henry Beattes, Jr., who was one of the best.

"Elmer," Dr. Beattes told me later, "your friend is suffering from hemiplegia." It was a fatal brain disease.

As the paralyzing disease progressed, I helped Pratt with his calls and worked with him on his reports so that he would not be dropped from the payroll at such a critical time. He soon reached a point where he could no longer make calls at all, so I made them for him. Then he became bedridden and within a short time he died.

After Pratt's funeral I had to go to New York to report to Schlicke, who by this time had lost some of his Prussian stiffness and become quite friendly to me. Whenever I visited he would take me out on the town, dining and drinking in posh cabarets, or to the theater in his chauffeured car. He lived in an elegant house in Brooklyn Heights, one of the most fashionable residential areas of New York at that time and, although married, behaved as if he was a rich bachelor. I had no idea what his salary was but guessed that it had to be at least $50,000 a year to support his life style.

In the course of our evening together, I made a bold proposal. With Pratt gone, the company had to fill his place soon, and

I told Schlicke that I not only could fill it but could continue with my own ethical detail work as well.

"No, Mr. Bobst, that would never work," Schlicke scoffed. "Doubling up like that has never been successful. Both the selling and detailing will be bound to suffer. I refuse to agree to it."

"Mr. Schlicke, I know it will work. I'm so intent on making it work that I will guarantee you and Mr. Saunders two things: Number One, you will receive the same number of reports from me each day on my calls to the medical profession. Number Two, I will guarantee that within six months' time I will sell at least three times the amount of business that you received from Mr. Pratt. Furthermore, I will not ask for an increase in salary."

"You think you can do that?"

"I don't think, Mr. Schlicke, I know I can do it."

Within four months I had quadrupled Pratt's volume and still maintained my own at the top of the company's American list. I was firmly entrenched in both sides of the pharmaceutical business. In the mornings I called on doctors. I devoted the afternoons to calling on wholesale drug houses, pharmaceutical manufacturers, and the important hospitals. I left home at 7:30 in the morning, and oftentimes made my first call on a doctor before he had finished his breakfast. I worked in the afternoon until about six o'clock, arriving home about six-thirty, and after a half hour at the dinner table, went to my desk to begin typing my daily reports, which had to be in the mailbox for the ten o'clock pick-up.

My best customer was Smith, Kline and French, which raised its original order for Digalen from twenty-five vials to a thousand at a time. My worst customer was the William R. Warner Company, which never bought a thing. Warner was owned and run by two brothers, Gustavus A. and Henry Pfeiffer, who had formed a kind of small-scale pharmaceutical conglomerate by branching out from a St. Louis drugstore that they owned to buy and combine a number of small drug companies. Although they placed all of their bulk orders with Mallinckrodt, Merck, and other producers, they were very friendly to me whenever I called and seemed to enjoy my visits. But they never gave me an order. Now and again they would invite me to lunch with them at the Manufacturers Club, and I would suppress my normally robust appetite to match their eccentric tastes for healthy dishes such as rice and prunes; but still no orders.

Twice a week, for a full year, I called on the Pfeiffers, and each time one of them would say, "How do you do, Mr. Bobst? Sit down." We would have a friendly chat, but when I would bring up business, the reply was always the same: "Well, we can't give you anything today, Mr. Bobst. You see, we're tied up pretty well with what we have."

One Saturday morning I was simmering over my latest failure with the friendly Pfeiffers when suddenly I decided that the polite fencing had to stop. I grabbed my hat and started out the door.

"Where are you going?" Ethel asked me.

"I'm going down to Broad and Wallace Streets to the William R. Warner Company.

"This is Saturday. They won't be open today."

"The Pfeiffer brothers will be there whether the offices are open or not. They don't pay any attention to Saturdays."

When I got to Broad and Wallace Streets the Warner Company door was locked, but I could see the Pfeiffers inside, working at their high, stand-up desks. I knocked and one of them let me in.

"Why, Mr. Bobst, what are you doing here? This is Saturday."

"That's right, this is Saturday," I said. "I came down to see you. I want to talk to both of you."

"All right, come in." He was a little taken back by the firmness of my voice.

"Now, Mr. Henry and Mr. G. A.," I began, "you know you've been awfully kind to me. I've been calling on you for about a year, twice a week, and you've been sweet, and you've taken me to lunch, and you've patted me on the back, and up to now you haven't given me a single order. *But today is the day!*"

"What do you mean?"

"I mean today is the day when you are going to give me

Gustavus A. Pfeiffer, of the William R. Warner Company. The author made one of his first sales calls on the firm owned by Gus Pfeiffer and his brother Henry. Three decades later, he became the company's president.

an order. That's why I came down here." I threw my affable sales techniques out the window and gave both of them a scolding for ordering products from my competitors that were no better than, and in some cases not as good, as mine. Suddenly it was as if they were learning about Hoffmann-La Roche products for the first time. By noon, when I left their office, I carried signed orders for $5,000 worth of immediate deliveries and $15,000 on contract for the future. Not long after that, their orders were running at the rate of $100,000 a year.

The Pfeiffer brothers went into business with the philosophy that it is cheaper to buy goodwill than to create it, and a lot

quicker. Their entire history had been one of reaching out, acquiring companies with single, good products, and integrating
them into their own. The operation soon became a large one,
with plants in Philadelphia and St. Louis. One day in 1915 they
called and asked me to come to see them. They had bought the
Richard Hudnut Company, the leading cosmetics and toilet water
maker in the country, and were building a new plant to enlarge
their activities in Philadelphia.

"Mr. Bobst, we haven't asked you to come up here today
to give you an order," Henry Pfeiffer began the conversation.
"We asked you to come because we want your ideas."

"How can I help you?" I asked.

"Well, we have bought the Richard Hudnut Company."

"Yes, I know that."

"And we're building a new plant here."

"Yes, I know about that, too."

"Forget about the plant," Henry continued. "We can sell it
as it is and still make money on it if we decide we don't want
it. It's not finished, but we can sell it. The question is, do we
move Hudnut to Philadelphia, or do we move William R. Warner
to New York?"

Without batting an eye, I stood up and reached for my hat.
"Give me your hand, will you please?" I said. "Goodbye, Mr.
Henry. Goodbye, Mr. G. A. You can move William R. Warner
any place in the United States, but you cannot move a cosmetic
and perfume company out of New York. It has to be in New
York — Paris or New York — or you'll lose your shirts."

So they bought the old Altman Department Store at Sixth
Avenue and 18th Street and moved their company to New York.
Their decision, in which I suppose I played at least a small part,
had a decisive influence on my life thirty years later. It made
me a fortune and a second business career that continues today.

● *Chapter Six*

● Carl Schlicke had his faults — many, as it turned out — but frugality was not one of them. Fortunately, he did not hold me to my offer to handle both Pratt's old job and my own at the same small salary I had been receiving. As my sales increased, so did my income. Ethel and I at last were able to move out of the rented rooms we had occupied for more than five years and rent a two-story brick row house in a quiet, middle-class neighborhood. Walton was growing strong and healthy, without a trace of the sickness that had made his first year and a half miserable. We tussled happily together and, in a rudimentary way, I even began to teach him to box. Ethel at last had the freedom and the resources to visit her lady friends in the afternoons or to entertain them at bridge, which made her happy. She was not too intellectually inclined; although I tried to interest her in the books that I loved and in my work, she preferred quiet social activities. In contrast to our early years of deprivation, it was a good life. But the house has unhappy memories, too.

The depression had not been kind to Mr. and Mrs. Rose, who had separated, and each came at different times to live with us, and to die. Mrs. Rose had contracted tuberculosis while visiting a wealthy cousin in New Jersey and became desperately ill. When she came to us, I brought in a full-time nurse and called Dr. William Maitland Robertson, the first professor of medicine

91

at Temple University and, incidentally, the first physician in Philadelphia to have an electrocardiograph machine. He did all that he could, but the disease overwhelmed her pleural sac with fluids. Dozens of times I sat and held her hand while she underwent the ordeal of aspiration, with Dr. Robertson sometimes drawing as much as two quarts of fluid from her chest. Although she had been implacably hostile to me when Ethel and I were first married, she became devoted to me then and called me her "guardian angel." But no amount of tender loving care or medical attention could save her. She went to sleep one morning after a wakeful, pain-ridden night and never awakened.

Ethel's father came to live with us after he had been stricken with a coronary attack. He was a jovial man who paid little attention to diet and was rather proud of his corpulent 220 pounds. Mr. Rose made it clear to Ethel that he wanted large portions at his meals. Food and prodigious quantities of beer were his pleasure. One night after a particularly heavy meal I heard him coughing oddly in the bathroom. When I got to him he was gasping for breath and I knew that he had suffered another heart attack. I relieved his gasping with aromatic spirits of ammonia and got him back in bed. But his pulse grew weaker and weaker, like a train going off in the distance. He looked up as Ethel came into the room, barefoot, and uttered his last words: "Daughter, get your slippers on."

My father, to whom Mr. Rose had become quite attached, preached at his burial service. I had by then persuaded Father to accept the call of a Lutheran church in Philadelphia. With Mother, Mildred, and Dorothy he moved into a rented parsonage in the same block as my own house, unaware that I had quietly arranged through the church to pay his rent. Not long after that I bought a home for him, and I still remember the proud look in his eyes when he told me, "Son, this is the first property that I have ever owned in my life." Father's new Church of the Reformation at Ontario and Venango Streets was a mission congregation of only sixty-eight members that had been about to disband before he agreed to come; exactly the kind of challenge that he cherished.

In Trenton, where he had remained for eleven years, he had increased the membership of St. Mark's Lutheran Church from 85 to 310, and the idea of beginning the struggle anew in Philadelphia appealed to him. The new church had some financial resources, but not many. The most that it could afford to pay him was $1,000 a year, less than he was receiving then in Trenton. Without telling him or my mother, I arranged with the church council to pay him $2,000 a year and made up half of the amount myself. It was the highest salary he had ever received, and neither he nor Mother ever learned that half of it came from their son. Until the time I left for New York, I never missed a service at his church.

My financial resources by then were growing at a moderate pace, partly due to my own foresight and partly due to the outbreak of war in Europe in 1914. The United States then produced no important pharmaceutical drugs or chemicals; all were imported, mostly from Germany. Imports dropped sharply with the British blockade, and by 1916 the sea lanes were so thoroughly cut that the Germans had to resort to a submarine shipment to get one valuable order of dyes and drugs to America. The submarine *Deutschland* ducked under the British blockade and finally entered Chesepeake Bay and landed in Baltimore. But it was not enough to make even a dent in the scarcity that was felt in America. Drug prices rocketed upwards due to shortages of plant alkaloids, aspirin, carbolic acid, sulfanol, veranol, argyrol, coumarin, saccharin, phenolphthalein, and other basic pharmaceuticals. Before the war I had sold saccharin for eighty-five cents a pound; as the war progressed the price climbed to twenty dollars a pound.

The first market to be hit was New York. I realized, when shortages began to develop there, that prices soon would shoot up throughout the country. Quickly I went to wholesalers with whom I had developed friendships and offered them premium prices for all or parts of their allotments of soon-to-be scarce pharmaceuticals. Because I had foreseen the crisis and began working on it before my competitors fully realized what was happening, I became expert in locating stocks of scarce chemicals and buying them up for Hoffmann-La Roche. Roche, as the company always has been known in the trade, agreed to pay me a 2 percent commission on these extroadinary transactions. I was buying up goods at relatively low prices, just a step ahead of scarcity, and Roche was profiting greatly from their resale after the prices shot upwards. It was not long before my commissions began to exceed my salary.

A typical transaction involved carbolic acid (phenol), which only one American company, Barrett Chemical of Philadelphia, had attempted to produce before the war. On one of my pre-war calls as a salesman, I had persuaded the manager of the company, a man named James, that Roche could supply him with imported phenol cheaper than he could make it. He had bought tons from me at twelve cents a pound. With the beginning of the wartime phenol shortage, I called on James again.

"I've sold you phenol at a figure lower than the cost of your manufacture," I said, "but that time is past. I know that you're now the only source of supply and that you have more customers than you can handle. But I would like to buy from you as much as you will let me have."

"Mr. Bobst, can you afford to pay the price we're getting?"

"I know what the price is. You're getting $1.25 a pound, and I can afford to pay it."

"I'll let you have a ton," James said.

Through my New York office I sold the ton of phenol to the Heyden Chemical company, which manufactured salicylates, used in the treatment of arthritis and rheumatism and for making aspirin. A pound of phenol produces about two pounds of salicylic acid which, of course, also was scarce. In return for the phenol, Heyden agreed to let me purchase most of its production of salicylates. Roche thus made a healthy profit in a rising market both on the original sale of phenol to Heyden and on the subsequent sale of the salicylates, and I earned a commission on each of them. The pattern was repeated many times over.

The intense activity of locating, buying, and reselling scarce pharmaceutical stocks brought me to New York often. I found it necessary to keep evening clothes ready for these fast overnight trips, because Schlicke insisted that I accompany him to clubs and restaurants that required dinner jackets and black tie. Again, I marveled at how he maintained such a rich lifestyle as the mere branch manager of a foreign company. I assumed that his salary and commissions must be extraordinarily large.

Whether it was from an overabundance of good living or a more prosaic cause, I do not know, but a severe physical disability caught up with Schlicke in mid-1916. He suffered a throat hemorrhage and was forced to take a six-week leave from his work in order to recuperate. As soon as he fell ill, I offered to help run the New York operation by spending one day a week in his office and accelerating my sales calls during the other four days. He didn't think I could manage it.

"I'll come to New York on an evening train, stay here all night, work the next day and return to Philadelphia, or go on to Baltimore and Washington if necessary," I told him. "While I'm here I can spend some time calling on the Pfeiffer brothers. They haven't given us any business since they moved the Warner Company to New York."

Schlicke went off to White Sulpher Springs to recuperate, and I took on part of his responsibilities. Although it was not the most important of the company's problems, I was anxious to get to work on my old friends, the Pfeiffer brothers. I knew that it was their purchasing agent, not they themselves, who had cut us off their order list. Within a few weeks after I restored personal contact with the brother-owners, Roche was filling orders for their Warner Company at the rate of $150,000 a year. But soon we lost their business again by a curious twist.

One of our products was Santonin, a human worm remedy which sold heavily in Asia, particularly in Japan. There was little market for it in the United States, not because it was expensive at $125 a pound, but because worm infections were relatively rare by then. One day a buyer for the William R. Warner Company came in and ordered ten pounds. The order surprised me, because it was more than Warner could possibly need for its U.S. markets. Puzzled, I packaged the Santonin myself.

A month or so later Schlicke greeted me when I arrived

at the New York office with the news that "I made a mighty good buy today." I asked him what he had bought.

"I bought ten pounds of Santonin, and do you know what I paid for it? I bought it for only $80 a pound — $800."

"Did you open the package yet?"

"No."

"Let me see it." He produced the package.

"Mr. Schlicke," I said, "I sold that very ten pounds of Santonin to William R. Warner last month."

There was only one way that the Santonin could have left Warner and returned to us at a thief's price. I went to see the Pfeiffer brothers the next morning and told them that their purchasing agent was a crook. After hearing my story and seeing the package and our sales and purchase sheets, they fired the buyer. But paradoxically, we received no further orders from the Warner Company. I was perplexed until I discovered that their new buyer was a friend of the old one and held his friend's fate against me and the Roche Company. After a couple of months of being frozen out of Warner orders, I went to see the Pfeiffers again.

"What should I have done in that situation?" I asked them. "Should I have been honest, as I was, or should I have kept quiet about someone who I knew was stealing from you? We had nothing to lose by keeping quiet. In fact, we stood to make a $450 windfall profit. We had nothing to gain by speaking out, except to help you. I did what I thought was right. As a result I seem to have lost your business."

The second buyer promptly followed his friend the dishonest one out of the Warner Company, and our orders were restored. My sales efforts were paying off in many other areas, too, and I began to have ideas of getting established on my own as a sales agent. Many of my customers, like the Pfeiffers, bought from me on a personal level without much regard for my company. I had received offers from other pharmaceutical producers to act as their agent, and I knew that I could earn more money as an independent operator than as a Roche employee. I told Schlicke that I intended to resign.

"You're going to resign?" he asked in astonishment. "You *can't* resign."

"I have to," I said. "You can't afford to pay me the money I can earn as an agent."

"I won't let you resign. I'd rather work out an arrangement. I'll give you the privilege of buying and selling anything on your own that is not in our line, not directly competitive. You can take any agency on the side if you want to, but please don't resign."

On those terms, I remained at Roche, while operating with rather large credits — $25,000 and more — as agent for companies such as Smith, Kline and French. By the time the U.S. declared war on Germany in 1917 I was doing rather well, which was fortunate. In addition to my direct family responsibilities to Ethel and Walton, and the secret subsidy that I provided for my father through his church, I was helping to support my brother Harry's wife and child. Harry had been so caught up with revulsion over propaganda pictures of German atrocities in Belgium that he had joined the British army in 1914. He had left his family with virtually nothing but his small military allotment to live on.

At the same time, my work had brought me into association with some of the social and business leaders of Philadelphia, many of whom became my close friends. I was invited to join the prestigious Poor Richard Club, Rotary, and other organizations, and I had become active as a campaign worker for the Republican Party. My political activities were an outgrowth of the reformist zeal that had led me to start preparing for the bar. Since I knew now that I would never carry out my first ambition, I became determined to do what I could, however small, to institute reforms in the corrupt government of my city. My opportunity came when an outstanding and honest judge named Pennypacker decided to run as the Republican reform candidate for mayor of Philadelphia. I went down to his campaign headquarters and volunteered to help raise funds for him.

Most of the people I knew — doctors, pharmacists, purchasing agents — were middle-class men from whom I felt lucky to get contributions of $5, or $10, or $20 for the Pennypacker campaign. But one of my acquaintances was a man named Freyhofer, whose family had founded the largest bakery in Philadelphia. He was as concerned about corruption as I was, and when I told him that I was raising campaign funds for Pennypacker, he sat down, wrote out a check, and handed it to me. I thanked him, assuming his contribution would be like the others. Then I looked at the check. It was for $5,000. I have since raised many millions of dollars for social and political causes in which I believe; in fact, the World War II bond drive in Essex County, N.J. which I headed, and still do, raised seven billion dollars. But I never again had quite the thrill that I felt when I turned in that first substantial contribution to Pennypacker headquarters.

When election day came along, the odds were in favor of the old city Political gang, because they were so firmly in control. By midnight, feeling disheartened over what I expected to be a resounding defeat for reform, Ethel and I went to bed. I was still awake an hour later when I heard the sounds of a brass band marching up Broad Street. It was hard to hear what they were playing. I strained to make out the tune and suddenly realized what it was.

"Thank God," I woke Ethel up, "We've won!"

"How do you know?" she muttered sleepily.

"The band is playing 'Onward Christian Soldiers,' that's how. If that Democratic gang had won, they'd be playing 'Hail, hail, the gang's all here, what the hell do we care. . .' "

Another Philadelphian who felt as I did was Howard Story, a tall, good-looking man who often was mistaken for Douglas Fairbanks, Sr. We became friends through the Rotary Club of Philadelphia and shared not only similar political views but similar tastes in dining and theater. During my years as a Roche saleman in Philadelphia we became inseparable, lunching together almost daily and even travelling together when his business engagements fit in with mine. He was the founding partner of a firm of newspaper representatives, Story, Brooks, and Finley, brokers of advertising for newspapers throughout the United States, and while still in his early thirties already had succeeded in putting away $200,000 in bond investments.

One day when I was on a selling trip to Baltimore, Howard telephoned me from Philadelphia. He had been urgently called home from Chicago because his sixteen-year-old daughter, Edna, had been stricken with what appeared to be appendicitis. "Please come back at once," he pleaded with me, "maybe you can be of help." I left for Philadelphia immediately.

When I arrived I went straight to the hospital and located the chief surgeon, whom I knew well. He shook his head hopelessly. Edna's appendix had been removed, but she was suffering severe surgical shock, and there was little hope that she would recover.

Howard and his wife were in a waiting room, weeping. "I never had Edna baptized," he said to me, "and it worries me now. Her condition is so grave."

I called my father, who hurried to the hospital and baptized Edna and accepted her as a member of his church. Then, because Howard and his wife were too distraught to stay in the hospital room, I sat by Edna's bedside and held her hand. She died as I sat there with her. It was a crushing blow to my best friend, who blamed himself for having been in Chicago when the appendicitis developed.

Later I went around to the surgical staff of the hospital to talk to one of the assistants at Edna's operation. "Did you see her appendix?"' I asked him.

"Yes," he ruefully replied, "and it was as clean as a whistle." The operation from which Edna died in all probability had been unnecessary. It would appear she was suffering from an intestinal type of influenza from which she probably would have recovered if properly treated. I never told Howard for fear that his guilt feelings would become even more pronounced. Her case, like many others that I had observed, had left me with the certain knowledge that medical diagnosis in those times was an uncertain affair, a matter in many cases of pure guesswork that led to many mistakes. As a result, I went out of my way to develop close acquaintanceships with the then small number of medical specialists, whose knowledge was far more advanced than that of general practitioners and surgeons. I wanted to absorb as much diagnostic and therapeutic information as they would pass along to me so that when the opportunity came I could put their needs to work in the pharmaceutical industry. Through these contacts and my continuous reading of medical disciplines I had the informal opportunity, in effect, to take a post-graduate course in specialties ranging from cancer to endocrinology that not only served me well in my business but actually saved my life many years later.

One of the basic medical phenomena that I knew from personal experience and that had been confirmed by every physician to whom I talked was the great healing power of the patient's confidence in his doctor. It seemed natural to me, a link in a way between salesmanship and medicine, because a doctor, like a salesman, will not find a responsive audience if he shows less than complete confidence in his product. This axiom was proven, almost perilously for Ethel, in 1919, the second year of the great flu epidemic that struck the United States. Thousands died all over the country. To come down with the flu was terrifying, because the patient knew that it might be fatal. From our upstairs bedroom window, Ethel and I could look out in our own neighborhood and see crepe hanging on the doors of victims whom we knew.

We should have been more wary, I suppose, when we visited Atlantic City one weekend with some of Ethel's relatives. Among them was an aged aunt who obviously was suffering from an upper respiratory infection with symptomatic running eyes and nose. Ethel sat beside her and permitted the old woman to kiss her. Back in Philadelphia two days later, Ethel came down with a severe sore throat. Within days she had developed an unrelievable abdominal pain. Fearful of the flu, I immediately called our physician, Dr. Herbert Smith, a professor at the Medical Chirurgical College of Medicine. I had long admired him because he was trained as a pharmacist before he entered medicine and wrote the finest and most sensible prescriptions that I had filled in my days as a druggist. He examined Ethel carefully, then turned to me.

"Elmer, three out of four physicians probably would diagnose Ethel's illness as appendicitis. It isn't. I'm positive that she has intestinal influenza. Instead of hitting the respiratory tract, it's hit her there." I was reminded of Howard Story's tragedy when a doctor mistakenly diagnosed Edna's intestinal infection as appendicitis and recommended the fatal operation. Smith was a wise physician, but there was not much he could do to treat Ethel's infection.

Our maid, too, was down with the flu, and with the epidemic at a critical level, I could not find a nurse available in all of Philadelphia. So I nursed Ethel myself night and day, and even kept a nursing chart of temperature and medications which I still have in my files today. Through the long nights of her illness I slept on the floor beside her bed, with a raised hand touching her arm so that I could feel her pulse and feverish skin. On the seventh day, her temperature reached 104 degrees. I knew it could be fatal unless a crisis came quickly. "If only I can get her to sleep tonight," I told myself, "the temperature will break." But she was bordering on delirium and could not sleep. Then I thought of two sample tablets of a new hypnotic drug that I had in my medicine cabinet. I called Dr. Smith and told him that I wanted to use the new drug — Veronal — to induce sleep, because I saw no other way to break her dangerous fever. "Go ahead, Elmer," he sounded discouraged, "I know of nothing else that can be done." She fell asleep promptly after taking the Veronal tablets. I lay down on the floor beside her and raised my hand to her wrist. As I stretched restlessly on the hard floor, aware of every pulse beat beneath her feverish skin, she slept soundly. Then at 4 A.M. I suddenly became alert to a new sensation at my fingertips. There was moisture on her arm. The fever had broken.

But the flu had a crippling aftereffect that left Ethel despondent and even afraid for her life. She developed a severe neuritis, an inflamation of the sheaths of the nerves, which gave way to such an incapacitating arthritis that I had to carry her from room to room and up and down stairs for many weeks. Fearing heart damage and other complications, I called, in succession, three noted professors of medicine from the University of Pennsylvania and Jefferson Medical College. One of them detected a heart murmur. The others saw grave complications but no way to cure Ethel's disabling condition. All three were worried, but their diagnoses were vague. The result, to Ethel's spirits, was devastating. She began to give up even fighting for recovery.

I was desperate to get at the cause and find a way to deal with her problem. My friend Dr. Henry Beattes, who was an outstanding cardiologist, rarely made outside calls, but I prevailed upon him to come to her. Ethel by now had almost accepted what she believed to be the inevitable. She feared that she was dying. When Dr. Beattes completed his examination, she asked him in a trembling, hopeless voice, "Doctor, do you think you can help me?"

"Help you?" he thundered. "Help you? I'll cure you or I'll take in my shingle!" At that moment, the cure began. She was relieved of her daily fear of death. The medicines he prescribed for her — tincture of iodine and tincture of iron (ferrous chloride) — were at best weak and probably worthless as remedies, but his confidence so uplifted Ethel that her own hope and confidence were rekindled. Still, she was disabled and suffering from severe pain. In an attempt to get at the root of the problem, I turned medical detective on my own. Recognizing that her troubles probably stemmed from viral complications after the flu, I sought a viral remedy, a vaccine tailored to her particular infection that would build antibodies so that her body could conquer the ailment. If I could retrieve a specimen of pus from any infection, I thought, I could take it to the most noted bacteriologist in Philadelphia and have an autogenous vaccine prepared. But her infection was so throughly diffused throughout her body that there was no prominent spot from which to take a specimen. Then I had a brainstorm. One of her wisdom teeth had been troubling her. I took her to our dentist. Hopefully, I brought along a sterile glass tube and cotton. When he extracted the wisdom tooth, there was a partial pocket of pus beneath it. I took a specimen and rushed it to the bacteriologist. From it, he produced thirty-six doses of autogenous vaccine.

Within half an hour after Dr. Smith gave her the first injection, she was able to move wrists and hands that had been almost frozen moments before. As he continued regular injections of the vaccine, she continued to improve. On Thanksgiving Day, in the same Atlantic City hotel where she contracted the original flu infection from her aunt, Ethel walked across the entire lobby floor without help. She was cured.

Not long after her recovery I visited Dr. Beattes in his office and he told me a story, strangely familiar, that underlined the vital importance of the patient's confidence in regaining health. "Elmer, I never told you that my grandfather was pastor of the Lutheran church in Kissel Hill that your father served," he said. "My grandfather once told me about his final sermon there. He ended it with these words: 'I have been preaching to you every Sunday for more than twelve years. But as I say goodbye to you, I must add that I don't think I've done you a straw's worth of good.'

"I heard that story long ago from my own father," I told Dr. Beattes, "but he never mentioned Pastor Beattes's name. He told the story to convey what he believed the pastor's meaning had been. To him it meant that if any good had been done in the church, it had been done by the congregation. The pastor was only the catalyst." Dr. Beattes, I thought, had performed the same role in his treatment of Ethel. He had been the catalyst in restoring faith in the future to a sick person who had almost entirely lost it.

By the time of Ethel's illness I had achieved such gratifying success with Roche and my own agency that we had no more great financial worries — and with fortune's help were never to have them again. I had bought my first car, a secondhand, 1914 four-cylinder Buick phaeton (for $750) and learned to drive by simply getting in it outside of New York and pointing it toward Philadelphia. (I had three punctures and had to fix them myself on that single journey.) It was the best car that I ever owned, and I include the Imperial Chrysler, Cadillac, and Rolls Royce that I own today. Ethel and I also bought our first house, which we paid for with money we had put away in war bonds. I had served during the war years on the Philadelphia War Chest Committee under the leadership of Edward Bok, the famed editor of the old *Ladies Home Journal* and author of *The Americanization of Edward Bok,* a classic autobiography, as well as a biography of his boss and father-in-law, Cyrus Curtis, whom I also knew rather well. Bok was a dignified man, destined to gain great wealth and power as head of the Curtis Publishing Company, which his father-in-law founded. But he was a forthright and practical man, too, who saw nothing remiss in publishing articles about syphilis and gonorrhea at a time in the early 1900s when mention of either disease was considered shocking.

While my agency and company business prospered, the Hoffmann-La Roche Company was having its troubles, unbeknownst to me or most of its other employees. The American branch under Schlicke, who had been semi-autonomous, was deeply in debt and operating at a loss of about $30,000 a month in 1919 and early 1920. To make matters worse, Schlicke had piled up a huge inventory of pharmaceuticals which had been rare during the war but were now in oversupply.

I was aware of the huge inventory and worried about it, but I had no idea that we were in real trouble, because Schlicke had been careful to preserve an appearance that all was well with the New York operation. He had even taken Ethel and Walton and me along on a two-car motoring vacation to Virginia where he wanted to buy a first-class riding horse, certainly not the behavior of an executive whose operations were on the brink of financial ruin. The trip, actually, was almost entirely carefree and delightful for the three Bobsts, but I had begun to find Schlicke's extravagance distasteful and no longer felt as kindly toward him as I had in our earlier years. At one of the highpoints of the journey we stopped overnight in Harper's Ferry, which had nostalgic importance to me. The following morning Schlicke's car broke down. It was apparent that he required a new axle and none was available in Harper's Ferry. He was terribly upset, so I located an axle by telephone in New York. Schlicke readily agreed to have a young shipping clerk in our office, Nelson Peterson, bring the axle to him by train. Young Peterson appeared the next day, and within an hour Schlicke's car was repaired. The clerk was such a bright and cleancut young fellow that I invited him to ride along for a few days in our car with Ethel, Walton, and me, and during that time he impressed me immensely with his curiosity and quick mind. Among other things I recall, he remarked on the fact that I was largely self-educated and asked me to give him a list of books that would help him to become the same, since he would never be able to enter college. I cheerfully obliged and a few days later sent him back to New York with a list of books and our best wishes. Not long thereafter, I was thankful that I had met him.

The company's directors in Basle were not as blissfully unaware of the depth of Schlicke's problems as were we who worked for him. In October, 1920, they sent a senior executive, Dr. H.G. Senn, to New York to solve what to them had become a catastrophic problem.

I was packing to leave Philadelphia for a sales trip to Baltimore when Senn telephoned. In a strong French accent, he explained to me why he was in New York. Before he let Schlicke or anyone else know he was there, he said, he wanted to talk to me. "Can you meet me here tonight?" he asked.

I explained that I was leaving for Baltimore, but he dismissed the trip as inconsequential and practically ordered me to entrain for New York immediately. I met him later that day in his room at the Commodore Hotel. Senn said that he and his fellow executives in Basle had been aware for some time that Schlicke's sales and earnings reports from New York had, to put it charitably, lacked candor. Apparently at least some of his high lifestyle had been financed by Roche, without the company's knowledge or consent. At the same time, there were practical business reasons for the company's sudden decline in sales and profits, mostly having to do with Schlicke's errors of judgement, such as his witless overstocking of post-war inventory. Senn came straight to the point and asked me to give him my views on the reasons for the company's decline. In less than an hour I drew a complete picture of our operations which, in my view, were overburdened by unnecessary overhead, too many untrained people on staff, and a total failure to economize when we knew that the war boom had ended.

Senn listened without comment, then said, "Mr. Bobst, will you take the job?"

I was startled. "What job do you mean?"

He was surprised in his turn. He thought I had been told of a decision by the Roche board of directors the week before to offer me the job of general manager of Hoffmann-La Roche operations in the United States.

"What is the compensation?" I asked Senn.

"Twelve thousand dollars a year and 5 percent of the profit of the American operation."

"What have you been paying Mr. Schlicke?"

"Fifteen thousand dollars and a percentage of the profits, guaranteed to be no less than $7,500 a year."

I was torn, not by money nor by loyalty to Schlicke, because he did not deserve it, but by the ties of Philadelphia. After almost two decades, beginning as a raw boy from Lititz, I had established firm roots in the city. Ethel and I loved our new house, a charming colonial on Lincoln Drive, near Chestnut Hill. She was born in Philadelphia and all of her friends were there. My independent agency was doing well and I knew that I could continue to prosper in Philadelphia regardless of the fate of Hoffmann-La Roche. Skeptically, I shook my head.

"I'm not sure," I said. "If I should decide to take on the management of the company here, the salary will have to be $15,000 and 5 percent, but I will not ask for any minimum guarantee. However, I'll have to think the matter over carefully and discuss it with my wife. I'll give you my answer within three days."

I returned to Philadelphia in the morning, still uncertain, and was greeted by an urgent message: Call Dr. Senn at the Commodore Hotel immediately. Senn was almost cryptic on the telephone: "Something dreadful has happened. Come back to New York at once." Feeling like a tennis ball in the midst of a volley, I met Senn again. There had been a grave slip in communications, he explained. Anticipating my agreement, he had cabled Basle the night before spelling out my tentative salary terms. The directors in Basle replied immediately, "Discharge Schlicke and hire Bobst." Unhappily, their cable was addressed to the New

York Roche office instead of to Senn at the Commodore. Schlicke had opened it, read it, and almost apoplectically confronted Dr. Senn to announce that he was consulting with his lawyer. At the moment, his office was unmanned.

"Now it is imperative that you take the job and move into Schlicke's office tomorrow morning," Senn said. "Your loyalty to the company demands this."

I felt as if I had no choice, but I told Senn and the company's legal counsel, Otto von Schrenk, that we would have to write and sign a contract before I would take Schlicke's chair. We worked on the details until three o'clock the next morning, when we finally produced a draft that satisfied Senn and me. It called for automatic renewal on October 15th of each year, with a clause requiring three months notice if either party wanted to terminate the agreement. In addition, it gave me full control of all American operations — more autonomy than Schlicke had exercised — and left me free to purchase from any supplier in the interests of the American operation. My compensation was to be as I had suggested earlier: $15,000 a year and 5 percent of the annual profits of the U.S. operation.

Sleepily, Senn instructed von Schrenk to draw up a formal document later in the day and advised me to show a copy to my lawyer before signing it.

"I don't have a lawyer," I said. "I'll be my own lawyer. And I prefer to write out the contract and sign it right now."

It did not occur to any of the three of us to note whether the 5 percent of profits was to be calculated before or after taxes, and that was the furthest thing from my mind when I took over Schlicke's office at 7:30 A.M., October 15, 1920.

Groundbreaking ceremonies for the present Hoffmann-La Roche plant in Nutley, N.J., November 1928. Holding the spade is Dr. Emil Barell, at that time president of the international Hoffman-La Roche organization. Others in front, from left to right, are Mrs. Barell, Mrs. Ethel Bobst, and the author.

● *Chapter Seven*

● One of my first acts upon becoming General Manager was to send for Nelson Peterson, who was still working in the shipping department and studying in his spare time. Peterson had all of the best qualities for a top-level assistant. He was the same eager, inquisitive fellow who had so impressed me on our auto tour; in addition he had a capacity for performing quickly any task that was required of him, and he was unusually quiet and discreet for a young man in his early twenties. He also was the only person on the New York staff that impressed me as possessing all the essential qualities of an assistant in whom I could place absolute trust, for the company was in far worse shape even than Senn had told me.

In addition to our staggering, and continuing, losses—$30,000 a month — the American operation of Roche had debts of almost $700,000, some of them appallingly overdue. Among other burdens, we owed $200,000 to banks, $150,000 to suppliers, much of it to Monsanto Chemical for purchases of saccharine and other products, and $250,000 in debentures to the parent company.

Hoffmann-La Roche in Basle was not then in a very strong position, either. It was still a relatively young company when I took over American operations, and the war, which had proved such a boon to U.S. sales, had been devasting to the European business.

The company had grown to modest size from an unpromis-
ing beginning in 1896 when Fritz Hoffmann and his father, a
wholesale silk merchant, founded it. Fritz, a lackadaisical student,
had left school and become interested in developing a chemical
firm. For a time young Hoffmann teamed up with a German
pharmacist to produce an antiseptic powder called Airol. Their
partnership soon dissolved, and the elder Hoffmann indulged
his son by establishing him in his own chemical works, with Airol
as his first product. He added flavors, some herbal remedies in
the form of crude drugs, and a few prescription pharmaceuticals.
The small company began to grow. The elder Hoffmann's wealth
gave free rein to young Fritz's two outstanding personal traits,
one of them good, the other bad. The first was an entrepreneurial
genius that led him to pioneer in risk-taking pharmaceutical research (with Father's backing) and in prepackaging prescription
drugs under brand names at a time when almost all prescriptions
were made up fresh by individual pharmacists. He foresaw the
revolution in packaged pharmaceutical specialties. The second trait
was Fritz Hoffmann's irrespressible yearning for the high life. Although he was married and had two sons, he made no secret of his
insatiable appetites for wine, women, and song, which became his
undoing in at least two ways.

Had Fritz Hoffmann been more abstemious, or at least less
impulsive, the company might have remained entirely in his own
family's hands, but he was not and it did not. He left his wife
in order to marry one of his other young women, and the price
of his divorce was a sizeable percentage of the shares of his company. He turned the interest over to R.A. Koechlin, his first wife's
brother-in-law, who was an officer of the famed Handelsbank
(Bank Commerciale de Basle) which, from that time on, exercised
a powerful influence on company affairs. And, ironically, his
company became better-known by his divorced wife's name than
by his own. Following Swiss custom, he had hyphenated her maid-
en name, La Roche, to his when they were married. The company
thus· was founded as Hoffmann-La Roche Chemical Works. A
few years later it marketed an orange-flavored cough syrup called
Siroline, which it sold in France under the trade name Siro

Roche. For the sake of uniformity, the name Roche was added to all Siroline packages and, ultimately, to all Hoffmann-La Roche product labels. Althrough the company — now one of the largest and richest pharmaceutical houses in the world — still bears its founder's corporate name (F. Hoffmann-La Roche & Co. A.G.), it is better known throughout the world simply as Roche, after his first wife.

Siroline, first marketed as a remedy for respiratory diseases and even tuberculosis, although it only suppressed coughing, was an instant success in Czarist Russia. Hoffmann established a branch office there, as well as offices in Paris and London, and an agency in New York. Despite his after-hours activities, he was doing well by the early 1900s. In 1904, a superb pharmacologist named Professor Max Cloetta, whom he had included on his board of directors, developed Digalen (the first injectable and standardized form of Digitalis), which was a world-wide success. Other discoveries followed. When the war began, Hoffmann-La Roche was doing almost as much business in ethical drugs as it had been doing in flavorings and basic pharmaceutical chemicals. But the war almost demolished both sides of the business. The Russian revolution eliminated Hoffmann's Czarist operations at a stroke, causing severe losses. The beginning of the first World War disrupted all European markets as well. The unfortunate geographic location of Roche's principal pharmaceutical production facilities made matters even worse. The main manufacturing plant was located in Grenzach, Germany, just a few miles from Basle across the Swiss-German border. At one point the Germans accused Roche of smuggling a drug called Pantopon, which contained all of the alkaloids of opium, across the border for sale to the allies.

The accusation, which was true, brought production of the plant almost to a standstill. The plant manager, Dr. Emil Barell, was arrested and held by the Germans under threat of execution. I was told that powerful political influences were brought to bear to save Dr. Barell's life and he was returned to his native Switzerland a couple of years later, but the effect of all these events had brought the company to its knees. Had it not been for the wartime profits of our American office, Roche might have gone under. As it was, the Basle executives had to scramble in 1919 to raise more capital in order to survive.

Hoffmann reorganized with about a half-million dollars of his own money plus a substantial investment from Koechlin, who actually had become President of Hoffman-La Roche, and a small amount from Dr. Barell, who was his favorite employee. Barell, the product of an impoverished and unhappy childhood, had somehow managed to win his university degrees in chemistry and joined Hoffmann early in the company's history. He became Fritz Hoffmann's assistant and constant companion, managing his affairs in the company and caring for him when he launched on his roguish escapades. As a result, Barell came to know more about Roche than any other executive. When Hoffmann died shortly after reorganizing in 1919, Barell became managing director, a position with which he was just becoming familiar when I became general manager of American operations in 1920. On both sides of the Atlantic, Basle and New York, we had trouble and we knew it.

It took me only a few days to discover just how bad matters were for us, but although I had no experience whatever as a top-level manager, I refused to believe our problems were insoluble. Not even the rueful forecasts of some of my Philadelphia friends dampened my enthusiasm. Howard Story, alone, tried to sound encouraging, but he told me later that he had expected me back in Philadelphia within a year. Other friends gave me a farewell dinner at the Goat's Club, a heckling organization like the Gridiron Club in Washington, and predicted imminent failure for me and Roche. Even Ethel said, "I don't think you can rebuild the company; it's gone downhill too far." There were actually only two people who were quite certain I could rebuild the company. One was my dear father and the other was myself. For myself, I was very much in the frame of mind that I had been when I sought a job from George B. Evans, knowing that he would turn me down. I was determined not only to do the job, but to do it better than anyone else. It was well that I had such confidence, because not many Roche employees shared it. Several good people quit the company at once when they realized the shape it was in. Others talked of resigning. One of them was a German named Conrad Reinheimer, an expert in the practical sub-dividing of rare chemicals and alkaloids who had trained under Merck of Darmstadt. "Mr. Bobst, I am a widower with seven children to feed," he explained to me in his broken English. "I can't afford to be uncertain of a job. What do you think of the future of this company?"

I looked at him in amazement, a reaction that I truly felt. "Why Mr. Reinheimer, we are going to go ahead. We are going to grow bigger and bigger. There will be no end to it." I was genuinely convinced that if I wanted Roche to succeed and worked hard enough at it, we would succeed.

"Mr. Bobst," he said, "I have faith in you and in the house. Bei Gott, I stick."

I moved as quickly as I could to cut overhead and reduce our losses. As his inventories had grown, Schlicke had felt the need for more space and had moved us to a five-story loft build-ing at 17-19-21 Cliff Street, between Fulton and John. The floors literally groaned under the weight of tons of unneeded materials: sugar of milk, quinine, bromides of sodium and potash, salicy-lates, saccharin, vanillin, coumarin, and other basics that had been scarce during the war but were now in plentiful supply. More supplies were pouring in under long-term contracts that Schlicke unfortunately had negotiated at wartime prices. It was as if we were under the spell of a demonic sorcerer's apprentice, refilling our pail faster than we conceivably could empty it.

I had no alternative but to cancel every supply contract on our books. Fortunately, most of the contract cancellations were amicably arranged with suppliers whom I had known well for years. A few were acrimonious, but I made it clear that I had no choice. No one sued.

Working night and day with Peterson at my side, I examined the job requirements of everyone in our offices and found that I could cut the staff to thirty-five, from about a hundred. At the same time, I moved quickly to shrug off the albatross weight of Schlicke's huge inventory. Pharmaceutical prices already had started to plunge from their wartime peaks, and I felt certain that the market would sink much farther still before it leveled off. My sudden distress sales hit the pharmaceutical industry like a whirlwind.

I had Nelson Peterson call Eastman Laboratories to offer them our five tons of bromides at a price of only sixty cents a pound, ten cents under the market price. They bought the lot. Next we moved all of the other items in our inventory, selling them at 10 percent less than the prices of the same products from Merck, Powers, Wakeman & Rosengarden (which later merged with Merck), Mallinckrodt, Monsanto, New York Quinine, and others. Word passed in the industry that the new young upstart at Roche had lost his mind. One of my friends quoted the great George Merck as clucking, "That young fellow is crazy for dumping his inventory." What Merck didn't know when he uttered the remark was that Roche would have gone bankrupt in a depressed market if I had not unloaded our supplies so quickly. Six months after I got rid of ours at sixty cents a pound, Merck's bromides were selling on the open market for sixteen cents a pound.

With the inventory cleared, I rented out three and a half floors, which paid for our building taxes and overhead, and I used the revenues from our clearance sale to pay off most of our debts. We were still losing money, but we were on a sound footing and ready to begin anew. One thing that I knew after the experience with the unwanted inventories was that I did not want to re-enter the bulk chemical business for a long time to come. Schlicke had been losing money on it to begin with. Now the market was depressed. We had gotten out of it in the nick of time. I decided to concentrate only on the sale of fine alkaloids and the development of a strong ethical specialty business. Roche by now had a number of good prescription products, all of excellent quality and packaged with the same fine attention to tasteful design as the first bottle of Digalen that had appealed to me before I joined the company. In addition to Pantopon, the pain-relieving opiate that had created such trouble for Dr. Batell during the war, there were other drugs, including an as yet unnamed non-narcotic sleep inducer that the Basle scientists had developed as a substitute for opiates.

The latter drug had not been marketed in Basle because of a conflict with another remedy which had been on the market for several years. The chemists responsible for the drug were disappointed when the company ignored their new development. Whether to molify them or to test me, I don't know, but Dr. Barell asked me to introduce the product to the American market. "This is your first opportunity to prove what you can do with a new product," he said, and settled back to await results. It was clear to me that he did not have much faith in the new compound, otherwise he would have brought it out in Europe first. But I examined it and found it quite remarkable.

It was a compound that fused allyl, isoprypyl and barbituric acid with a pain-relieving element called amidopyrine. Amidopyrine was slightly in excess in order to have a true molecular relationship for a perfect compound. (It was because of this fact that eventually the AMA Council on Pharmacy and Chemistry refused to accept the remedy for publication in its new and non-official remedies.) But with my background as a pharmacist and my growing knowledge of the fairly advanced knowledge in therapeutics, I recognized immediately that the compound would have great value to physicians who were treating wakeful patients in pain. A sleep inducer is no good if pain persists, because the pain keeps the patient awake; conversely, a pain reliever alone will not induce sleep. I had full confidence that the two components of our new drug would exert a synergistic effect; one helping the other against pain and insomnia. I knew that if I tested it responsibly, named it well, and marketed it intelligently, it could be a great success.

Searching about for a name, I was influenced by the demands of the Council on Pharmacy and Chemistry of the AMA, which had decreed that the names of prescription products should not baldly indicate their areas of medical usefulness, but rather their chemical components. Thus I chose Allonal as the name of our new compound; *al* for allyl-isoprypyl-barbituric acid, *lon* for amidopyrine, which is a pyrazolone derviative, and the final *al* because it was more or less accepted as a proper ending for hypnotic remedies such as, for examply, veranol and others. Besides, I loved the Hawaiian expression, *aloha*, which was appropriate.

Then I went to Dr. Francis Dercum, professor of neurology at Jefferson Medical College in Philadelphia. I had known him since my days as a detail man and knew that he was one of the most respected neurologists in the United States and certainly one of the best-known. He had treated President Woodrow Wilson after his first stroke. I explained the make-up of the new drug to him, and he agreed to undertake clinical testing at Jefferson and other institutions with which he was connected. Within a very short time, Dr. Dercum and several of his colleagues reported their excellent results with Allonal in a professional journal.

My marketing campaign followed a pattern I already had developed in my very first effort to get the Roche American operations back on a profitable footing. I had been determined during our first deep cost and inventory cutting period to concentrate sales efforts on a single promising Roche product which had not been doing too well on the American market. Our sales of Pantopon, still used today, incidentally, as a more effective and less dangerous pain reliever than morphine, lagged at about $12,000 a year. I brought in a chemist from Switzerland and had him make a year's supply in our Cliff Street laboratory, using stocks of raw materials on hand. The package was designed with great neatness and graphic taste. I made a special point of emphasizing our packaging when I called in our detail salesmen — seven of them since I had abandoned the calling — for a training course in sales which I conducted myself. "When you're talking to the doctor, take what you're talking about and hold it up in your left hand, like this," I said, displaying a package of Pantopon. "Break the seal, nip the carton, and take out the ampule. He'll see that it has been packaged with care and love, and he'll feel, correctly, that the product is made with the same care. You gain strength, and the name of the product registers. It will make a tangible impression on the doctor's brain, because he will be using two of the wonderful faculties that God has given to everyone, namely the power of sight and the power of hearing."

My advertising campaign was mainly in the form of direct mailings to physicians and, incidentally, was the beginning of an institution that I built on throughout my pharmaceutical career. The idea of writing product letters to physicians was not new — Roche had been doing it for years, sending heavy chemical and pharmacological product descriptions which most doctors could not understand — but my approach was entirely different. I wrote a catchy headline at the top of the letter, often one that had nothing whatever to do with medicine. One that I recall, headlining a letter about infectious diseases, was "My Father Hung His Prince Albert Coat on the Clothes Line." Another, not too subtly leading up to the absence of "drug hangover" from Allonal, was "The Morning After."

Under the headline was a chatty letter that always began, "Dear Doctor," and opened with a literary allusion, a reference to some topical and often non-medical subject, or a reminiscence of my own. One of them, for example, began, "Back in my early drugstore days, when Essence of Pepsin was frequently prescribed, my boss used to send me to a butcher shop about once a month to buy fresh rennets." I went on to discuss "butcher shop endocrinology" and concluded, naturally, with a description of Roche's great advances in modern hormones. The doctors were asked to write for samples of our new products. Since I signed the letters, "Elmer H. Bobst," the responses were often personal and directed to me.

After years of dry laboratory descriptions from pharmaceutical houses, physicians apparently were delighted to receive something less opaque and boring, for many thousands of them replied, and hundreds who had never met me were moved to begin years-long exchanges of correspondence as a result. At the beginning my mailings — at least one a week — went to about 30,000 doctors, but in time the list grew to 140,000. Later I added many thousand more recipients of "Dear Doctor" and "Dear Nurse" letters with special mailings to the dental and nursing professions. The letters became the single most powerful selling tool in the Roche advertising arsenal, widely copied not only in the pharmaceutical business but by other direct mail advertisers, as well. But at first Barell and his colleagues in Basle were appalled by them. When they received the first one concerning Pantopon, they cabled an urgent plea that I stop this undignified promotion effort before it hurt the company's reputation. I ignored the cable for a few weeks while I tabulated the results of my mailing. Then I wrote to Barell:

"Our requests for samples in the past have been averaging about 5 percent, on postage-paid orders which we provided. My first mailing brought back 10 percent, and I made the doctors pay for their own one-cent stamps on the return card." When my mailings began drawing responses as high as 20 percent, Barell's protest sudsided, and he began to hint that he would like me to come to Europe soon to pass along my marketing techniques to the executives and salesmen there.

My final marketing tactic with Allonal concerned its price, which, incidentally, is the source of one of the much-touted "secrets" of the present-day Hoffmann-La Roche Company's high profits. (The Swiss company never reveals exact sales and profit figures, but *Fortune* magazine in August, 1971, made what I believe to be an accurate guess: on sales of more than $1.2 billion, Roche netted at least 16 percent, probably more.) Competitive products that were not as good as Allonal were selling on the market at a price of fifty cents for a dozen tablets. Although it cost no more to produce, I knew Allonal was better. So I coined the slogan "Makers of Medicines of Rare Quality" for all packages and promotion and charged a dollar for a dozen tablets.

The motivation for doubling the price of Allonal was not a crass one, although it obviously increased profits materially. We had already begun laboratory experimentation in the U.S. operation of Roche, trying to create new and better drug compounds for medicine. Such research is extremely expensive and highly risky (less than one experimental compound in three thousand ever reaches the market and the manufacturer loses every research penny he has put into the rest). But research is essential both to medical progress and to corporate growth. The only economic means of financing it is through the profits of successful products. Therefore one must price his products as high as a competitive market will permit. With Allonal my price was twice that of the competition, but my product was better, and I reasoned that the basic yardstick by which Americans judge quality is by price: if it costs more, it must be better. The Hoffmann-La Roche Company subsequently applied my pricing philosophy and my "Rare Quality" slogan to all of its international products. The result was that it pioneered successfully for many years in pharmaceutical research and grew to be one of the largest and most capital-rich companies in the world.

My first letter concerning the new pain-relieving sleep inducer was as chatty as its forerunners, but I went straight to the point in my headline, because it was news: "A New Non-Narcotic Remedy for Pain and Insomnia." The reaction was astonishing. Requests for samples of Allonal poured in by the thousands, and the product was in the black as soon as it was introduced on the market. Sales quickly built up to more than a million dollars a year. From a starting point that was close to bankruptcy when I took over on October 15, 1920, the American operation of Roche was off and running as a growing concern. By the end of 1921 our loss had been cut to $12,000. In 1922 we had more than $200,000 in profit.

The achievement did not go unnoticed either in Basle or in New York. I was offered the presidency of an American pharmaceutical company. Although sorely tempted by a rather large salary offer, I had begun a pattern of growth at Roche that I wanted to continue. I wrote to Basle of the attractive offer and added that if I could justifiably do so I would prefer to remain with Roche. As an inducement the directors voted to let me buy 1 percent of Hoffmann-La Roche, a surprising concession on their part. Roche shares — there are only 16,000 voting shares in the company today — had been closely held and are still jealously guarded. The majority remain in the hands of the heirs of the early holders. The cost of my 1 percent, 80 of the then 8,000 outstanding shares, was $24,000, which I paid out of my 5 percent commission on American profits. Basle also agreed, after a struggle, that my 5 percent was to be calculated before taxes.

It was a good bargain for both of us. By 1923 I was able to contribute 12½ percent of Roche-New York's gross income as our share of Basle overhead and managed to give them an additional $300,000 of dividends on our profits, something that no foreign operation had done before.

Barell and his group were more than pleasantly surprised; they were overwhelmed by the quick turn-around and the sudden flow of money from New York to Switzerland. Among our debts in the New York office had been $250,000 in debentures owed to Basle headquarters. At the time of our worst troubles, the directors had so despaired of ever receiving payment on the debentures that they literally tore them up and threw the scraps away. I saw it as a debt that had to be paid, however, so I had new debentures printed and sent them to Barell. Within a few years, largely on the profits of Allonal, Digalen, and Pantopon, I had paid them off.

Pantopon, like Allonal, had taken a sharp sales turn upwards when we began to market it with my informal sales letters. Our detail men boosted it, too, but at best a detail salesman can make only about 1,700 calls on physicians a year; with only seven detail men in the field, we reached relatively few doctors so directly. Our best salesman was the United States mailman. From a slow start at $12,000 a year, Pantopon sales rose sharply to $750,000 and would have gone higher still had there not been a wise legal limit placed on the amount of opium we could import for manufacturing Pantopon.

By this time in the early 1920s, the free-wheeling sales of narcotics that had prevailed when I first became a pharmacist had been curbed by Congress in the light of growing knowledge of their dangers and abuse. A series of narcotics laws, beginning with the Harrison Act and culminating in the Jones-Miller Act,

---

*(After a stock split, my holding advanced to 160 shares. For purposes of comparison, on the rare occasions that a share of Hoffmann-La Roche is traded today, it sells for $45,000.)

banned some and put the others under strict controls. The laws were designed to prevent the sale of opiates to the public except by unrefillable prescription. It happened that on the day the law became effective, Roche had a large shipment of opiates that had not yet been cleared by customs, although I already had paid a considerable duty on them. Under an administrative interpretation of the new law, I couldn't get the opiates out, nor could the government return the duty that I had paid.

The opiates did not matter to me, but we could not afford to lose the duty, so I went to Washington and began haunting the offices of Secretary of State Charles Evans Hughes, Secretary of the Treasury Andrew Mellon, and Secretary of Commerce Herbert Hoover. These three headed what was called the Narcotic Commission. Finally, after I had spent several hours in his waiting room, Hoover agreed to see me. I found him sitting behind his desk with his head propped on one arm. Without changing position he said, "What's your problem?" He sat up and made notes as I explained my plight, then said, "I'll see that you get relief." Within ten days our duty payment was refunded. More than a quarter of a century later, I found myself seated beside then former President Hoover at a banquet table. It was 1949, the time of the Truman Administration's "5 percent" influence-peddling scandals. I reminded Hoover of our first meeting, which he did not recall. "Did you get relief?" he asked me. "Thanks to you," I said, "I did." He smiled and asked me, wryly, "Did it cost you 5 percent?"

I was happy to see the new limitations applied to opiates, particularly to heroin, which we realized by then was devastating in its addictive affect. But my colleagues in Basle apparently were dismayed by the restrictions. Without sharing their secret with me, they decided to evade the drug controls if they could. Other pharmaceutical companies in Europe did the same. Congress could control American importers, but it had no jurisdiction over European producers, who remained free to sell their products to anyone who ordered them. When I found out what was happening, I was shocked beyond words.

I knew, of course, that Roche had produced sizeable quantities of narcotic drugs before the new laws, because I had imported and sold them to wholesale druggists and pharmaceutical houses. But when the restrictions were applied, no further large orders went through my office, and I was pleased that we were out of that business. Then, one day, I received an unexpected warning from the Commissioner of Narcotics in Washington. He told me that illegal opiates were being shipped by my company and others to Mexico, Canada, and the United States. Unless the shipments stopped, he said, all Roche imports would be cut off, regardless of their nature. I was appalled. Although I knew that there was a traffic in illegal drugs, I had no idea that my own company headquarters in Basle was involved in it.

As it happened, the warning came just when I was preparing to sail for my first visit to the company's Swiss headquarters. I vowed before boarding my ship to force a showdown.

● *Chapter Eight*

● The headquarters of Hoffmann-La Roche in Basle reflected the principal mental attitudes of the men who ran it; near-fetish for secrecy and a rather gloomy prospect of human nature and the world. The offices were the faintly disguised major and minor rooms of a palatial old house, once the home of a well-to-do Swiss family, that was surrounded by a high-walled fence whose gate was manned around the clock by a dour concierge. It was apparent, even to a casual observer, that the company liked to keep a close eye on its employees. The rather extensive grounds of the main house and laboratories included a smaller dwelling that was occupied by two company executives and their families; across the road under observation from the main house was a large plot of ground subdivided into small lots for the employees' vegetable gardens.

When I arrived there for the first time, in 1923, the company's tendency towards overbearing watchfulness was as much on my mind as the narcotics problem. Although I had been promised autonomy in running the American operation, Barell had appointed a brilliant but irritatingly ambitious former German professor of chemistry to be in charge of "liaison" with my business affairs. Professor Dr. Otto Eckstein had travelled the world over, spoke seven languages, including Chinese, and had become an "expert" on American business by teaching briefly at the Univer-

sity of Chicago. With Barell's patronage, he had set out to take
control of all Roche international sales promotion, including
mine, and his constant prying into my affairs had begun to annoy
me. Thus, my second most important reason for visiting Basle
was to settle, once and for all, the question of who was to run
the American company, me or Barell's ingratiating surrogate.

To my surprise, Eckstein met me when I checked into the
Drei Koeing (Trois Rois) Hotel and invited me to dinner that evening at his apartment. I accepted out of politeness and appeared
at the appointed hour. He handed me a drink.

"Now, Mr. Bobst," he began in flawless Cambridge English,
"we are going to have a council meeting tomorrow. I thought
you and I might go over the situation and clarify matters." He
smiled, as if anxious to strike some kind of a bargain.

"Doctor, I have come all the way from New York to attend
this meeting," I answered him slowly. "I will say what I have
to say there. I do not intend to discuss anything relating to it
with you tonight."

"Well, as long as you're here, I don't see why you shouldn't,"
he shrugged.

"I'm your guest and you're my host," I said. "I don't think
it is proper for a host to insist that a guest do something that
he doesn't want to do. So if it is a matter of your insisting on
talking business, then I'll take my leave." I remained through
dinner, but the evening was an unpleasant one.

The next morning, while visiting various offices in the Roche
headquarters building before the meeting, I came across a cryptic
telegram. It read, "SHIP AT ONCE 30 KILOS OF M-
HYDROCHLORIDE AND 9 SMALL KEGS OF SODIUM BI-
CARBONATE. MARK THE ONE CONTAINING THE
STUFF." The telegram had been sent from a New York hotel.
I recognized it at once as an underworld order for morphine,
which the purchasers were gambling would slip through customs
under the guise of sodium bicarbonate. By the time the council
meeting began, I was hot with fury over this fresh evidence of
my company's perfidy. But the Eckstein matter was first on the
agenda.

Barell called the meeting of his top executives to order and nodded to Eckstein, who took the floor with a large sheaf of letters and papers. He spoke at length on the urgency of subordinating the foreign agencies of Roche to headquarters management in matters of advertising and promotion. Both subject matter and policy must be controlled from Basle, he emphasized. Other agency managers were cooperative, he cited from the letters in his hands, but the American manager was not. He pointed to me and declared that I was rebellious, that I had refused to submit my material to him before using it, and that my letters and advertisements — all of which I wrote myself — were undignified and were hurting the reputation of the company. Eckstein sat down with a satisfied smile and Barell called upon me to reply.

"Well, Dr. Barell, I'm not prepared with any documents or letters," I said. "I don't think I need any. I don't need them because the situation is simple. I took hold of this business in 1920 when it was in trouble. Now, three years later, I've paid off the debts and rehabilitated the company to a considerable extent. I've sent you the 12½ percent of gross income we pay as our share of your overhead, and I've sent you $300,000 of dividends, something you never received before. I've started to pay off the debentures we owed. I've done this through my own ability and initiative. I like the job. It has been a great challenge, and I want to continue.

"But the good professor here would like to run me. He would like, figuratively, to have a long cord reaching from Basle to the chair in my office on Cliff Street, and he would like to pull the cord and have me jump. I want to make it clear to you, to him, and to the other gentlemen here that if he tries to pull such a cord, he'll find an empty chair. I will not be sitting in it. If I stay at my post, I don't want to have any further correspondence with Dr. Eckstein. It's only aggravating, perhaps to him, certainly to me.

"I want your agreement that I will operate without interference, and then I have something else to say."

Barell agreed without argument, and his executives followed suit. He was a straight-laced Germanic autocrat who ran the company with an iron fist, but he kept an open mind, at least in those days, and he was not about to destroy what was becoming his most profitable subdivision just to satisfy the ambitions of an opportunistic subordinate. I took the floor again.

"Now, gentlemen, we've dealt with one problem that was responsible for my coming over here. I have another problem, a far more serious problem, on which I must have action."

Barell, a large man who wore a full beard and baggy clothes to make himself look older than his forty odd years (presumably to please his wife, who was twenty years his senior), shifted his weight and looked up at me with surprise. "What is it?" he asked, as if nothing could be more serious than the matter just settled.

"It is the selling of narcotics to Americans. I am aware that you have been shipping narcotics to illegal purchasers in Canada, the United States, and Mexico. It must stop."

"Mr. Bobst," Barell began like an indulgent parent explaining the facts of life, "you did not know this, but we make $200,000 or more each year on those sales. We get a dollar, sometimes two dollars, more per ounce from those purchasers than through normal channels. Why must it stop? It's perfectly legal for us in Switzerland to fill any orders that we receive."

"Filling orders may be legal here, Dr. Barell, but it is not legal to sell them in the United States, and I do not care to be identified with a business that seeks to make a profit out of destroying my fellow man, my own fellow citizens."

Barell bristled and his fellow executives were on the edges of their chairs. "You are wrong, Mr. Bobst. We will not stop. You cannot stop us."

"No, you're wrong, Dr. Barell," I said. "If you don't stop, the United States government will prevent you from importing any pharmaceutical products into the country. Furthermore, as I said, I will not remain with a company that deals in illegal drugs which destroy the Americans who use them."

Barell exploded with a German obscenity, one of the few that I ever heard him use, relegating the United States to a vulgar fate. He did not realize that I understood.

"No, the United States will not do that, Dr. Barell," I replied calmly. "**It will do exactly** what I told you. If you attempt to carry on this trade that is degrading this company, there will be no Roche in America."

The meeting broke up in turmoil without arriving at any resolution of my demand.

The next day an uncommunicative Dr. Barell took me with him to Zurich for a business meeting. He did not mention my demand of the day before until we sat down to lunch together in a little restaurant on the market place. Only then, he looked at me quizzically and said, "You wish to make a stand on this narcotics question?"

"I certainly do," I said. "Please believe me, I want to help this company, not to hurt it. Yesterday I told you of my own repugnance concerning these narcotics sales. I meant what I said, sincerely. I personally do not care to be identified with a company that makes money out of destroying my own people. I think you can understand that. But quite aside from my own feelings, the government of the United States is aware of this problem. The U.S. Narcotics Control Commission knows what you are doing. If you persist, we will not be able to import anything at all. The government can enforce that."

Barell was a logical man with a good mind, and he obviously had taken seriously my report that the U.S. government would retaliate against Roche if it continued its illegal sales.

"Well, what do you want from me?" he sighed.

"Last night in my hotel room I drafted a statement," I said, taking a folded paper from my pocket. "I'm not a lawyer, but I am sure that if you sign this statement it will have legal force. It says that 'The firm of F. Hoffmann-La Roche of Basle, Switzerland, henceforth will accept no orders from nor furnish any narcotics to illegal purchasers in Mexico, Canada, or the United States.' It's that simple."

Barell carefully put his signature beneath what I had written, then asked, "What will you do with this?"

"I intend to deliver this agreement to the United States Minister in Switzerland. He will forward it to the Department of State in Washington. A copy will be sent to the Narcotics Commission.

It will remain there as evidence of our intention never to engage in this traffic again."

I did as I said, and, so far as I know, the handwritten document is still in the files of the Narcotics bureau in Washington, forty-eight years later.

(My allusion to this episode of nearly fifty years ago has been mainly to indicate that the narcotics problem existed even then. But, fortunately, during those days it was found mostly in the "red light" districts of American cities, instead of being an epidemic involving both youths and adults throughout our country, as it is today.)

During the days about which I have been writing, the Swiss had not as yet signed the agreement with the League of Nations that controlled the sale of narcotic drugs. Also, it must be borne in mind that other European drug companies were unrestricted in this respect and consequently took advantage of the premium prices paid for the narcotics sold in countries where controls existed.

Dr. Barell, as I discovered when I came to know him, was not at heart an immoral man. He not only sympathized with my abhorrence of the narcotics trade, he privately agreed with my point of view. But in business affairs, Barell acted as if he was utterly amoral. Although privately they might abhor certain behavior as questionable on moral or ethical grounds, if there was no Swiss law against that behavior, or if the law had loopholes that permitted profitable digressions from it, Barell and the directors would engage the company in it. They held to two ethical standards, one for their private lives and another for business. As private citizens they behaved honorably and obeyed the laws; as businessmen they seemingly sought to evade laws if the company stood to make a profit. The distortion of their morality was a never-ending source of headaches to me as the head of Roche-America, for they saw no reason why I, too, couldn't adopt the same standard and act against my own conscience by evading instead of legally avoiding tax regulations.

I was as conscientious as any American businessman in my efforts to avoid paying unnecessary taxes by taking such write-offs as we were entitled to receive and by taking care in the planning of capital investment, expansion, and other deductable items. But to attempt to evade legitimate American taxes not only would have been a violation of my own conscience, but foolish as well, for the simple reason that evaders usually get caught. Truthfully, in my opinion, my Swiss colleagues found it very difficult to distinguish between what we term tax evasion and tax avoidance. From its beginning, in fact, the Swiss company was structured in such a way as to reduce payment of taxes to the absolute minimum.

These methods of avoiding or evading taxes were commonly followed by many firms abroad.

Although a Swiss company, Hoffmann-La Roche's international activities were conducted under the umbrella of a Lichtenstein holding company called SAPAC, an acronym for Societe Anonyme de Produits Alimentaires et de Gellulose. Each share of Roche stock actually carried with it a presumed share of SAPAC, but these shares were not issued. Instead, there was a large set of coupons, representing the unissued shares, that could be clipped and cashed in at the required intervals. These coupons, as has been the custom in Switzerland, did not bear the name of their owner. To avoid Swiss taxes, all of the company's foreign earnings went into this Lichtenstein tax refuge. SAPAC's "headquarters," nothing more than a financial forwarding office, was shifted to Panama during the war. The last I heard, it was chartered as a Canadian corporation with headquarters in Montevideo, Uruguay.

My profits, of course, went to SAPAC only after they had been fully taxed by U.S. federal, state, and local governments, a fact which seemingly irritated my Basle friend no end. I shall never forget one memorable occasion during a visit to Basle when I explained in exasperation that even if I wanted to evade American taxes, which I did not, the Internal Revenue Service would never permit it.

"Why can't you treat your revenue department in the same way that we treat the Swiss government?" one of the Basle executives innocently inquired. "When they come to see our books, we refuse to show them. Instead, we give them just a digest indicating the profits and the amount of taxes that we will pay."

In my twenty-four years of management with the company, I never fully convinced the Swiss that we simply do not do business that way in the United States. Ultimately, it was Dr. Barell's own failure to appreciate the niceties of the American free enterprise system that led to my final and total break with him. But for many years after the time of my first visit to Basle in 1923, we were close business friends, and as long as he left me alone to run the American operation as I thought it should be run, we remained so.

Once my two major problems were cleared away, my first European trip became a pleasure. The aristocratic and powerful Mr. Koechlin, who was then president of Handelsbank and president as well of Roche's four-man board of directors, took a liking to me and invited me to his home, a friendly ritual that was repeated a number of times, much to Barell's chagrin, whenever I visited Basle. The Swiss observed strict protocols of social class. As a successful American I apparently qualified to mix socially with the local artistocracy. Barell, however, had struggled up from humble origins, a fact that he was never permitted to forget. Koechlin would work closely and cordially with him in business, but if he saw Barell on the street or at a social function he would not even acknowledge his existence, and he would never deign to invite Barell into his home.

In a way, I suppose, Barell had his revenge at the office where Fritz Hoffmann's oldest son Emmanuel, a fine and handsome young fellow, was learning the business in a junior position. Barell ran his office like a Prussian riding master, and as long as Emmanuel, who was Koechlin's nephew, worked for him he had to toe the line. During my first visit, Emmanuel and I became close friends. We used to go out together in his elegant new Mercedes automobile, but no matter where we went he had to be in early, because Barell insisted that he must report for work, like the other employees, not a minute later than 7:30 A.M. Nine years later Emmanuel was still enduring Barell's strict work discipline, even though he had inherited about one-third of the company when his father died. One night in 1932, Emmanuel drove to Geneva to attend a wine fest. He was racing along the road back to Basle in the early hours of the next morning in order to be at his desk by Barell's strict starting time when he fell asleep at the wheel. The car hit a train that was standing at a station. He died two days later. We had become such close friends by then that I felt his loss as deeply as if it had been Mahlon Yoder or Howard Story.

Barell was an excellent administrator, in the classic European tradition, but he had no talent for sales or sales promotion and was honest enough with himself to acknowledge it. During my first European journey he urged me to visit each of the company's dozen branch offices of Western Europe to conduct courses in marketing and salesmanship. I was pleased to do it and delighted to learn that, in return for sharing my sales techniques with the Europeans, the company would pay me a bonus which came to the equivalent of the dividends on 100 shares of Roche stock. The trip lasted eight weeks. Fortunately, I had prepared for a long absence before leaving New York. In those days of leisurely shipboard travel, quick trips to Europe were out of the question. The ocean crossing alone took seven days. I had carefully instructed Nelson Peterson and my secretary, Miss Mae Murray (an invaluable business associate who remained with me, in all of my careers, for forty-nine years) in how to handle matters during my absence. They could reach me by mail and cable, but our problems were few and they handled them well, so the business travel in Europe was like a vacation for me even though I worked every day. I had time to visit both great and obscure art galleries, and even bought a few inexpensive paintings which became the beginnings of eventually a sizeable number of Impressionists and 18th-century English canvasses.

I was charmed by all of the European countries, with one exception. Germany both depressed and frightened me. The country was then reeling under the blows of the runaway inflation that followed World War I and led eventually to the rise of Hitler's fascist state. When I arrived in Berlin the mark was at its lowest ebb. In order to have enough cash with me for a modest

day's activity, I had to carry a briefcase filled with German currency. In the evenings I would empty the briefcase on my hotel
room bed and cull out the small denomination notes, because
they were virtually worthless. I gave them to the hotel employees.
For the equivalent of two American dollars a day — I have forgotten how many thousands of marks that was — I hired a chauffeured Mercedes limousine to go about the city.

I shall never forget the vivid illustration of inflation's ruinous
effects that came one evening when I joined Hoffmann's former
Czarist manager, a White Russian named Salle, and his son for
dinner at the elegant Bristol Hotel on the Unter den Linden.
We sat down to a full seven-course meal, including caviar and
vodka (my first taste of that tasteless alcohol; I hated it), still
wines and champagne. The check for three of us came to the
equivalent in marks of seventy American cents. I handed the
waiter an American dollar bill and told him to keep the change.

"Please don't make jokes with me, sir," he said, "When you
cannot mean to give me so much." There was no irony in his
voice. He meant what he said. To him the thirty-cent tip, millions
of marks worth of solid American money, was astronomical. "We
need food in my home. We take eggs or butter as our salary,"
he said.

"I'm not fooling," I told him, "that's your tip."

To my embarassment, he fell on his knees, in gratitude. I
had seen, literally, how inflation can bring a nation to its knees.
It was a lesson I never forgot, a lesson that I have recounted
on more than one occasion to my close friend, Richard Nixon.

● *Chapter Nine*

● On February 14, 1924, my father took down his well-thumbed copy of Charles Lamb's *The Essays of Elia* and turned to one of his favorite pieces, "The Superannuated Man." After reading it over as he had many times before, he carefully wrote this note on the title page:

"Charles Lamb retired at 50 years of age. I expect to retire at 77 years, 4 months and 15 days next Sept. the first. My dear boy Elmer offers to help to support me. God bless him and all my dear children and fine wife. This essay inspirited me."

Although he did not know it, he already had begun the last year of a full, eventful, and spiritually rich life. He had not ranged widely over the world, except in his restless mind; he had never achieved great prominence, except among those who had seen him and heard his voice; and he had accumulated no wealth, except in the currency of his soul. Not long before he began to look forward to retirement, we visited Atlantic City together and took a long stroll on the boardwalk. He was in a reflective mood, not at all disturbed by his advancing age; rather, he was pleased with what he had done with his years. He was still as devoted to my mother as he had been when he first met her in Harper's Ferry almost half a century before. He had raised five children in a loving environment that enriched them more than material wealth could have done. Kate was raising her own family in Lititz. Mildred, a lovely girl with a fine figure, a beautiful face, and a talent for music, was happily married to the son of a successful Trenton jeweler. Dorothy, also beautiful and musically talented, had married a college teacher and, like her sisters, was happy. Harry, who had served as a cavalryman, a tanker, and a sniper in the British army, had suffered terribly and been deafened in the war, but he was making a new life for himself as a pharmacist in a drugstore that I helped him to establish. My father was proud of all of us, but he was most proud, I think, of the degree to which he had managed to touch so many lives other than those of us closest to him. He was reflecting on these things when he turned to me on the boardwalk and said:

"Son, I saw in the paper today that a wealthy man died and left $50 million to his wife. As for my wealth, it is non-existent as far as dollars are concerned. I have spent more than 40 years now in the ministry, and I don't think that in all those years I've received a total of even $40,000 in salary. But wealth and peace of mind cannot be evaluated in terms of money. They must be judged rather by the knowledge of what you have done in the world that is worthwhile in respect to your fellow man.

"Through the many years that I have worked in the Lord's vineyard, I compare myself to a painter who can take a rather drab picture produced by one of his pupils and with a few masterful strokes of his brush bring life into it. I feel that I have been able to touch the lives of men and women many times and have changed them from a Godless life into one that was saintly. That knowledge to me is of far greater value than a great fortune."

It was to us, too. If you live long enough, the events of your life have a way of completing themselves, like broken circles seeking logical closures, coming full cycle. It happened that I had read the same obituary as the one my father referred to, and I knew its wealthy subject. It was only a few years later that I saw the young widow who had inherited his $50-million fortune. I watched as she heedlessly flung an obviously valuable mink coat onto the dirty deck of a passenger liner and hurried into the first-class salon to drink and dance with one of her new beaus. The large inheritance, to her, had been only a ticket to pleasures that she chased but never really found. Later I noted without surprise that she had died of dissipation. The inheritance of those of us who received something from my father was entirely ethereal, but it was far more valuable than hers.

Aside from his bitter experiences in the Civil War, Father's life was a studious and quiet one, but it was not without noteworthy occasions. Among other things, he had seen the greatest and the worst of Republican presidents and a few other national leaders in between. As a boy infantryman, he had been awestruck by the lanky figure of Lincoln just a few yards away on an army parade ground. The experience made a vivid impression upon him. Less salutary, however, was his meeting of Warren Gamaliel Harding. The latter was my doing. Harding, then a United States senator, was to address my Rotary Club in Philadelphia, and I invited my father to come and hear him. I was chairman of the entertainment committee and responsible for the senator's care. I introduced my father and said, "You're now shaking hands with a man who in my opinion is going to become president of the United States." The prediction seemed logical to me because Harding was prominent, personable, handsome, and seemingly forthright, all prime presidential qualities. Had I known of the irresponsible and even fraudulent influences to which he would later be subjected, I would not have welcomed him so ebulliently.

Father also met Teddy Roosevelt, whom he almost idolized. When the news accounts of Roosevelt's victory at San Juan Hill were first printed, I remember my father saying, "That young man will be president some day." The only time Father ever deviated from voting a straight Prohibition Party ticket was when TR ran for the presidency. He was thrilled to shake the Rough Rider's hand when I took him to a political reception in Philadelphia one election year.

While he saw each of those presidents only once, he made it clear to me that he had seen far more of Woodrow Wilson than he ever wanted to. As one of the leading clergymen of Trenton, Father often was asked to give the benediction at major public events. He also was Trenton's most articulate veteran of the Civil War and as such was asked to address the Fourth of July gathering in the city's principal park every year. In the course of these events he often shared a carriage or a platform with Wilson, who was then governor of New Jersey. "Son," my father said, "he may be a good governor, but he's a rebel." Wilson had grown up in Stanton, Virginia, where his father was an Episcopal clergyman. I visted the Stanton church once while Wilson was president and asked the aged sexton there if he remembered the illustrious son of his former pastor.

"Oh, I remember the president very well," he said. "When he was a young man he used to ask me for the key to the church. Then he would go in there and make orations to the empty pews."

On one of the occasions that my father had to appear at a public function with Governor Wilson, a famous opera singer was asked to open the festivities with the song, "The Beautiful Isle of Somewhere," a sentimental ballad alluding to heaven. Wilson followed her to the podium and, speaking extemporaneously, derided the sentimental lyrics of her song. His rude remarks made my father furious and convinced him that Wilson was a cold and heartless man. My father appreciated sentiment and was wary of those who were suspicious of it, because sentiment to him was only the sweet coating of a rich and loving soul.

From the time that he left the army hospital at Annapolis in 1865 until the autumn of 1924, my father was never seriously ill, never let sickness keep him from his pulpit. But suddenly, not long before the date he had set for his retirement, his health inexplicably failed. I rushed to Philadelphia and worriedly brought five specialists whom I knew to examine him. None of them could arrive at a diagnosis. One day Father had been hale and hearty, invigorated from walking four or five miles to visit sick and troubled members of his congregation, and the next he was ill. He was not in pain, but he could not retain food or water, and it was clear that he was dying of acute dehydration. Each of the doctors shook his head sadly and shrugged, "Your father is suffering from old age." We know now that there is no such thing as dying of "old age" — even the most ancient human's death can be attributed to a more exact cause—but medicine then was still far more of an art than a science, and there was nothing that they could do to save him.

On November 22, 1924, he got out of his bed at home, brushed aside the protests of his nurse, and went to the bathroom to shave himself with an old-fashioned straight razor. Then he returned to his bed and sang, as loudly as he could, three stanzas of Billy Sunday's famous crusade hymn, "Open wide the windows, open wide the door, and let a little sunshine in." He died the following day.

Father's church was filled to overflowing with his congregation and with friends of all creeds and races. Six clergymen offered eulogies at the funeral service, and most of the audience followed the cortege to Laurel Hill Cemetery. His coffin was raised over a grave, beneath a newly-planted pine tree on a hillside overlooking the Schuylkill River. A United States Army guard fired a formal salute, then the coffin was lowered as an army bugler blew taps in honor of the Reverend Isaac Walton Bobst, former private, Sheridan's cavalry.

*The original entrance to the Hoffmann-La Roche plant in Nutley, N.J.
The building and grounds served as a design prototype for other attractive complexes built by corporations in the expanding phamaceuticals
industry.*

● *Chapter Ten*

● One day in 1928 my old friend Charles Cameron from the Roth-well and Cameron drugstore in Philadelphia came to call on me in my New York office. He needed help. I had known Charles Cameron since 1906, when I first made my rounds as a rubber goods salesman while studying for the preliminary bar examinations. It was during one of these calls, in fact, that he interrupted me and said, "Doctor, you are a registered pharmacist?"

"That's right," I answered.

"Filled many prescriptions?"

"I certainly have."

"I need a manager very badly," he complained. "I have two managers now. Neither of them is worth very much. I'm taking a course, a special course in bacteriology at the Philadelphia College of Pharmacy, and I can't be here all the time to watch them. Would you consider replacing one of them?"

"What do you pay your managers?" I asked him.

"I pay them fifteen dollars a week. I also have a good young man to work around the store and make deliveries."

"You tell me these managers are not worth very much?"

"Not much. I don't think they're any good at all."

"If you want to get rid of both of them and let me take over both jobs for twenty-one dollars a week, I'll give it a serious thought."

"You think you could handle both jobs? We do a pretty big prescription business."

I wouldn't want to take it if I wasn't sure I could run it," I said. "I'd expect you to give me a hand in the afternoon when you get through with your schoolwork."

"Oh, I'd come back," he said. "I'd be here."

So I went to work for him, running the store. When Ethel and I decided to elope to New York, I borrowed twenty dollars from him. By the time Walton was born in 1908 we had become good friends, and a couple of weeks after Walton's birth his own son, Charles Sherwood Cameron, Jr., was born with the same obstetrician and nurse in attendance. We saw one another from time to time, and as Charlie's young son grew I was particularly impressed by his lively spirit and intelligence. By the mid-1920s, however, events had taken a bad turn for Charlie. His drugstore had failed.

"I've come here because of necessity," he told me that day in 1926. "Since the store went down I've had a position with the Nestlè company calling on doctors, but they're going to discontinue detailing."

"How much were you getting?" I asked him.

"I got sixty-five dollars a week. I have to find something to replace it, because I'm trying to get my son Charles through college and into medical school. Maybe you can help us find a medical school."

"All right, I'll try. But what about yourself?"

"Well, I thought you might be able to use me."

"Charlie, I'm sorry, but I don't think it's good policy to have close friends come to work for me." That was hard for me to say, but I meant it. "But I have a friend who is head of Schering and Glatz, Dr. Edgar Sampton, and I happen to know that he needs someone of your experience and ability. I'd like you to see him."

"Well, Doctor," Charlie always called me "Doctor," "I'll see him now, today, or any time."

Charlie's high stiff collar was a little frayed, and his necktie did not go with his suit. "Now Charlie, I don't want you to feel hurt by what I'm going to say," I told him. "Up the street from here is one of those chain stores. I wish you would go there and get a different collar and shirt, and a necktie whose color will be in sympathy with your coat. Then you'll find a barber shop near the subway entrance. I want you to go down there and get a trim and have your nails manicured."

"I've never had my nails manicured in my life!"

"Well, you're going to have them manicured today."

While he was out, I called Edgar Sampson and praised Charlie to the heavens. "He knows pharmacy from beginning to end. He knows medicine; he's well up on it. He's taken a special course in bacteriology at the College of Pharmacy in Philadelphia. Wonderful character, personable, intelligent. Writes a very fine letter." Sampson wanted to see him that afternoon.

Charlie came back looking better than I had ever seen him. I handed him a Schering and Glatz catalog so he could study their products before he went for his interview.

"If he asks me about salary," he said, "What shall I tell him?"

"Ask for eighty-five dollars a week."

"Eighty-five dollars?" He was shocked.

"Yes. I told him you're a crackerjack. I told him you could become his assistant. I talked you up to the heavens. You're no cheap man. Eighty-five dollars."

Sampson called me at home that evening to tell me how much Charlie had impressed him. "I'm going to write him and ask him for a little more information about himself, though," he said.

The next morning I called Charlie to tell him that he would receive a letter very soon from Edgar Sampson. "I want you to send it to me immediately, special delivery," I said. "I'll write your reply to it."

Within two days the letter came. I wrote an answer and sent it to Charlie to mail to Sampson. Three days later, Edgar called me. "You know, I've got a very intelligent letter from that man Cameron," he said. "I'm impressed with him."

"Edgar, you know I wouldn't send him to you unless he was good," I said.

Charlie was hired at eighty-five dollars a week and soon got a fifteen-dollar raise when he became Sampson's assistant. Not long after that, through friendly relations with the faculty, I helped his son Charles, Jr., gain admission to Hahnemann Medical College in Philadelphia. I did not realize it at the time, but through my small efforts affecting their two lives in the 1920s, I had set in motion events that would affect my own life almost two decades later. The circle of life's events, once again, had begun to close.

● *Chapter Eleven*

● The activities of Hoffmann-La Roche in the 1920s brought me nearer than ever to my friends in the medical profession. The closest of these was Dr. Morris Fishbein, editor of the *Journal of the American Medical Association* and the most perceptive and powerful polemicist in the history of American medicine. No one since Hippocrates and Galen has done more to strengthen the standards of the profession and to demolish quackery, nor has any doctor since Morris braved more public controversy without wavering one inch from his values and ideals. He was a superb leader and spokesman for a profession that, for many years, deeply needed his wise council. He is still active and remains one of my closest friends today.

Morris told of our meeting in his autobiography, *Morris Fishbein, M.D.*, and I think, perhaps, that he pictured some of my activities at that time more objectively than I can describe them. He wrote:

"I first met Elmer Holmes Bobst in Chicago in 1920, when he had just taken a position as an executive of the Hoffmann-La Roche company. He wanted to become acquainted with the officials of the Council on Pharmacy and Chemistry and the executives of the AMA . . . The campaign which the AMA was waging through its Council on Pharmacy and Chemistry for raising the standards of the drug industry brought many pharmaceutical

143

manufacturers to Chicago for fuller information on standards and requirements. Dr. Simmons, then the editor of the *Journal,* . . . conferred with these visitors but only with suspicion and grave doubt, like diplomats working on an armistice.

"One time Theodore Weicker of Squibb, visiting Dr. Simmons, asked specially to see me. [Morris was then assistant editor.] I was called in but only after Weicker left. Dr. Simmons warned that communication with pharmaceutical manufacturers was about the same as Faust trying to make a deal with Mephistopheles. When Elmer Bobst, much younger (at age 36) and far less prepossessing in manner or appearance than Theodore Weicker, arrived, Dr. Simmons was cold and angry . . . I told him that I saw no reason why anyone could not maintain his honor and his integrity in communicating with any visitor. I could listen to any representative of any agency . . . .

"During the next few years I came to know Elmer Bobst well. He could play bridge or poker or golf purely for the fun of the game and never for particularly large stakes. He enjoyed the theater as I did. He enjoyed good books as I did. He enjoyed genial companions with good food, good drink, and good fun . . .

"Then in 1924, an incident occurred that cemented our friendship . . . at the [AMA] meeting in Atlantic City . . . Elmer Bobst proposed that a few of us with our wives stroll the Boardwalk . . . We came to the Silver Slipper Club . . . As we sat in the Club, a delegate from Iowa came in, accompanied by a handsome young woman whom he brought to our table. Pointing to [AMA president] Dr. Haggard, he said: 'I want you to meet our president,' and she said, 'Why, Mr. Coolidge, I never thought to see you in a place like this!'

"This was the origin of the annual Silver Slipper Club. A dinner on Wednesday night after other AMA meetings had ended included a fine supper, excellent entertainment, and the opportunity for a few hundred people concerned with many different aspects of medicine to meet socially . . .

"The taint of commercial influence was never alleged. The officers of the Association, including the members of the board and their wives and the directors of many of the councils and bureaus participated . . .

"In view of the extensive political activities in organized medicine, the umblemished repute of this social event may be considered one of the marvels of the age . . .

"Elmer Bobst liked to be master of ceremonies . . . essentially a sentimental man [he] liked to burst into song, invariably some sweetly sentimental ballad which told of the delights of life and happiness in 'the good old days.' "

That was a fair description and a flattering accolade for a happy social occasion which I planned and hosted every year. The Silver Slipper dinner party, honoring the incoming president of the AMA, remained an institution at the annual medical meetings for thirty years, and its guests included virtually all of the most important men in medicine in the United States and the world. Obviously it offered a ripe opportunity for commercial exploitation by my company, but I never allowed even a hint of salesmanship to touch the event. I invited only two Roche people to attend: my remarkable medical director, Dr. Ralph Shaner, who was a member of the AMA, and my loyal secretary, Mae Murray. The only mute, but I must confess, powerful, promotional aspect of the affair was simply the unacknowledged awareness of the distinguished guests that the party was hosted by the president of Roche-America and in later years, Warner-Lambert.

The Silver Slipper parties were totally relaxing affairs in which everyone put away the cares of the profession and simply had a good time. Only one of the parties ever bordered on tension. That was in 1949, after the AMA House of Delegates, meeting again in Atlantic City, voted to muzzle Morris Fishbein as the outspoken editor of the *Journal*.

Morris had firmly stood his ground for thirty-five years with the AMA, fearlessly going after quackery and applying his own powerful talents as a speaker and writer to upgrade medicine and associated fields, including pharmacology. Because he was both outspoken and effective, he accumulated as many enemies as friends in and out of his profession. Serious efforts to unseat him from his post as *Journal* editor and to silence him as a spokesman for American medicine began in the mid-1940s. What Morris called "medicine's civil war" had reached a fever pitch by 1948. In 1949 the House of Delegates finally passed a resolution that could have no effect other than to force his retirement from the *Journal*.

The resolution stunned all of Morris's closest friends and angered some of us. I sat up talking with him until 3 A.M. the night after the vote, then retired for a short rest before preparing for the Silver Slipper party the following night. Before I left his room, Morris said, "Anna and I are coming to your party, but please, don't make any reference to yesterday's events."

"I'm always more or less controlled by how the spirit moves me at the time, Morris," I replied.

The festivities began with a cocktail party at 10 P.M., followed by a supper, during which I took over as master of ceremonies and prepared to introduce the five or six acts of entertainment— singers, bands, and celebrities from Broadway and Hollywood. As I rose to begin the entertainment, I thought of the great service Morris Fishbein had rendered to medicine, and how we had worked together to make the pharmaceutical industry what it had become, the handmaiden of the medical profession. His adversaries were in the audience. Every physician in the room was a present or potential user of my firm's products, and influential far beyond his own practice. The most politic course for me as head of Roche would have been to remain neutral, to say nothing. I had no taste for neutrality.

Spotlighted on the stage, I held up the evening's program and spoke into the public address system. "This headline reads, 'Silver Slipper Party in Honor of the Great Men of Medicine! I want to say the printer has made an error. The party tonight is not in honor of the great *men* of medicine. It is in honor of *one man* of medicine who in my opinion has made the greatest contribution of anyone to medicine in this country. His name is Dr. Morris Fishbein."

My remarks were met by several seconds of stunned silence. Then the audience broke into sustained applause. Anna Fishbein rushed up to the platform, threw her arms around me, and kissed me. The next morning Morris and I were strolling along the boardwalk on the way to the exhibition hall. For a few minutes he was silent, then he turned to me, eyes characteristically bulging in his jolly, round face, and said,

"I know no other one person heading any pharmaceutical enterprise in this country who would have the goddamned guts to say what you said about me last night."

Morris relinquished his post at the AMA *Journal,* but he continued to write books and hundreds of magazine articles in support of what he believed. As I write this I take some satisfaction in knowing that he outlived most of his critics and is still going strong. He is, in a way, like the subject of one of his own favorite stories about an old man who, when asked how he felt, replied, "Fine, I am eighty years old and I haven't got an enemy in the world."

"How can that be?"

"I've outlived all of them."

One of Morris Fishbein's most energetic causes was the Council on Pharmacy and Chemistry of the AMA. He was deeply committed to establishing high standards for the pharmaceutical industry and to elevating the profession of pharmacy from its sometimes ignoble role as a lowly medical middleman to that of a respected health care profession.

I was thoroughly committed to both causes long before meeting Morris. My early years as a pharmacist had led me to reflect on the sad state the profession was reaching. More and more we were wearing the dirty apron of the soda fountain instead of the white coat of professional excellence. Pharmacy increasingly had become alienated from medial practice and standards. In ancient times, the apothecaries of Greece, Rome, and Roman Britain were usually physicians and surgeons as well. Early British history mentions one court apothecary, William de Stanes, who was at the same time a physician, an ordinance supplier, a vintner, and a dispenser of remedies. By 1672, the Society of Apothecaries included both practitioners and chemists, and together they founded the pharmaceutical industry when the society opened a laboratory to manufacture remedies for London physicians, surgeons, and apothecaries. The society did a brisk business selling the remedies in bulk to apothecary shops, the forerunners of modern drugstores. By the nineteenth century the society had split in two, with the pharmacists going into their shops and the practitioners into medicine. The separation of professional pharmacist from professional physician has grown wider ever since. I wanted to narrow that gap, and in those days I already had begun working on a plan that I hoped would accomplish my dream of bringing doctor and pharmacist close together again for the benefit of health care generally.

I was not in a position to do much about the professional excellence of individual pharmacists in the 1920s, but I was in a position to do something about the pharmaceutical industry, and I moved as rapidly as I could to lead one of its first major revolutions.

I had been conscious ever since I began calling on pharmaceutical manufacturers of the downright unhealthy conditions under which most of them worked. Roche-New York was typical of the industry as a whole. When I first entered the old offices on Fulton Street the windows of its small medicinal "mixing" room were open to all of the dust and grime of the city. Hygienic standards were rudimentary. Our loft building on Cliff Street was no improvement. Delicate pharmaceutical manufacture took place above ancient wooden floors from which dust rose with every vibration. Rats and mice infested the walls and crawl spaces of the building. Some of our production involved volatile chemicals that presented a constant danger of explosion and fire. I vowed as soon as I took over the Roche operation in New York that as soon as we could afford it, I would lead the industry out of the unsanitary quagmire of city grime and dirt in which it worked and create a clean and modern home for medicine in beautiful surroundings.

On the last working day of each year, beginning with my first in New York, I gathered the Roche staff at Whyte's Restaurant on Fulton Street for a summing up of past activity and a forecast of the future. Each year I sketched for them my dream of building a beautiful new Roche complex in a quiet, pastoral setting. And each year Aubrey Lobell, an English accountant whom I had brought in to establish cost controls and up-to-date financial record-keeping, quipped, "It sounds damn' good, even though I doubt it will ever happen."

Lobell, of all people, should have known better, because he saw the figures in our books. Our sales and profits were increasing at a rate of 33-1/3 percent each year. By 1925 I had paid off the $250,000 in debentures owed to Basle, and by 1928 we had done so well, principally with Allonal, that I sent a scout out into the countryside to look for land in a clean and stable community. He located a site in Nutley, New Jersey, fifteen miles from Manhattan. It was an old and settled community in the Passaic Valley at the foothills of the Orange Mountains, with good schools, an honest and well-run city administration, and no smoke, noise, or heavy industry. I spent one day tramping around its fields, gathering cockleburrs on my pantslegs, and decided to buy twenty-two acres on a hill overlooking the town.

Emil Barell sailed to New York for the ground-breaking of our new offices and plant. I was startled when I met him on the Hudson River pier where his ship docked. His elderly wife had died a few years before and he had married a much younger woman. Apparently freed of the need to look older than he was, Barrell had thrown off his baggy suits and shaggy beard. When he walked off the boat I did not recognize him. He was nattily dressed, like a Berlin dandy of the period, and wore only a neatly-trimmed mustache which exposed a rather weak-looking mouth and chin. His new wife was a charming and beautiful Russian-German opera singer whose mother was Jewish, a fact that figured largely in all of our lives when World War II began.

By that time, Roche-New York had restructured as a wholly-owned, independent subsidiary corporation of F. Hoffmann-La Roche, Basle. I was no longer general manager, but president of the American company. My salary had been increased appropriately to $28,000 a year, plus my 5 percent of profits. We were doing well in a booming economy, and the directors in Basle were happily looking forward to the certain day when the American company's profits would dwarf those of the parent company itself. That day already was taking shape in Nutley, New Jersey. I had arranged to build and equip the new plant entirely out of capital and retained earnings without asking Basle for funds, issuing securities, or taking a mortgage or any other long-term debt. The directors were so pleased with our progress, in fact, that they gave me permission to draw up plans for one of the most liberal employee pension and insurance programs in any industry and the first ever introduced in our own. I established the employee benefit program just as the Depression got under-way. The new plant, however, came first.

At the ground-breaking, I spoke to the assembled guests and employees, who now numbered 180. "We shall not be satisfied with mere success," I told them. "We pledge ourselves to an even greater aim. We shall strive by ever-increasing study and research to make this institution a notable factor in guarding the life and health of the nation." I sincerely meant what I said.

The new plant site was not far from Montclair, where Ethel and I had bought a comfortable house on South Mountain Avenue that had been built some years earlier by one of Thomas Edison's partners. Ethel loved the house and the quiet life we established for ourselves there; but she was exasperated, I think, when I came home in the evenings that year with dreams of building and ground plans under my arms and spread them on the floor to sketch in the broad avenues and pleasant gardens that I wanted our company's new "research park" to have. With an architect's help, I personally planned the interior and exterior layouts of the buildings as well as the drainage of the grounds and the three acres of landscaping, complete with evergreens, pin oaks, flower gardens, two clay tennis courts, and a greenhouse to supply flowers for the reception room and early vegetables for the employee cafeteria.

The building contractor doubted whether he could meet my deadline when I told him in November, 1928, that I wanted everything—the main building, power house, manufacturing laboratory, research laboratory, and garage — ready for occupancy by June 15, 1929. I goaded him. He worked through the winter, using 125 blazing salamanders to keep concrete pillars and walls from freezing, and the job was near to completion by spring.

Nelson Peterson, who never had a title other than "Mr. Bobst's assistant" until he became president of the company himself some years later, helped me plan the move. "We're going to write this out like a military logistics problem," I told him. "We will quit work here on Cliff Street at Friday noon. Then I want every piece of furniture and equipment moved to Nutley and in position so that each secretary and billing clerk can be in his place with his unfinished work before him at 8:45 on Monday morning."

"That's a tall order," Peterson said.

"Yes, it is, but that's what we're going to do. You will stay at Cliff Street to supervise things here. I will be in the new building, directing every load as it comes in, telling them where it should go, from top to bottom."

After a weekend that was almost sleepless for both Peterson and me, we watched with pleasure as the employees arrived at 8:45 A.M. Monday and found their desks just as they had left them three days before, only in a new place. At noon they had their first meal in our new company cafeteria, which we subsidized so that their food cost far less than its true value. And at 12:30 we shipped our first order from the new plant.

Within a few days a reporter from the New York *Times* came to see what we had done. Suburban and rural industrial parks have become common since World War II. It is no longer unusual to find major industrial corporations working quietly in attractive low buildings behind garden landscapes. But in 1929 such a development was revolutionary. "The exterior architecture represents a new trend in factory design," the reporter wrote of our main building with its attractive facade of residential-style windows. "The usual unsightly water tanks will be concealed in a beautiful tower. Travertine stone walks, terrazzo marble floors . . . A scientific library . . . richly panelled in oak, will contain a most comprehensive collection of books and works devoted to chemistry, medicine and allied professions."

When the landscaping was finished, Roche-Nutley looked

more like a small university campus than a manufacturing plant, and our gardens were so lovely that I named the complex "Roche Park" and arranged to use that as our post office address. Among other flowers, the grounds were well-planted with white and red carnations, my mother's favorite flower. When I brought her there for the first time she was far more interested in enjoying them than in touring the marvel of industrial progress that her son had wrought.

We had no sooner settled into the new quarters than I realized that our steady progress and growth would demand a great deal more room for expansion around Roche Park. As quietly as I could, I bought up another 100 acres adjoining our land and made plans to develop it with the same garden-like atmosphere as the original plot. It was my intention, and remained my intention wherever I went thereafter, to make our work environment so attractive that both the employees and I would be reluctant to leave it when the work day ended.

● *Chapter Twelve*

● The Depression decade of the 1930s produced many great ironies, but few were more vivid than the extraordinary medical progress that filled those otherwise terrible years. While an international bear market dragged down the economies and living standards of every country on earth, a bull market in pharmaceutical and medical discovery began to revitalize mankind.

One by one the four deadliest killers of children — diphtheria, whooping cough, scarlet fever, and the combination of measles and pneumonia — were conquered. Typhoid fever and blood poisoning became curable diseases, as did pneumonia, tuberculosis, and the once invariably fatal pernicious anemia. Pharmaceutical and medical discoveries have accelerated at a far greater pace in more recent years, but in many ways that great decade of discovery was the most exhilarating of all to those of us who worked through it. It was the dawn of a new age, and we knew it; sooner or later, we realized, *all* of the great scourges of mankind would be conquered. We were thrilled to be in on the beginning of this momentous war for humanity.

Pharmacology had not yet reached the sublimely esoteric levels of knowledge to which brilliant microbiologists and organic chemists have brought it today. Discovery still was a matter of painstaking experimentation with chemical compounds, and educated guesswork, the kind of intuitive research to which a self-educated pharmacist such as myself could make a contribution. Wherever we looked there was something to be done.

One major health problem that concerned medical researchers and pharmaceutical manufacturers alike was the widespread incidence of goiter among the inland and mountain people of many nations. It was endemic to a broad "goiter belt" of the United States that spread northward from West Virginia to the Great Lakes region and westward to Oregon. For centuries the source of this grotesque, tumorous enlargement of the thryoid gland remained a medical mystery. It was as common among the hill tribesman of southeast Asia as it was among the plainsmen of South Dakota, and equally debilitating. The usually non-malignant growths often protruded like half-swallowed melons from the throats of their victims and weighed ten or fifteen pounds. Among other scientists then working to isolate its source was Dr. David Marine, professor of pathology at Columbia University and director of laboratories of Montefiore Hospital in New York.

In the late 1920s I had become deeply interested in the mystery of goiter after observing an effective experiment that was being conducted in Switzerland, where the ailment was common. School children there were being given small chocolate tablets containing a new derivative of iodine called iodostarine. They showed no tendency toward goiter. When I returned to the United States I read all of the available literature on goiter and began to seek out endocrinologists with special knowledge of the thyroid gland. When Dr. Marine's experiments with fish proved conclusively that this hideous thyroid enlargement, common to inland and mountainous regions, was caused by the lack of iodine in water and food, I went to see him and had several extended conferences with him concerning the problem and its apparent cure.

It was a short step from this preliminary preparation, buttressed by my observations in Switzerland, to a new Roche tablet, rich in a very soluble iodine, called Idostarine, which, if taken daily, would prevent goiter. I publicized the ailment, the treatment, and our new product as vigorously as I could with letters to community officials, school boards, health officers, and physicians. Working at home on Sunday afternoons — when I composed most of my promotional material — I wrote educational pamphlets as well as advertisements for the professional journals. Because it was strikingly effective, the medication was almost immediately successful in the areas most affected by iodine deprivation. It remained successful for a time. Then someone discovered that the condition could be more easily and far more inexpensively forestalled by simply adding iodine to common table salt. Goiter virtually disappeared as a major medical problem in much of the world, and Idostarine disappeared with it. It was one of the many cases in pharmaceutical history of the introduction of a product that works, only to be superseded by something cheaper that works better. When iodized salt appeared, Roche lost its investment in Idostarine and any future profits that might have accrued from it, but I was grateful that I had been able to do as much as I had to bring this wretched disfigurement of the human body to an end.

There have been many similar cases of promising discoveries overwhelmed by even better new discoveries, a fact of life in the pharmaceutical industry. Perhaps it would be well to recount a famous one here as a reminder, to some critics of my industry, that the seemingly high prices of our products are not unconscionable but are necessary to pharmaceutical progress. As I have noted before, less than one in a thousand new experimental compounds successfully reaches the market. It must carry within its price structure the cost of those necessary failures — necessary because, if they are not attempted, the successful one may not be found. To those who claim that better-directed pharmaceutical research conducted by government instead of competitive business would be more beneficial and would reduce the staggeringly expensive failure rate, I suggest that they observe the rate of pharmaceutical discovery in the Soviet Union. Since 1917, when the Communist government took over that nation's drug industry and began its "beneficial directed research program," not one significant new drug has resulted from original Russian research. So far as I am aware, the other Communist countries, including China, have had no better luck. The competitive pharmaceutical industry of the Free World has discovered hundreds.

The most famous case of expensive pharmaceutical failure concerned vaccines against pneumonia, a serious preoccupation of every major drug company in the 1920s and early 1930s. There were then thirty-two known varieties of pneumonia, and the pharmaceutical research laboratories spent literally hundreds of thousands of man hours and millions of dollars in their attempts to isolate vaccines that would be effective against them. The disease was a major killer, and the researchers literally were running a race against death. Usually pneumonia ran its course quickly, so unless the vaccine specifically tailored for that particular variety of the disease was administered within thirty-six hours, it was no use. Working cooperatively, the medical profession, government, and industry established 26,000 special diagnostic centers where specimens from pneumonia victims throughout the United States could be rushed for analysis to determine which of the thirty-two varieties the patient had in order to quickly select the correct vaccine. The planning was as involved as that of the Normandy invasion, involving countless police relays for the rushing of specimens and vaccine. Lederle even established the world's largest rabbit breeding farm in order to insure sufficient serum for the many vaccines.

After these elaborate and incredibly expensive preparations had been made to conquer pneumonia, a series of unlikely events in Europe converged to make all of then unnecessary.

Dr. Gerhard Domgk, a research director of the Bayer Company in Germany, had been working with a red dye called Prontosil that his company produced. He discovered accidently that the dye killed streptococcus in mice. It happened that while he was puzzling over this strange effect of the dye, his daughter Hildegarde pricked her finger with a knitting needle and came down with septicemia, deadly blood poisoning. Domagk, desperate in the face of his daughter's grave condition, took the gamble of experimenting on her with the miraculous dye. It worked. Subsequent experiments with it proved equally miraculous. Young London mothers always had suffered a high mortality rate from puerperal fever after childbirth; with Prontosil the mortality rate dropped almost to zero. But no one knew what ingredient in the dye was responsible for the cure.

Chemists in the Pasteur Institute in Paris began taking the dye apart and soon found the magic ingredient. It was sulphanilamide. As it happened, sulphanilamide was almost unknown, but it was not new. It had been discovered originally, and patented, by a scientist named Paul Gelmo of the Vienna Institute of Technology. But neither Gelmo nor others familiar with his discovery ever realized its remarkable curative value. They did nothing with it, and Gelmo's patent expired at about the same time as the Pasteur Institute discovery in 1935. Suddenly, sulfanilamide became the most valuable pharmaceutical on earth. Since it was in the public domain, every pharmaceutical house, including all of the American companies that had invested millions in the now obsolete new pneumonia vaccines, jumped into the race to produce it. The situation reminded one wry industry observer of a limerick:

An epicure dining at Crewe
Found a very large mouse in his stew;
Said the waiter: "Don't shout
"And wave it about,
"Or the rest'll be wanting one, too."

Overnight, every penny that the pharmaceutical industry had invested in their painstaking vaccine cures for pneumonia washed down the drain; a new product that not only cured pneumonia but many other diseases as well, took its place. And because of the intense competition, its price was within the reach of everyone. The rediscovery and rapid spread of sulfanilamide saved millions of lives and without question altered the course of history. Among others who probably would have died without it was Sir Winston Churchill, who was twice so gravely infected with pneumonia early in World War II that his doctors agreed sulfanilamide was the only thing that saved him.

The story of pharmaceutical discovery is not always so arcane, but often it can be as involved as a Simenon mystery story. Sometimes I like to compare research, unfavorably, to searching for a needle in a haystack. The pharmacological researcher has the harder task; while the haystack searcher at least has the advantage of knowing there is a needle somewhere, the scientific researcher must often proceed without even an inkling of what he is looking for.

I played a part in one of these searches with a Roche drug called Prostigmine. Our scientists in Basle had developed the drug while searching around for a substitute for strychnine as a poison to control rodents and wolves that had been preying on calves and sheep in the American West. In their search for a new toxic substance, they synthesized a powerful nerve-stimulating compound known to opthalmologists as "eserine" or "physostigmine." The new product was called Prostigmine. It had no effect on the predatory animals in the West, but the scientists found that its nerve stimulus promoted intestinal activity — peristalsis. They thought that it might be useful as a bowel stimulant in difficult hospital cases. English physicians tested the drug but found that its effects were inconsequential.

I had arranged for similar tests of Prostigmine in New York, Philadelphia, and Baltimore, with the same results. But after reviewing our reports and those of the British physicians, it occurred to me that perhaps we had put the drug to the wrong use. Although it had not been effective in producing the desired bowel activity, there was no doubt that Prostigmine was highly active in increasing peristalsis, by which the intestines contract rhythmically to avoid painful accumulations of gases. From long experience with surgeons, I knew that after all types of abdominal surgery, post-operative gas pains usually cause more distress to the patient than the operation itself. And I knew that the pains were caused by what might be termed the surgical shock to the nervous system controlling the gastro-intestinal tract, blocking peristalsis and permitting the build-up of numerous gas pockets. With this in mind, I wrote letters and brochures promoting the routine use of Prostigmine following abdominal surgery. It worked. Almost overnight the drug found its way into every hospital. Physicians soon began its prophylactic use *before* surgery, and it became a matter of pre-operative routine throughout the United States. The demand for the drug was so heavy, in fact, that I had to build a new manufacturing laboratory in which to produce it in Roche Park.

Some time later, in mid-1935, I read a provocative article about Prostigmine in the *Proceedings of the Royal Society of Medicine* by Dr. Mary Brodhead Walker. This English lady physician had spent many years studying myopathies, various forms of progressive degeneration of the nervous system. Sometimes myophatic degeneration is rapid, sometimes slow. Once of these myopathic diseases is myasthenia gravis, a fatal atrophying of the muscles, which was then thought to be extremely rare. It was utterly unknown to me. Dr. Walker's article reviewed its history and noted that the treatment of choice in the past had been curare, the poisonous plant extract that South American Indians use on their arrow tips to paralyze enemies and wild game. Dr. Walker had come across Prostigmine and experimented with it as a substitute, because curare did not work especially well. The Prostigmine, however, proved to be very effective.

I took the article to my own scientists and had them dig up all that was known about myasthenia gravis. They found that fewer than a hundred cases had been reported in medical journals and advised me that any effort to promote Prostigmine as a therapeutic agent for myasthenia gravis would therefore be pointless and commercially wasteful.

I disregarded their advice. In my next mailing to doctors about Prostigmine, I added a little slip stating that the drug had proven of value in the treatment of myasthenia gravis in England, citing Dr. Walker's article. I noted, also, that physicians found it difficult to determine the differences between myasthenia gravis and other myopathies; but that if any physician wanted to direct a request to me, personally, I would send him some ampules of Prostigmine with which he might determine whether the myopathy he was treating was myasthenia gravis or some other type of nerve degeneration. I repeated the message in my next signed column of the *Roche Review,* a regular periodical that we had, by then, begun publishing.

My scientific colleagues and I were astonished when I received more than eight hundred letters. It soon became evident to us and to doctors all over the country that myasthenia gravis was not such a rare disease after all. One clinic in Boston eventually reported more than seventy cases, and many others turned up elsewhere. Prostigmine became the drug of choice in their treatment. Unhappily, it is only a therapeutic agent, not a cure. Yet it provides victims of the disease with years of near-normal life that they would not otherwise have. I think that I was justified in feeling some pride in the role I played as we learned of case after case in which a totally incapacitated, almost deadened victim of the disease arose fifteen minutes after an injection of Prostigmine and performed such feats as hefting a large dictionary over his head. If I had not had both the scientific curiosity and the informally acquired medical knowledge to move forcefully after reading Dr. Walker's report, the drug may not have reached those patients at all, certainly not for years, by which time many of them would have died.

I think that the medical knowledge that I acquired during my career was my most valuable asset as a businessman. Without it and my training as a pharmacist, countless opportunities would have passed me by unrecognized. I worked at acquiring knowledge by voraciously reading medical books and journals, but much of my information came to me informally from my friendships with skilled physicians and medical researchers. One of them was Dr. Carl de Sajoux of Philadelphia, an early specialist in what was then known as the field of "internal secretions." He was a pioneer endocrinologist and author of a number of books on the endocrine glands — thyroid, pituary, adrenals, and others — that secrete vital hormones into the body's system to perform myriad essential tasks, many of which still are unclear. I made frequent sales calls on Dr. de Sajoux and became so enthralled by his descriptions of hormone activity that he carefully explained his work to me and cheerfully shared his knowledge and speculations. This led me to read not only his work but that of other endocrinologists and to follow developments in the specialty as they were published in professional journals. By 1938 I was almost as conversant in the field as the specialists themselves, and it served me well when I bumped into Morris Fishbein in the lobby of the Waldorf-Astoria one December day.

I had not known that Morris was in New York, so our meeting that day was pure coincidence. Another man was with him. Morris introduced him as Saul van Zwanenberg, president of the Organon Company of Oss, Holland, one of the leading producers of estrogen (female) and androgen (male) hormones. The scientific director of his company, in fact, had first isolated testosterone, the hormone that stimulates development of masculine characteristics, from the testicles of a bull. Van Zwanenberg, apparently impressed that I was a close friend of such an illustrious person as Morris Fishbein, invited me to his hotel suite to chat. We had a knowledgeable discussion about hormones, their impact on medicine, and the role his company had played in synthesizing them. It was an extraordinary meeting of minds and interests. Before the chance meeting ended late that night, we had agreed to form a business partnership and laid down the general terms of our agreement. I would form a subsidiary of Roche-Nutley to be called Roche-Organon, jointly owned by van Zwanenberg's company and ours. I became president of it. Under our agreement, Roche-Nutley held all U.S. rights to Organon's production. They would ship the products to us in bulk. Our joint subsidiary, Roche-Organon, would prepare them in capsules or other therapeutic forms, and we would promote their use as prescription items among American physicians.

It fell to me, as it always had, to write the principal mailings on each of the new products. The first was Neo-Hombreol, a synthetic testosterone. So little was known then about testosterone's therapeutic uses that I was in something of a quandary over how to go about introducing it to physicians. There was no doubt that the drug had a definite effect in stimulating the development of male characteristics. It occurred to me that as a man ages there usually is a certain diminishment of his most prominent masculine traits; muscle tone often slackens and sexual interests wane. There was little solid evidence then to prove that these characteristics of aging were connected with hormonal changes in the body, but neither was there evidence that they were not. Informed hypotheses suggested that perhaps they were, because it was known that hormone production diminishes with age. As I mulled this over at home on a Sunday afternoon, after a particularly vigorous round of golf, I thought of the earnestness with which men seek to recapture their lost youth as age carries them through what amounts, I think, to a "male climacteric," a change of life. The greatest historic symbol of that search for youth, I thought, was the Spaniard, Ponce de Leon. I reviewed the story of the great explorer and then sat down to write my first "Dear Doctor" letter about testosterone.

THE LAND OF BIMINI

Dear Doctor:

No doubt young Juan was greatly admired by all the young ladies of Servas as he matured, for he was a fine looking lad, with a splendid physique and possessed of a daring personality. His adventuresome spirit forced him at a very early age to take a hand in the Moorish Wars, and he was only 33 years old when it led him again to persuade Columbus to let him go along on his second trip to the new world.

By the time the estimable Juan had conquered the Island of PUERTO RICO and had settled down to the rather soft and engaging life of its governor, the first shadow of old age started to fall across his pathway. As his vigor began to wane, the Indian legends about the Land of Bimini and its wonderful spring of waters with their marvelous curative powers intrigued him more and more. And soon thereafter, Juan Ponce de Leon set forth on his memorable search for the so-called Fountain of Youth. When Ponce de Leon began his quest of the youth-restoring waters, he was just about fifty years of age.

Yes, just about the period of man's life when the downhill journey becomes significant. Is it due to the rapid decrease of the male sex hormone secretion at middle life? More and more physiologists and endocrinologists are coming to that conclusion. A study of the clinical characteristics of the male climacteric, embracing physical, psychological, and functional changes, leads rather definitely to the conclusion that proper administration of testosterone propionate can play the same role in man as does estrogen therapy in the menopause, or female climacteric. Testosterone propionate, which we are making available under the name of Neo-Hombreol, is the active, chemically pure, crystalline propionate salt of the male sex hormone, identical in every respect with the same substance derived from natural sources and with the added advantage of synthetic production.

We suggest the experimental use of Neo-Hombreol for combating the annoying symptoms of the male climacteric. Treatment should be started with injections of Neo-Hombreol. For maintenance purposes we then suggest the use of Neo-Hombreol Ointment which is now available in a most accurate dosage form called The Dosule. We will gladly send you a 3-day supply of Neo-Hombreol Dosules if you will make use of the enclosed card.

Sincerely yours,

Elmer H. Bobst,
President

The response was almost incredible. We received more requests for free samples of Neo-Hombreol than for any pharmaceutical we had ever introduced. It was from some of the replies that the doctors, somehow, had picked up the idea from my letter that the Dosules would have a regenerative value in cases of impotency. A surprising number of the physicians, in fact, indicated that they intended to try the medication on themselves, in the interests of scientific inquiry, of course. But some of the medical people chided me for being just a bit too overenthusiastic on behalf of my product. One of them was Morris Fishbein.

Morris permitted neither time nor our close friendship to stand in the way of his professionally conservative reaction to my letter. The very next issue of the AMA *Journal* featured an editorial in bold type entitled, "Elmer Bobst Goes to Town." He repeated "The Land of Bimini" letter in his editorial, then somewhat scathingly denounced its implied thesis as totally speculative.

I did not have a chance to see or talk with Morris after the editorial appeared until the annual Silver Slipper Club dinner following the AMA meeting in St. Louis that year. When he saw me, he rushed over, smiling, and said, "Now Elmer, don't you be upset."

"I'm not upset, Morris, but don't ever do it again," I replied jokingly.

I was perfectly happy about the whole thing. What Morris did not know was that his editorial focused so much added attention on my "Land of Bimini" letter and our Roche-Organon product that sales almost doubled. He had helped me far more than he realized, and the incident did not create a ripple on the calm surface of our friendship.

In time, our success with testosterone put my business philosophy to an acid test. Two other companies, Ciba and Schering, were engaged in hormone production and each of us had been asked repeatedly to license our products to still more American drug companies so that they could sell testosterone, too. We refused, and the Department of Justice decided to step in on the grounds that our Europe-based companies were violating the antitrust laws by freezing out other competition. In the course of the proceedings, I was called before a federal judge in Newark. The judge came straight to the point.

"You have refused to give a license to Parke, Davis, to Abbott, and to others. Is that correct?"

"Yes, that's correct, your Honor," I said.

"You're in conflict with the Sherman Act," he said. "Why won't you give them a license?"

"Because if I did that, those newcomers in a very short time would be underselling me, and my profit would disappear. They would be able to undersell Roche-Organon because they have spent nothing on promoting or developing the product."

"Well, it's my intention to force you to give licenses. Now what do you think of that?"

"I suppose you have the right to enforce the law as you see fit," I replied, "but I'm not going to give licenses."

"You mean that you will subject yourself to arrest by not complying?" The judge was incredulous.

"No," I said, "I won't comply, because I won't be in the business".

"What do you mean by that?"

"I mean that if you insist on licenses, I'm getting out of the hormone business immediately. I will not engage in any business where I cannot make a profit. I would not be able to make a profit if my product is licensed. As far as I am concerned, it is that simple, your Honor."

We never did grant licenses, although we did have to accept a consent decree and a $3,000 fine.

The decade of the thirties also saw some personal changes in our lives. Although it was depression time, Roche-Nutley had grown both in sales and profits every year, and my income had grown accordingly. My assets passed the million-dollar mark at some point in the early thirties, so we were no longer bound as we had been by severe financial boundaries. On a personal level, too, we were more free to do as we pleased than we had been in our early days.

Walton was fully grown, six feet tall, athletic, and handsome as a movie star. In fact he looked rather like Richard Arlen, the actor. He had finished prep school, where I am afraid that he devoted more energy to football, track, and tennis than to academics. Then he completed two years at Brown University. But the academic life still did not suit him, so he came to Nutley to begin learning the operations of Roche from the ground up. I put him to work in the shipping department in 1929. He worked his way slowly and diligently, through every department of the company. By 1939 he was a knowledgeable and effective junior executive, director of sales and promotion for Roche-Organon, and not too much affected, I hope, by the shadow of his father.

My mother was comfortably settled in a spacious Philadelphia apartment that was the first luxury she had known since her childhood in Harper's Ferry. When I procured it for her, she objected that it was "far too toney," but I knew that she loved it and made arrangements for her to have it for as long as she lived. She was happy there with her Philadelphia friends and had the freedom to come and go as she pleased in a chauffeured car that I provided. In the summers she took a room in the elegant old General Sutter Hotel in Lititz and visited her old friends.

Ethel and I had become extremely fond of our life in Montclair. But I was not altogether satisfied with our house there. For one thing, we entertained frequently, and the size of the house limited the number of guests we could have. For another, I had a taste for larger, landscaped gardens, and our lot was not a spacious one.

One evening in 1936 Ethel had invited some guests of whom I was not especially fond, so I politely excused myself and went out for a walk. I had a destination in mind. There was a particular house in Montclair called "Highwall," which had appealed to me for several years because of its gracious architecture, its location on the highest hill in town, and its generous acreage sweeping up the terraced brow of Montclair's Old Eagle Rock. The house had been built for and was occupied by Everette Lee DeGolyer, the nation's leading petroleum geologist, who had brought in the great Amerada gusher. There was a rumor in Montclair that he was planning to move to Dallas to be nearer his important oil interests. I decided to go to his house and ask him if the rumor was true.

DeGolyer came to the door when I rang, and after I had introduced myself he said, "Yes, I've known of you. Come in."

He invited me into his library, a large panelled room with an extremely high, mottled ceramic ceiling, a balcony and floor-to-ceiling walnut shelves containing more than five thousand volumes, many of them rare. As he handed me a drink, I said:

"I have heard a rumor that you are thinking of disposing of your house. I've been looking for a larger house with more grounds, and I thought I would find out if there is any foundation to that rumor."

"Mr. Bobst, there is. I love this home. But since I brought in the Amerada well, I've been overwhelmed with business. I have to fly to Texas at least every two weeks and it's a chore. As much as I hate to leave this house, I feel that I should move to Dallas."

He showed me through the place. From its position just

*The north side of "Highwall," the author's former home
in Montclair, N.J.*

below the brow of Eagle Rock it had an unobstructed view of New York City and the surrounding country. It was huge, but warmly relaxed and comfortable. The twenty-eight rooms of the house included servants, quarters, a seventy-foot living room, a dining room panelled in French walnut, and seven fireplaces, a few of them deeply recessed and big enough for five-foot logs. I loved it.

"Do you have any idea of the price you want?" I asked when we returned to the library.

"It doesn't mean much what I get for it if I can sell the house to someone who will love it and take care of it. That means more to me than money. I'd like to have the privilege just to drop in and look it over when I come back here from time to time. I think $100,000 would be a fair price."

I doubt if the DeGolyer house could be built today for less than $2 million, and I am sure that it was worth more than $100,000 then.

"I can assure you that if I purchase it, you may have the privilege of visiting the house. I would welcome you as a guest at any time. If you wish to have a gentleman's agreement, I'll shake hands on it and you can feel that I have bought the property."

"You mean you want to do it right away? Now?"

"Yes, that's the kind of fellow I am. I do things that way. It doesn't take me long to make up my mind." We shook hands, had another drink, and I went home.

When Ethel's company had left she gently scolded me for leaving her alone. "Where in the name of sense did you go?"

"Oh, I went up there and bought a house."

"You didn't buy that big house on the hill?"

"That's exactly what I bought."

"You *really* bought it?"

"Yes. It's a deal."

"Oh!" she cried, and refused to speak to me until bedtime. But by the time we were ready to decorate and move in, she loved it.

I was ebullient and sometimes a little impulsive in those days.

One day, during my lunchtime, I walked into a Lincoln automobile showroom in Montclair and listened patiently while a salesman tried to interest me in a plan to help finance a new car. "I'll take two. One of these and one of those," I said, pointing to two new-model Lincolns. "And I'll pay cash. I want to show my faith in the economy of this country." They were happy times, at work and at home, and this was in 1932, the height of the Depression.

Heavyweight boxing champion Jack Sharkey, left, with the author at the funeral of Dr. Wilfred Fralick, specialist who attended many boxing figures. At right rear is Max Jacobs, dominant boxing promoter of the early thirties.

● *Chapter Thirteen*

● My reputation in the pharmaceutical industry had been built entirely on ethical drugs, but such modest public attention as I received came to me not as the promoter of the vital prescription drugs that I helped to develop, but as what Fortune Magazine called "The Vitamin King." The vitamin boom, too, was a phenomenon of the thirties, one that revolutionized the science of nutrition and restored the health of many million people who were deficient in one or more of these essential basic nutrients. One by one, following the discovery of natural vitamin A in 1918, the pure chemical vitamins were isolated, identified, synthesized, and mass-produced. Eleven Nobel Prizes were awarded between 1928 and 1937 to successful researchers in the field, and all of us in the pharmaceutical industry were active in supporting the research.

One of the important vitamin discoveries of the early thirties was that of ascorbic acid, an ingredient of citrus fruits and some vegetables that had long been known to informal "folk medicine" as essential to the prevention of scurvy. Sailors had for centuries carried limes and other citrus fruit to ward off scurvy on long sea voyages. English ships drew their supplies of fruit from the "Limehouse" district of London, which thus became the birthplace of the unflattering term "Limey" for British sailors. The German marines aboard sailing ships found that sauerkraut prevented scurvy. It contains a fairly sizable amount of ascorbic acid; that is why German sailors were often called "Krauts." The ascorbic acid in these fruits and vegetables also is vital to other metabolic processes, including the rapid healing of sores and wounds, and has a defense quality, too, helping to guard against certain infections, such as colds.

In searching about for economical ways to produce ascorbic acid in its pure form as vitamin C, and more important still, to synthesize it, a few of the pharmaceutical companies looked for the richest natural sources of the substance. Extracting ascorbic acid from citrus fruits, such as lemons, was extremely expensive. Sweet pimientos and some other vegetables also were expensive sources. I came across one of the least expensive of the rich natural sources quite by accident and in an utterly unlikely place, the Yukon territory.

Ethel and I, along with some close friends, had taken a vacation through parts of the United States and Canada and finally a sea voyage from Vancouver to Skagway, Alaska, where thousands of amateur miners converged, many of them to die, in the great Gold Rush. During our visit I happened to stop in what had been a saloon with a gold-dust-buying section, frequented during those early days by drunken prospectors and prostitutes. In this relic of the old days, I fell into conversation with a wizened sourdough who would talk just as long as anyone supplied him with drinks. He was a colorful character, short, stocky, and so weatherbeaten that it was impossible to guess his age, although it obviously was beyond the sixties. As I asked the bartender to set them up, the sourdough began telling me how difficult it had been to get together a grubstake in order to go out into the wilds to a stake claim. He would have to spend many weeks in his search for gold.

"What did you take along?" I asked him.

"Not much," he said. "Not much variety, anyways. Smoked meat, flour, and Irish potatoes, mostly."

"Why Irish potatoes?"

"Oh, you had to have them. They were dear. Cost a dollar apiece up here then. But you had to have em."

"Why did you have to have them?"

"Because of the scurvy, had to have 'em to keep from gettin' the scurvy."

I had never before heard of potatoes as a major source of ascorbic acid, which they must have been if they were used by the miners to forestall scurvy. When I returned to Nutley, I asked our laboratory researchers to investigate. They reported back that potatoes were a rich source of vitamin C. Nutritionists later discovered all of the marvelous qualities of that humble tuber, which is now recognized as the only human food that contains all of the nutrients necessary to sustain life. Unfortunately, extracting vitamin C from the potato or any natural source proved to be impracticable. A few companies tried it, particularly Merck & Co. but their products were too expensive for the market. The real race among the pharmaceutical houses was to discover a commercial means of synthesizing vitamin C. As it turned out, the race went down to the wire with Roche in the lead and Merck, Pfizer, Abbott, and Parke, Davis breathing down our necks. It was a dramatic and exciting affair.

I had concluded one of my periodic visits to Europe, in 1936, and was in Paris, with Emil Barell, getting ready to return home the next day. We had just finished an elegant "going-way" dinner at my hotel, the Crillon, when Barell announced in his ponderous, heavily accented English.

"Mr. Bobst, I want you to come with me to the men's room."

"The men's room?"

"Yes, I'll tell you why when we get there."

Puzzled by his mysterious air and half-wondering if he required help to relieve him of some after effect of our splendid dinner, I followed him into the empty men's room.

Barell looked furtively around as if expecting to be attacked. He opened the door of one of the toilet stalls. Then he entered and motioned for me to follow. I suppressed a mixed urge to laugh or to run for the safety of the dining room, but he appeared to be so utterly serious that I joined him in the closet-sized booth. Barell carefully closed the door. Sighing with relief, he reached carefully into a vest pocket and extracted a small, sealed bottle. He held it gently in both hands.

"Here," he whispered, "is the active culture for fermentation of vitamin C. We have synthesized it. When you get back, you can start with this culture and make it grow as far as you want to."

It was a serio-comic situation, but it accurately reflected the urgency and secrecy with which all of us had been working to develop a practical synthesis. Barell had been guarding the invaluable vial for days, fearful that an agent from another pharmaceutical concern would seize it. He had waited until the eve of my departure to entrust it to me, and then had gone through an act straight out of Eric Ambler to pass it along.

The race to synthesize ascorbic acid had begun in 1932, after Dr. Charles Glenn King and his team at the University of Pittsburgh had isolated and identified its natural chemistry in lemons. Roche in Basle had given a grant for experimental work on synthesis to Dr. Thadeus Reichstein of the University of Zurich, In less than four years, Reichstein found the answer to synthetic production.

His process began with a form of dextrose, a very low grade of sugar, that became the fermentation bed for several special strains of friendly bacteria. In the tiny bottle that Barell gave me was a culture of the micro-organisms which, on fermentation, oxidized sorbitol to a ketone sugar called sorbose. This, when heated in an acid solution, rearranged to form ascorbic acid. In effect, the tiny bottle contained a base, like a baker's first cake of yeast, that would grow to produce as much vitamin C as we wanted to make.

I guarded it carefully on the sea voyage home. The slightest contamination by other bacteria would ruin the culture. Rather than risk contamination and to avoid explanations that my competitors might overhear, I slipped the bottle through customs in an inside pocket of my coat. At Nutley we took a fairly large laboratory that had been used for mass production of strychnine, no longer profitable, and converted it to become the home of the valuable culture. We began marketing small quantities of the product to pharmaceutical houses just as soon as we were able

to do so, even before our application on the Reichstein process
was approved by the U.S. Patent Office. In the meantime, our
competitors had been moving too.

Both Merck and Pfizer, long experienced in the techniques
of fermentation, somehow obtained information on the Reichstein
process. As Roche-Nutley went into production, both moved into
the early stages of synthetic fermentation. It was clear that they
would soon follow us on the market with what I believed to be
essentially our product. As soon as I learned of their moves, I
went to see the heads of the two companies, George Merck, Jr.,
and John L. (Jack) Smith. My message was plain.

"You know the day will come when I can legally stop you
from producing ascorbic acid," I said. "We have not yet cleared
the Reichstein patent in the department, but I could easily make
your operation unprofitable for you right now. I could do that
by underselling you, and we all three would lose money. I don't
want to do that. You can go ahead until the time when the patent
is issued. Then we'll consider giving both of you a license based
on a proper royalty."

Another threat came from Dr. Charles Glenn King, the dis-
coverer of vitamin C. King and his associates, with the backing
of Parke, Davis, Abbott Laboratories, and Pfizer, had produced
a crystalline substance that proved, after guinea-pig testing, to
be a synthesis of vitamin C. Dr. King and a partner, encouraged
by their backers, filed a patent application on their process. The
King application had the effect of creating a legal interference
which blocked ours while the two processes were studied. Intrigued by King's approach, our scientists at Roche-Nutley tried
a number of times to produce ascorbic acid by following his formula. Every one of the attempts failed.

Dr. King was a fine gentleman and a wonderful scientist,
but there was clearly an uncertainty about the viability of his process. It wouldn't work; at least not on a commercial basis. Yet
his application for a patent was blocking our patent petition. It
was a frustrating bureaucratic stalemate, and I felt that I had
to find a way to break it. First, on the basis of our tests of the
King process, I convinced his industry backers that their efforts

were futile. Then I invited Dr. King to meet with me.

"We have tried to produce ascorbic acid by your process and have been unable to do it," I told him. "You know, of course, that Reichstein has successfully synthesied vitamin C in Zurich and that we alone have been able to produce it. We have world rights to the process.

"Now your application has been standing as an interference against our petition for a patent. I can tell you frankly that I have spoken to your supporters in the industry. I think I have convinced them of the futility of keeping the Reichstein patent from issue by the department."

Dr. King replied with graceful and understandable caution. He explained that he had no personal financial interest in the matter, because he had insisted that the full benefits of his work must go to the University of Pittsburgh. He firmly believed that academic scientists working on graduate programs should not personally profit financially from their discoveries. "If there is anything in it for the university, well, so much the better," he said. But he felt the matter was one for the patent attorneys to settle. We parted cordially. I was confident that the Reichstein patent eventually would be granted to us, so I immediately stepped up our production efforts and began to construct extra facilities for the production of 15 to 20 million ounces of ascorbic acid a year. I may mention at this time whereas the amount we were to produce appeared to be enormous, that the new facilities of Roche will have a production that will run into several thousand tons of ascorbic acid per year.

Dr. King cheerfully discussed the problems of his process with an associate of mine, Robert C. Alberts of Pittsburgh, just a year or so ago. According to Alberts, he explained that the King process had two crucial weaknesses. "It was clear that our synthesis would be too expensive as a complete process, King explained. And we were deficient in one of the intermediate stages. We produced the vitamin, and we checked it out by animal assay, but we did not succeed in isolating in pure crystal form osone or alpha ketonic acid . . . But Reichstein actually isolated the ketonic acid. He was a really great organic chemist, and this, sugar chemistry, was his field." Dr. Reichstein later won a Nobel prize for other work in suprarenal cortex hormones. And Dr. King went on to a distinguished career at Columbia and as executive director and later president of the Nutrition Foundation. When our patent dispute finally was settled in Roche's favor, I had our company make a sizeable contribution to his laboratory at the University of Pittsburgh.

When the patent award came through, I called Jim Kerrigan, president of Merck, and Jack Smith of Pfizer. "I'd like to take you out to dinner at the '21' Club," I told each of them.

"What's up?" Smith asked. "Anything special?"

"Yes, something very special. We're going to talk about vitamin C. I have the patent and I'm ready to talk."

After a few drinks, we got down to business. "Now, you're both producing vitamin C and you're doing very well with it, aren't you?" I asked.

"Yes, we are."

"You'd like to continue, wouldn't you?'"

"Yes, we would."

"Well, you know that Roche has exclusive rights through the Reichstein patent. I can stop you. But I wouldn't want to do that. I'm ready to come to terms."

"Can we talk about it between ourselves?" Kerrigan asked.

"Fine. I'll get up and go to the men's room." I dawdled in the men's room for five minutes and returned. "Did you talk it over?"

"Yes," Smith said, "we're willing to pay 5 percent."

I put on a pained expression. "Look, if I had everything to say about this, I might agree to a 5 percent royalty. But I've got Barell over there. He's claiming that the world rights come to the Roche company abroad, and he's getting 10 and 12 percent from other companies." That was true enough, but I knew that Barell would agree readily to 5 percent from America. "He's going to kick like the devil at 5 percent," I continued, "and I don't think he'll agree. I don't want to get into a fuss with him. I'll settle for 7½ percent, and if he says anything, I may tell him to go to hell."

They readily agreed to my figure, probably because they knew they were liable for the payment of back royalties if I pressed the point. As a result, Roche-Nutley collected from $500,000 to $800,000 a year in royalties from Merck and Pfizer throughout the seventeen-year life of the Reichstein patent. In a sense, the story that began for me during a few furtive minutes in a men's room in Paris reached a conclusion of sorts while I waited in the men's room at the "21" Club in New York. The contents of that tiny four-ounce bottle that Barell slipped to me in the cramped Parisian stall was the original base, the mother element, of literally thousands of tons of vitamin C that Roche has produced since.

In the same time period, the mid-to late thirties, we were working with equal competitive vigor and had developed about half of the complex steps necessary for the synthesis of vitamin B1, thiamine, which is essential in the prevention of beriberi and the maintainance of proper metabolic functions. But with this vitamin, I soon felt the shoe on the other foot, and it pinched. Merck won exclusive rights to the first viable method of synthesis, developed in 1936 by Robert R. Williams, a Bell Telephone Laboratories scientist. Williams had first become interested in vitamin B1 while working in the Philippines in 1912. It was there that he first linked the presence of beriberi among the natives to their diet of polished rice. The thiamine in rice grains is concentrated in the outer husks, which are stripped away in polishing, much as nutritious bran is removed from wheat. Williams decided to experiment with a filtrate of a watery extract of the outer husks left over after rice polishing. Many years later, when I served with him on the board of directors of the General Aniline and Film company, he told me of the results of his first clinical investigation with rice. He was in a small Filipino village where beriberi was common among infants. Late one night, after making the filtrate of rice hulls, he went to the hut of a peasant family whose month-old child was blue in the face and gasping for breath. The parents were resigned to losing their baby to beriberi within a few hours. By candlelight, Williams fed the infant the watery substance that he had made, squeezing it into the child's mouth through an eyedropper. The next day he returned, expecting to find the baby dead. To his astonishment, the child was alive, vastly improved and cooing happily.

Williams spent many years after that attempting to synthesize thiamine, and finally achieved his goal with some assistance from the Merck Company, whose scientists helped him in developing two phases of the complicated synthesis. At the request of his employer, Bell Laboratories, he assigned his rights in the discovery to a foundation called the Research Corporation, which applied for a patent in the process and gave Merck an exclusive license to produce thiamine.

Stymied in our own efforts to complete the synthesis of thiamine independently, I made a number of overtures to Howard A. Poillon, director of the Research Corporation, hoping that he would agree to grant Roche a production license, too. He rebuffed me again and again, as he did every other pharmaceutical company that came to him. If I was ever to produce thiamine, I would have to find a way to get around this seemingly impregnable obstacle. The trouble was, there was no straightforward way to do it. But I had an idea that I might succeed in working a "poker bluff" on Poillon and Merck if I could develop the several hidden cards that I knew were available to me. The first of my "hole" cards was Roche's own development of about half of the intermediate stages of thiamine synthesis. By following our own process through to the end, we could make thiamine, but not economically enough to compete with Merck. Our process was not well-enough advanced, even, to warrant attempting to block the Research Corporation's pending patent on the Williams process. However, if our process for the first half of synthesis was coupled with another pharmaceutical company's process for the second half, the two together might come close to producing a competitive product. I knew that Sterling Products Company, which was affiliated with I.G. Farben of Germany, had rights to the second half of the process, because the German company had succeeded in developing it. Sterling did not intend to go into thiamine production, but nevertheless had filed, if only for the record, an interference against the Research Corporation's patent application. If I could get Sterling to give me the second half, I could join it to my half and at least appear to be ready for thiamine production under a process that would compete with Merck's. But I knew that Merck could prevent me from getting it on the market unless I somehow won the approval of Poillon and the Research Corporation.

After word passed around the industry that I was attempting to put together Roche and I.G. Farben developments to create my own production process, George Merck stopped me one day at the Chemists' Club in New York. "You know, Elmer, we will stop you from making this," he said.

"George, I don't think you will," I replied with bravado. "If I did, I wouldn't be building facilities for making thiamine, and that's what I'm doing."

To complete my hand and strengthen it, I got Dr. William Weiss, president of Sterling, to let me have the I.G. Farben half of the process, and to give me his power of attorney, as well, to use his patent interference against the Research Corporation patent application. I was now in a position to prove not only that I could make thiamine, but that I could cause the Research Corporation and Merck a long legal delay in receiving their patent, because I could use Sterling's patent interference against them. With this poker hand — frankly, it was a weak one and I doubt if it would have won the pot if they had decided to fight me — I bypassed Merck and called on Poillon. I told him candidly that my two halves made a whole and that I was going to produce thiamine, come hell or high water. I told him that unless he granted his approval, thus legally clearing the way for me to go into production, I would block his patent application with the interference for which Sterling had given me power of attorney. He could fight it out in court, I said to him, but I planned to forge ahead.

The news upset Poillon considerably, and he asked me for a day or two to think it over. That Saturday evening he called me at home and asked to visit with me on Sunday morning. He came to my home in Montclair.

"What royalty is Roche willing to pay to the Research Corporation?" he asked. "Merck is paying 12½ percent."

"You know that I have an arrangement with Sterling," I replied. "I have to pay a percentage to them for their half of the process. Therefore I do not feel that Roche can afford to pay you more than 7½ percent."

Dr. Poillon groaned, but it was that or the prospect of a protracted legal battle, something that I relished even less than he did, because I was almost certain that he would win it. But my bluff worked. He reluctantly accepted the figure and granted approval. I had taken a huge risk and won.

Soon, Roche-Nutley became the leading producer of bulk vitamins in the United States, supplying about 50 percent of the market. But at first we did not market vitamin specialties, either in liquid or capsule form, which had become widely prescribed by the medical profession. We sold only in bulk quantities to other pharmaceutical houses which handled the promotion, packaging, and distribution under their own product names. In time I decided that we were overlooking an important part of the business, surrendering the public marketplace to our competitors, many of whom were entering it with our basic product under their names. We made plans to market vitamin specialties under our own name, but when we advised our parent company of our plans, we found we were completely blocked from entering the most profitable market of all, that of multi-vitamin capsules.

The impediment was Dr. Barell's doing. He had made a deal of which he was inordinately proud to supply the Swiss Nestlé Company with five vitamins for a "multi-vitamin" milk product. Nestlé planned to add the vitamins to a canned condensed milk as well as to a cocoa butter candy that they called "white chocolate." In exchange for the exclusive supply order, Roche agreed not to market any multi-vitamin specialty in any country where it would compete with Nestlé. Furthermore, we were supposed to handle the Nestlé products in America. There were two things wrong with Barell's agreement from the American point of view. First, not many people used condensed milk in this country, so there was little market for the Nestlé product. Second, cocoa butter will not stand up to the extreme changes of climate in our

south and southwest, therefore the candy would not be a marketing success, either.

I pleaded with Barell to change the agreement.

"We've made a deal with Nestlé," he said. "It's a contract."

"You had no right to make such a contract for us."

"Why not? You're part of the company," Barell replied.

"No, we are a company over here, a corporation, of which
I am president. We happen to have a relationship, obviously,
but we will run our own company And I will not market these
products. They will fail."

I remained so adamant that Barell finally realized that he
could not sway me. He went back to Nestlé and won their agreement to change the contract, excluding the United States. We
were free to proceed and I was anxious to get started.

Five companies then sold multi-vitamins: Merck, Abbott, Up-
John, Squibb and Parke, Davis. Each of them produced similar
capsules containing vitamins A, B1, B2, C, and D. At the time,
neither vitamins A nor D had been synthesized and both were
extracted from fish oils, mostly from cod and sharks. All five
of the producers relied on a single processor, the Gelatin Products
Company of Detroit, to encapsulate their multi-vitamins; thus,
all were about the same in size and dosage. Gelatin Products was
owned and run by Robert Scherer, who invented the encapsulat-
ing machine. I knew him well, had worked with him in the past,
and had a good business relationship going with him at the time,
because Roche was supplying him with $2- to $3-million worth
of multi-vitamin ingredients a year. But before going to Scherer
with plans to encapsulate a new Roche multi-vitamin, I decided
to analyze my competitors' products to see if we could come up
with something better.

I called in Nelson Peterson and the scientist in charge of
our applied research laboratory. Together we examined the five
competing products. A couple of the capsules were round and
the others were shaped like footballs, but all were equally large.
The philosophy seemed to be that the larger the capsule the more
important it would appear to the public.

I noted the number of miligrams of each of the five vitamins in each capsule. These measures, too, were about the same, but in every case the weight of the vitamins was only a small fraction of the content of the capsule. The rest was mineral oil.

I took a knife and cut each capsule in two. All five with their natural vitamins A and D smelled strongly of fish oil, a disagreeable odor that led to an even more disagreeable taste when the vitamin swallower belched. Clearly the multi-vitamin capsules could use some improvement, and I saw how we could leapfrog our competition by doing two relatively simple things. I drew a small circle, about a third the size of the competing capsules, on a piece of paper and handed it to my chief scientist. "I want you to go to Detroit and talk to Bob Scherer at Gelatin Products. Tell him to make us a capsule no larger than this, and tell him to do it in strictest confidence."

I sniffed the fishy capsules again. "We're also going to do something about this," I said. "We will use the best fish liver oil we can get, but it's still going to smell and taste of fish. Tell Bob Scherer that I want him to put a fraction of a drop of oil of peppermint into the mixture. When people burp, I want them to burp peppermint, not old fish."

He came back about a week later with a capsule that was slightly larger than the circle I had drawn on the paper. "Take it back," I said, "it's too big." After a second trip to Detroit he returned with a perfect, small capsule. I cut it open and it both smelled and tasted of peppermint, not fish. "Now we're fixed," I smiled, and we began to get ready for production.

As with most of our products, I wrote the advertising and promotion and created the brand name myself. I decided that we would not refer to our multi-vitamins as capsules. We would call them Vipenta Pearls: *Vi* for vitamins, *penta* for five, and *pearls* for 'Pretty as a pearl.' A bit corny today, perhaps, but it was effective then.

I wanted my first "Dear Doctor" letter about Vipenta Pearls to be an arresting one. Reaching back into memory, I recalled the monstrously large capsules that I used to sell as a pharmacist for the treatment of gonorrhea. The huge capsules were no cure for the disease, but they relieved the pain of it. I remembered

how strong men would come into the store, take one look at
the large black capsules, blanch, and exclaim, "Good God, Doc,
do I have to swallow those?" I recounted the story under the
heading, "The Threatening Glare of a Big Black Capsule," in
my first letter to physicians.

Among other things, I also called in our sales representatives
for a little training. We had prepared a special vitamin container,
a round box, for their sales kits. "When you call on the doctors,"
I said to the salesmen, "show them this round pillbox and say,
'Now, Doctor, you see the six crosses on the lid of the box? You
may wonder what they mean. Well, I'd like to show you. Each
cross represents a different multi-vitamin capsule.' You open the
box and show the six capsules. 'Now, Doctor, suppose that each
one contains exactly the same amount of the five different vitamins. And suppose that you have to take one. Tell me frankly,
which one you would take.'

"Naturally he will take the smallest, because it's the easiest
to swallow. Then you say. 'That's the one everybody chooses.
Think how a child feels, Doctor. The one you have chosen, the
small one, is the Vipenta Pearl. It contains not only all five vitamins, but it contains double the amount of vitamin C. (We were
producing so much vitamin C that we could afford to
double the quantity.) Furthermore, your patients won't complain of fish oil burp. We add just enough peppermint oil to
take away the bad taste. If you would like to taste for yourself,
try one.' "

The detail men hit the road, and my first mailing about
The Threatening Glare went to 135,000 physicians. My second mail-
ing carried the headline, "When The Swallowing Apparatus Goes
Into Reverse." The product was in the black immediately.

Within a few months, pediatricians began calling for Vipenta
in liquid form so that they could prescribe it for infants. Recognizing a ready market, our chemists set to work immediately, but
they could not get all five vitamins to stay in solution; one or
two of the components would precipitate soon after mixing. This
was one of the many cases in which I figuratively slipped on my
pharmacist's coat and went into the laboratory myself. I went

through all of the solvents the chemists had tried, then made a druggist's mixture that they had not attempted, using pure alcohol with about 7 percent glycerine. It worked. But after two or three days in solution, the vitamin A and C began to oxidize and disappear. The problem stumped us at first. Finally, by flushing the bottles with carbon dioxide to rid them of oxygen in both the mixing and bottle-filling processes, that problem, too, was solved. Overnight, Vipenta Drops became a household name to young American mothers. Again, Roche was off and running ahead of the competition.

Our greatest competitive coup in the vitamin field, however, came as the rumblings of approaching war began to swell in Europe. It began with a visit to the United States by Emil Barell in 1938. He brought with him a draft contract between Roche-Basle and the Millers Association of England under which Roche was to supply thiamine to fortify British flour and bread. I took one look at the contract and leaped to the obvious conclusion: if thiamine were good for British bread, it would be good for American bread, too. I immediately contacted Donald Davis, president of General Mills, whom I knew socially as a fellow member of the Boca Raton Club in Florida. "There is a movement afoot among the millers of England," I wrote, "to increase the use of flour and to enrich its nutritional value by adding B1, thiamine. This is the vitamin that is milled out almost entirely when you take the bran away from the wheat grain. It has occurred to me that you could be the first American manufacturer to restore the vitamin values to the wheat by adding thiamine." Davis was interested enough to meet with me in the old Ritz Carlton hotel in New York, but he was uncertain about my proposal.

"Elmer, I'd like very much to be the first in this field," he explained, "but thiamine costs $1.50 a gram. When I talked to my board chairman, Mr. Bell (James F. Bell, who exercised control of the company), he said, 'Why, that would mean an increase of at least forty cents on the barrel of flour. We can't possibly afford that. It would take us out of competition.' "

"When do you have your next board meeting?" I asked.

"We're going to meet the day after tomorrow."

The author, right, with Wendell L. Willkie in Paterson, N.J., during Mr. Willkie's campaign for the Presidency.

"Well, I want to ask you to bring the subject up again. Tell the board members that you have arranged with the most important manufacturer of thiamine and other vitamins in the United States to buy it at half price. We will sell it to you at seventy-five cents a gram if you will use it in your Gold Medal Flour and all of your cake and breakfast specialties."

Davis was delighted when his chairman and board agreed to my proposal. I had shaved our price awfully thin, but the vast increase in volume of thiamine sales that followed more than compensated for it. Soon we added riboflavin (B2) and niacin to the flour fortifier. It was only the beginning. When the U.S. entered the war in 1941, I went to Washington to see M. Lee Marshall, former board chairman of Continental Baking, who was the government-appointed czar of the flour industry. "Thiamine is the source of strength and endurance," I reminded him. "The armed forces will benefit if the flour that they use is fortified with it." Soon the Army, Navy and Air Corps were using fortified flour, and after a nation-wide campaign among political leaders in each of the states it wasn't long before state health laws began requiring vitamin-fortified flour. The laws were largely my doing, and I am proud to take credit for them.

The laws presented a problem for small millers, however, for most of them did not employ chemists or processing experts who could control the proper vitamin content to be added to their flour. I found a solution in the unique capacities of a well-known firm in Belleville, New Jersey, called the Wallace and Tiernan Company. Mike Tiernan, a close friend of mine, was an inventor who dealt in millers' supplies, and some of his special products were used by most of the millers, small and large. One was a Dutch compound called Agene that chemically aged flour, and another was a special bleach that whitened it. I suggested to Mike Tiernan that he prepare a carefully-measured, ready-mixed packet of vitamins B1, B2 and niacin, which Roche would supply, and sell it to the millers along with his other specialties as an easy and accurate means of fortifying their flour. He picked up the idea, and soon Roche vitamins were fortifying the flour of the small mills as well as the big ones all over the United States.

We began to make thiamine and other vitamins literally by the ton.

Vitamins and vitamin-fortified foods are accepted today as necessary elements of a healthy diet. While some people quibble over how much of each vitamin is enough, no one doubts that they are essential. To learn how important they are, one need only look at surveys by the Department of Agriculture and the Food and Nutrition Board of the National Research Council, National Academy of Sciences. The Food and Nutrition Board annually publishes Recommended Dietery Allowances, listing the amounts of seventeen basic nutrients, including all of the vitamins, that are essential to a healthy diet. People, unfortunately, ignore the Board's advice. The Department of Agriculture, in a 1970 survey, discovered that only half of the U.S. population actually eats a diet that comes up to the Recommended Dietary Allowances of essential nutrients. At least 27 percent of all Americans, rich and poor alike, according to the survey, are deficient in vitamin C; a quarter of all teen-agers, those who need it the most, are deficient in thiamine; and deficiencies in the other vitamins and nutrients are widespread — in the best-fed country in the world!

Unhappily, such surveys were not available in the thirties and early forties, when the pharmaceutical industry and a few nutritionists worked so hard to make the nation vitamin-conscious. Paradoxically, the strongest resistance to our efforts came from the leadership of the American Medical Association, including my good friend, Morris Fishbein. Always conservative in matters of public health, the AMA consistently condemned the growing popular consumption of vitamins as an undesirable form of self-medication. Vitamins, the AMA leadership felt, should be prescribed only by doctors after careful diagnosis. Multi-vitamins, especially, were to be condemned because they represented self-medication with a "shotgun prescription." The AMA leadership later learned that they had been much too sanguine about national undernourishment in the land of plenty, but in those years they were adamant. After fortified flour was introduced, the AMA announced that "The average American on today's diet needs no vitamin supplements. The use of reinforced bread takes care of most of the deficiencies."

One member of the medical profession who strongly disagreed with the AMA position was Dr. Tom Douglas Spies, a plain-spoken Texan engaged in pellagra research at the Hillman Hospital Nutrition Clinic in Birmingham, Alabama. Tom Spies had proven that the key vitamin deficiency in pellagra was nicotinic acid, the source of the B-complex vitamin, niacin. After performing seeming miracles with it on pellagra victims, he extended his concern to the whole field of vitamin deficiency. Spies, who unfortunately did not have the statistical evidence that is abundant today, believed correctly that a high percentage of Americans, rich and poor, consumed such an unbalanced diet that they were bound to suffer at least some degree of vitamin deficiency. Other nutrition experts and the AMA scoffed at his notions. The vitamin producers, naturally, took him seriously, but so did many other intelligent people in and out of the scientific community.

Since Spies lacked the research money to prove his thesis, many of us joined together to help him. With Charles F. "Boss" Kettering of General Motors and a broad-based group of mostly disinterested business and professional people, we founded the non-profit Spies Committee for Clinical Research and pledged to support an annual research budget of $150,000 for five years. The Spies effort stimulated other research, and soon there was no further doubt about the need for mass-consumption of vitamins. These days the great vitamin war of those decades is all but forgotten, its only reminders the occasional skirmishes of food faddists such as Dr. Linus Pauling who perhaps unwisely has recommended massive doses of vitamin C to ward off colds. (Vitamin C *is* a "defensive" vitamin that *helps* to combat colds, but it also is an acid, and a rather strong one. Those who consistently take heavy doses of it risk gastro-intestinal damage. I base this statement on my own long knowledge of ascorbic acid and its influence on the human system.)

The Spies Committee effort also turned a strong spotlight on another kind of deficiency, this one in American medical education. It was found that only a small handful of medical schools

Two old friends meet at the Waldorf: Bernard Baruch, right, and the author, who was there to receive awards from Columbia University and the American Medical Association.

even bothered teaching courses in nutrition. Thus, most physicians were found to be as ignorant as laymen in the field. In order to begin correcting the deficiency, a group of us from the Committee began a fund-raising drive to establish a $500,000 Dr. Tom Spies Chair of Nutrition at the Northwestern University Medical School, with Tom as its first occupant and department chairman. Starting with $150,000 that I donated, the rest of the money came quickly. It was the first department of its kind in the country. Happily, the example was followed by Harvard and other medical schools.

One of my friends in this period was Paul De Kruif, the controversial science writer who was Sinclair Lewis's silent collaborator on the novel *Arrowsmith*. I had known Paul since the twenties, when he was becoming famous in his own right as the author of *Microbe Hunters* and many other popular books and articles about science and medicine. Unfortunately, he had a tendency at times to go overboard in his writing and report medical speculations as if they were facts. At one point I gave him most of the basic factual material for a book called *The Male Hormone*, which was sharply criticized by some of my endocrinologist friends. But by and large his work not only was good but extraordinarily popular. One article by Paul in the *Reader's Digest*, of which he was a contributing editor, could accomplish more for public health education than a million-dollar publicity campaign.

Morris Fishbein also was one of Paul's friends. In fact, it was he who introduced De Kruif to Sinclair Lewis, thus setting in motion their collaboration. Paul received no author's credit for his work on the novel, but Lewis assigned him one-fourth of the book's royalties, because he created all of the fictional Dr. Arrowsmith's medical background. For the most part, Morris enjoyed Paul, but he became frequently irritated with him for his tendency to report, breathlessly, medical facts that had not yet been proved. Often Paul was dead wrong, and the public was misled. But more often he was right, and it was on one of the right ones that he and Morris parted for good.

De Kruif was an enthusiastic champion of Dr. Spies and his

precious vitamin theories, and he wrote about them in the *Reader's Digest*. I was delighted, of course, but Morris Fishbein was furious. Along with the rest of the AMA leadership, he thought the mass-consumption of vitamins was a mistake. Morris retaliated with an editorial in the AMA *Journal* that accused Paul of overstatement and lack of objectivity.

When they next met, Morris was having lunch in the Norse Grill of the Waldorf-Astoria in New York. Paul came into the room with Tom Spies, whom Morris greeted warmly. Paul stared straight ahead and refused to speak. Neither of them spoke to the other after that for years until one night when Morris, Jack Smith of Pfizer, and I were having dinner in one of the upstairs rooms at "21". Someone told us that Paul De Kruif and Tom Spies were dining together in the next room. I urged Morris to go with me to say hello to them. The meeting was cordial, not warm, and although they saw one another a few times afterwards, their deep friendship never resumed. It was one of the casualties of the vitamin war.

● *Chapter Fourteen*

● Oliver Wendell Holmes, my *very* distant cousin, once wrote only half in jest that "Science is a first-rate piece of furniture for a man's upper chamber, if he has common sense on the ground floor." I had worked ever since my first apprenticeship with Dr. Bethel to furnish the "upper chamber" and took justifiable pride in the accomplishment, because my scientific knowledge during those exhilarating years of pharmaceutical discovery was invaluable. Fortunately, I had some solid furniture on the ground floor, too: the happy congruence of a good genetic heritage and the common sense of my mother and father, whom I naturally emulated. I had grown up as a practical child, the son of practical parents who taught me to use the critical faculties that God had given me and to act with an eye to the future and a sense of compassion for my fellow man. These qualities are the nucleus of what we call common sense. They cannot be acquired like knowledge, in a classroom, but come entirely, I think, from heritage and upbringing. What common sense I possess, therefore, is the lingering, lifelong gift of my mother and father, and I am as grateful for it as I am for the love in which they enveloped me.

Although I lack Holmes' eloquence, I have always known the truth of his epigram and have striven to use common sense to the fullest throughout my several careers. Never was it more essential to me than in my closing years at Hoffmann-La lRoche. An impractical man, or a rigid, doctrinaire thinker in my position then would have cracked like a glass pane in the face of the battering from Basle.

My business affairs were never placid—no senior executive's are—but for most of my years with Roche they were a source of enormous pleasure to me because they were crowned so often with success. The frequent and natural concomitant of success, however, is envy and resentment, such as I believe motivated Dr. Eckstein, when he first goaded me to my declaration of independence from Basle in 1923, and later motivated others in the European headquarters.

Roche-Nutley's remarkable record of growth in the 1930s, when we succeeded in increasing sales and profits by about a third every year, naturally put us in a powerful position in the international company. By the end of the decade we were responsible for almost two-thirds of the revenues generated by Hoffmann-La Roche; the tail had grown much larger and more successful than the dog. Actually, this should have been a happy state of affairs for the headquarters company; and among the directors and stockholders, it was. But senior executives in Basle apparently viewed our growth with a certain amount of alarm, for they feared that it jeopardized their own well-paying jobs.

My first hint of this kind of insecurity in Basle came rather early in the game. In 1928, before I bought the Nutley property and began building on it, I had become acquainted with Walter Chrysler and a few other major financiers at Palm Beach, where Ethel and I vacationed. One of them was a founder of Hornblower and Weeks, who had been watching with increasing interest the growth of Hoffman-La Roche, particularly our American subsidiary. Other financial firms, including Blair & Co., also had taken notice. Roche still was relatively small then, but it clearly was destined to expand enormously. On the basis of conversations that I had with these financiers in Palm Beach, and later in New York, they decided to back me in an attempt to buy the entire Basle company. They were willing to go as high as $25 million. At that time it was probably more than Roche was worth; just six years earlier when I bought 1 percent of stock for $24,000, the entire company was valued at $2.4 million, and while Roche had grown, it had not multiplied tenfold. Nevertheless, the opportunity looked so good that the financiers were willing to pay a premium price. Along with a representative of Blair, I sailed to Europe with the offer in hand. Naturally I went to Barell first, even though his personal financial stake in the company was a small one and he had no voice on the board of directors. He was, after all, the company's manager. But Barell was afraid to communicate my proposal to the president, Koechlin, who also was president of Handelsbank. This powerful man, Barell said, would react with fury. By this time I had Koechlin's friendship, something that he had never deigned to grant to Barell, so I took the proposal to him myself.

Koechlin discussed the proposition quite amiably; he was even flattered by it. But in the end he said, "Mr. Bobst, I will not be able to sell the company to American interests. It would be against the principles of Switzerland, I'm afraid. The government would never permit it." He mused for a moment after closing out the offer, then added:

"I understand—all of the directors understand and appreciate what you have done to build the entire company as well as your operation in America. If you want, I will agree to sell you the American company for $5 million."

I was surprised and delighted by his counter-proposal. My companion from Blair, who represented the financial interests behind me, was intrigued, too, but we could not give Koechlin an answer until we had discussed it with our American backers. I felt that Koechlin's proposal was fair and would be good both for the American company and for Basle. It would free me to expand our business in America entirely on my own. It also would require continued firm cooperative links with Basle, from which the Swiss would profit. I suspected that Barell might take it hard, however, so I decided to discuss it with him before proceeding any further. Despite my occasional business conflicts with him, I considered Barell my friend and did not want to violate our friendship by taking an independent course that obviously would affect him without at least explaining my intentions first.

Dr. Barell was in his office, converted from the former master bedroom on the second floor of the baroque old headquarters mansion, when I reported to him the results of my talk with Koechlin. As I talked his face registered astonishment, then shock, then deep fear, in that order. I knew that he would be surprised by what I considered my extreme good fortune, but I was not prepared for the completely emotional outburst that followed. The straight-backed autocrat with the tough exterior who had faced down countless threats to his position in the past went through an instant metamorphosis. Suddenly he quivered and broke into tears. "Please, you must not do it," he cried, "It will ruin us. You and I must stay together. We work best together. We must remain together. Please!" My attempts to convince him that a truly independent American company would not mean the end of the world, nor of Emil Barell, only met with more tears and a more urgent plea. I was so swayed by his outburst that I actually believed the move would, in fact, break his spirit if not his capacity to carry on.

I relented and called off the negotiation. It was probably the greatest mistake that I ever made.

For a time the mere fact that I had possessed the power to gain complete independence and had not taken it gave me a natural psychological edge in my dealings with Basle. The rapidly growing profits of the American company gave me even more leverage, so I was not too bothered by interference with my management during the thirties except on occasions such as the multivitamin dispute with Barell. Roche-Nutley and I benefited, in fact, from extremely cordial relations with our European headquarters during this period. As a result, I did gain a partial stake in the American company. It came about in the same way that I won my original right to purchase 1 percent of the parent company in 1922—an attractive chance at another job.

I was approached in 1938 with an offer to assume the presidency of one of the largest of the American pharmaceutical companies. Had I been interested only in money and prestige, I would have jumped at the offer because it was a plum. In addition to a truly tempting salary—my earnings from Roche at the time exceeded $300,000 a year—I would have received a very sizeable block of stock at a special low cost. It was tantalizing, but I was having too much fun running Roche-Nutley to want to make a break to another company. Nevertheless, I told Barell about the offer and suggested that since I had turned down such a handsome opportunity, the Swiss should permit me to purchase at least a part of my own American operation. Barell took my suggestion to the Roche board of directors. They, fearful of my leaving the company, agreed to let me buy 5 percent of Roche-Nutley for a figure which was considerably below actual value in my opinion. There was a condition that if I wanted to sell my shares I must offer them first to them.

Thus, everything seemed to be coming up roses, on the financial and business side, at least. My personal fortune was not great, but it was comfortably into seven figures. I had invested prudently in stocks at a time when the market was low—General Motors at twelve dollars a share, Phillips Petroleum at fourteen—and my annual income from salary and 5 percent of profits in the American company was quite substantial, almost embarrassingly so when President Roosevelt began publishing the taxable incomes of the top incomes every year. I was on the first five list every time. Little of my income came from dividends on Roche stock, however. One of the Basle company's so-called "secrets" is that it has always skimped on dividends, resulting in an enormous accumulation of capital within the company; so much in fact that Hoffmann-La Roche is probably the only major company in the world today that finances all of its capital needs out of its own resources, never from banks or public money markets.

As World War II approached, however, common sense told me that a time for change in the operations of Roche was fast coming. After the Anschluss with Austria and the weakness of Chamberlain at Munich, I had no doubt that Hitler would try to bite off all of Europe. That Switzerland would be spared as a neutral nation seemed doubtful. And Hoffmann-La Roche was pathetically vulnerable. The Basle headquarters compound was

less than a mile inside Swiss territory, on the German side of
the Rhine River. Quite aside from the damage that war would
do to Basle's business operations, a German invasion of Switzerland would put our entire company in Nazi hands, thereby threatening the very existence of Roche-Nutley, the company's subsidiaries and agencies in Canada and Latin America, and its interests
in the Far East. Even before the threat became imminent, I began
to make plans to put an American flag over all of these international interests, for the protection of the Swiss owners as well
as of their far-flung subsidiaries.

But as Hitler's armies marched, the focus of my concern
became Emil Barell, himself. In 1939, frightened by the same possibility that I had foreseen, Basle had set up an emergency company headquarters in Lausanne, on Lake Geneva, hoping that there
would be more security there than on the German border. The
Swiss thought that if Germany tried to invade, the Nazis might
quickly take the part of Basle in which Roche headquarters lay,
but if the bridges were blown up across the Rhine, which is swift
at that point, the invasion would be stopped. Actually, it was
clear enough to me that if the Germans invaded they would take
Lausanne just about as easily as they would seize Basle, with the
same end result to Roche.

I telephoned and cabled Barell repeatedly, urging him to
leave a small managing committee behind in Lausanne and flee
to America, for his own safety and that of his wife and daughter.
Barell's young Jewish wife and their daugher were the crux of
the matter. As long as the threat of invasion existed, both were
in great danger. Barell and the board responded by sending me
several million dollars in cash and 87 percent of the company's
shares, with myself as nominee for safekeeping. Finally Barell
consented to bring his family, but by then, the dark days of 1940,
movement was not so easy. America had all but shut her doors
to more refugees, and those who were admitted had to go
through difficult and time-consuming procedures. Anxious to get
my friend and his family out of Europe before it was too late,
and to give Barell the freedom to run the international company
from the safety of America, I took the most practical step that

I could. I went to Congressman Fred Hartley (noted for the Taft-Hartley bill), chairman of the House Committee on Immigration and asked for his help. Hartley felt a sense of gratitude toward me because of some assistance that I had given him during a particularly tough political campaign in 1938. When he learned how distressed I was over Barell and his family, he went out of his way to help cut the red tape that was holding them in Switzerland. He also helped me to gain American asylum for a number of scientists, many of them Jews, who had been working for Roche in Switzerland and other European countries.

The Barells sailed on the last boat out of Genoa, the *S.S. Manhattan.* Within two weeks they were temporarily resettled with Ethel and me in our home in Montclair. It was the beginning of one of the worst periods of my life.

Almost as soon as he was settled in my house, where he remained for six or eight weeks, I began to unfold to Barell my plans to save the company from German domination. It seemed to me that if Hitler took Switzerland, our American company probably would survive by, in effect, seceding from Roche and placing ourselves under the control of the U.S. Alien Property Custodian for the duration of the war. But our ties to other Roche subsidiaries would be cut. The other subsidiaries would be completely at the mercy of the Germans. To forestall this grim possibility, I suggested that Roche-Nutley should purchase 51 percent of the Basle subsidiaries in Canada, Mexico, Brazil, and Argentina and, through agreement, take over the supervision and supply of the various Roche agencies around the world.

Such a move would put all but Basle under our corporate wing in Nutley, but it would not guarantee the protection of the American flag to all of our interests. The only way to do that, I reasoned, would be to create American shareholders in Roche-Nutley by issuing stock. It then would be truly an American company and not merely a subsidiary owned almost entirely by foreign interests.

Barell enthusiastically supported the idea, under which I would run the American company and he would run the international interests until the war ended. But when he communicated the plan to the four-man managing committee of senior executives whom he had left behind in Lausanne, they became afraid for their own jobs. All four had long made clear their resentment of the growth and power of Roche-Nutley, and my plan looked to them like a death knell for their own futures. Actually it was nothing of the kind, nor did I stand to profit from it in any way. I was merely trying to protect the company from the devastation that war might bring. The wisdom of my course was amply demonstrated after the United States entered the war.

Although the managing committee objected to the plan, the board of directors, particularly two of its members named Drs. Brugger and Weiland, did not. They expressed full confidence in Barell's judgment and mine. As a result, we consummated the purchase by Roche-Nutley of 51 percent of the Argentinian, Brazilian, and Canadian subsidiaries and made a long-term contract to supply and service all of the Basle agencies in the western hemisphere. We also contracted to supply and service other Basle agencies and companies in the Far East. This much was essential, with or without an invasion of Switzerland, due to blockades, because Basle was no longer in a position to supply and service the companies and agencies as it had before the war.

With the purchase agreement and contracts made, Barell and I moved next to register our new stock offering with the Securities and Exchange Commission in order to vest the company with American ownership. Our first step was to issue 10,000 preferred shares, worth $2 million. Since I already owned 5 percent of the American company, I did not plan to purchase any of the shares myself. I did, however, want Nelson Peterson and a few other senior executives, including my leading scientists, to have a chance to buy some of the shares at market price. Barell wanted a thousand shares for himself, at brokers' price, which I considered unnecessarily greedy.

The committee of executives in Basle, however, became more alarmed than ever when we filed our registration statement and began preparing the necessary documentation to meet SEC requirements. First, they were frightened over the loss of complete control from Basle. Second, they were loathe to let the SEC look searchingly into the details of their international operations. They had never let the Swiss government see their books, and the mere thought of the Americans taking a good look was more than they could stand. They dispatched Fuchs, by flying boat from Lisbon, to make an urgent last-minute appeal to Barell. Barell was unmoved . . . at first. But when it came time to supply information to the SEC, the seeds of doubt that Fuchs had planted began to sprout. Barell was every bit as loathe as his Swiss executives to reveal what Roche-Basle had always considered its private business. He was intent on ignoring, or evading, the reasonable legal requirements of the SEC. Frustrated and deeply disappointed, I finally asked Hornblower & Weeks, which was handling the stock matter for us, to withdraw the application from the SEC. Come what may, we would have to endure the problems that the war and foreign ownership brought us.

Barell at this time was titular president of Hoffmann-La Roche International. He had been given the title in 1938 after I had prevailed upon the directors to grant it to him. But he was not president of Roche-Nutley, and his presence there soon created an awkward morale problem, not only for me but for all of the employees. They worked for me, but they were constantly being asked to do things by the other "president," and the results often were total confusion. The whole atmosphere of Roche Park, once a place which many of us hated to leave at the end of the work day, began to change materially.

At first I hoped that our morale problems were mere "settling pains" that would disappear as Barell and a coterie of Swiss executives whom he brought along with him settled down and learned to work harmoniously with us. Until 1942, despite the agonizing ordeal of our on-again, off-again SEC registration, I still had that optimistic hope, for aside from his intransigence and frequent contradictions of my orders to my own people, my personal relations with Barell remained quite friendly those first two years. Both of us acknowledged our increasingly difficult clashes at Roche Park as "office problems," yet continued to act on the outside as warmly as we always had. However, unbeknownst to me, the pressure of his Swiss colleagues was pushing

Barell so firmly in opposition to me that a break was inevitable. When the explosion finally came, it was titanic; but several bizarre incidents preceded it to make the end, for me, far from completely unhappy.

Our minor clashes were too numerous to recount. Typical of them was Barell's approach to plant expansion. As much to give him something to do with his time as anything else, I had turned over to him the responsibility for planning and overseeing the construction of new laboratory facilities. Over my strenuous objections, he favored Swiss architectural and construction methods with expensive materials that not only looked grotesque but cost three times what was necessary, took twice as long to build, and were inefficiently laid out. He disliked my esthetically appropriate and secure ornamental iron gate and had it replaced with a stout factory gate so he could preserve the feeling of "secrecy" he valued so in Basle. He contradicted my orders, even to Nelson Peterson, my top executive. And he instructed his own people, particularly a man named Ritz whom he had placed in charge of our foreign division, to withhold information from me.

The situation already was becoming intolerable when one day he airily described to me a scheme for secretly getting back into the narcotics business. It seemed that a Roche chemist in Basle had gained knowledge for extracting morphine from the straw of opium poppy plants, an extraordinary achievement since previously opium had to be extracted from the sap receptacle of the poppy flower itself, then refined into morphine. With this discovery in hand, Barell wanted to smuggle poppy seeds to Argentina, set up some poppy plantations, and begin harvesting straw to produce morphine outside the rules of the Geneva Convention on narcotics and the U.S. Narcotics Control Commission. I was appalled.

"Absolutely not!" I told him. "I can't understand you, Dr. Barell. What you propose not only is immoral, it is in direct conflict with rules and regulations in the United States which control narcotics. We are an American company."

To reinforce my warning to him, I had Nelson Peterson draft a long memorandum that made very clear to Barell the

U.S. government's attitude toward the absolute control of narcotics. Narcotics production by any American company was flatly forbidden, and that was that.

Barell had a younger brother-in-law named Hans Oldenberg who worked for the company but operated completely outside my ken. Not too long after I had forbidden any further actions concerning poppy plantations in Argentina, young Oldenberg and Barell slipped off to Canada without even hinting of their plans or their mission to me. A confidential source, however, eventually filled me in on what they had done there. They had picked up a shipment of poppy seeds and transshipped them to Argentina.

Some time later, my old and close friend Harry Anslinger, the able U.S. narcotics Commissioner, called and asked me to come to Washington. When I arrived he told me that Roche not only had planted acres of poppy seeds, but the first crop was almost ready to harvest.

"Elmer, I know you too well to put the blame on you or your management." he said. "I would like to have your instructions to have our agents in Argentina burn the crops and destroy any possibility of future growth. If you will agree, I'll be satisfied to let the matter rest." I agreed immediately. When I returned to Nutley I called Barell and Oldenberg in and gave them a tougher verbal licking, I think, than I have ever given anyone in my life. Even my father could not have delivered a more devastating sermon to a cathedral full of sinners.

"We have a fence around this plant and a guard on the gate," I concluded. "If either of you engage in any action of this sort again, I will instruct the guards to lock you out for good."

But we had not heard the end of the poppy episode. It was recalled for us just a few weeks later when, after a shattering experience, we were called before the Alien Property Commission in Washington. Because my stock plans had not gone through, Roche still remained an almost entirely foreign-owned company. Its only American ownership was my 1 percent. Consequently, after the U.S. entered the war, Roche came under the routine scrutiny of the Alien Property Commission. In the first days of the U.S. war effort, the company's traditional secrecy had placed us under a cloud of suspicion: the officials in Washington suspected that some of our "hidden" ownership might be in German hands, which, if true, meant we would definitely be taken over by the Alien Property Custodian. (All of Roche and SAPAC shares were bearer shares, unrecorded by the owner's names. This is legal in Switzerland although not in the U.S.) The government people knew and trusted me and my team at Nutley, however, and were reassured by my authority as nominee for 87 percent of the Roche stock and by my firm intentions to continue running Roche-Nutley as an American company. Until Barell's insane attempt to secretly produce narcotics, we were trusted and largely left alone by the government.

But very soon after my unnerving talk with Harry Anslinger, at least fifteen Treasury agents moved in and demanded all of our books and files. I had nothing to fear and nothing to be ashamed of in my own operations, but heaven alone knew what secrets the files of Barell and his cohorts contained. For all I knew they might be perfectly innocent, aside from the poppy episode, but I doubted it; with the Swiss executives' records of tax trickery and amoral business behavior, it seemed to me more likely that their records would be damaging. They might ruin the reputation of Roche in America—a reputation that I had labored more than thirty years to build.

I moved as rapidly and as practically as possible to reassure the government that Roche-Nutley would remain an American company under loyal American management and that Barell's misbehavior had been curbed. Fearful of being taken over by the Alien Property Commission, I decided the quickest way to the top was through my old friend Basil O'Connor, a close friend and confidant of President Roosevelt. I went immediately to Basil, explained the mess that Barell had created behind my back, and pledged my own word and reputation that there would be no repetition, because I would not permit it. Apparently he communicated my plea to President Roosevelt, because within twenty-four hours the treasury representatives were recalled from Roche

Park.

Shortly thereafter, however, Barell and I were called to appear before the Alien Property Commission in Washington. Barell, sensing that he would have to defend himself against me, brought along a lawyer to advise him. The interrogation, which focused entirely on Barell, was conducted by a firm and wise former judge who was a member of the commission. He questioned the Swiss executive sharply about his interference in my business operations at Nutley, then admonished him to cease interfering immediately, because any attempt to superimpose his Swiss management upon my American management was completely unacceptable to the U.S. government. For the sake of emphasis, he reminded Barell that the Swiss company had sent to me, as its nominee, 87 percent of the Roche shares, which gave me complete control of Roche-Nutley as well as of all other Roche interests. Barell's lawyer was speechless, but he had not yet heard the worst.

The former judge next read aloud Harry Anslinger's report on the poppy episode. Barell paled. Even the commission members were surprised by the appalling tale.

Mr. Bobst," the chairman of the commission asked me, "were you aware of this action?"

I told him of my shock at Barell's first mention of the idea and added that I had flatly forbidden it.

"Did you put that in writing?"

"Yes, I gave him a long memorandum clearly explaining that the action he contemplated was against the law of our land."

The chairman then turned to Barell and gazed steadily at him with barely concealed contempt. "I want you to know that you owe your presence in this country to the kindhearted action of Mr. Bobst, because of his fear that Hitler would at any moment enter Switzerland; the United States of America offered you a place of refuge against actions that might have been taken by the Germans against your wife and child, and maybe yourself.

"You have abused the kindness of Mr. Bobst by your untoward actions almost since the time of your arrival. You have caused trouble and problems with which this commission has had to deal. Now you have willfully broken our laws with respect to the narcotic poppy seeds which you sent through Canada to the Argentine.

"I want to tell you, Dr. Barell, that if you wish to stay here any longer, you will have to behave yourself and conduct yourself as a foreign citizen should when taking refuge in this country during war. If you don't, you will either get the hell out of our country, or else you shall be interned."

For a time, Barell seemed chastened by the experience, but it was not long before he was again interfering with my management, contradicting my orders, instructing his own men to withhold information from me, and generally lacerating the cooperative spirit of our Nutley employees by his autocratic demands. In a sincere effort to reach some kind of understanding with him, I wrote him a long and carefully reasoned five-part memorandum in which, as gently as possible, I tried to open his eyes to the problems he was creating.

On the question of the frequent chaos that had resulted from conflicting views and orders by Barell and his Swiss executives, I acknowledged that some confusion was inevitable. "No one can expect the Nutley organization to absorb a dozen or so important gentlemen from foreign countries with limited knowledge of English, possessing foreign ideas, education, training, and an absolute lack of knowledge of American psychology without causing great confusion. Particularly is this the case when from the beginning, unfortunately, some of these gentlemen adopted a hypercritical attitude toward American workmen, executives, chemists, and American ideas and methods . . . there has been, and there continues to be, growing complaint against what is considered continual unwarranted criticism. And this complaint is aggravated because of the total lack of praise or sign of appreciation coming from those who continually find fault . . ."

On Barell's supervision of the building program, which ultimately cost us about $20 million in lost profits due to his tedious delays in getting necessary production facilities finished, I wrote:

"I honestly do not consider it practical for a Swiss architect, regardless of his skill, to step into a new land of which he knows nothing and take complete charge of plans, the execution of which entail the expenditure of millions of dollars . . . In Switzerland, materials are on the whole relatively high and labor relatively cheap. In America, the reverse is the case . . . I am prepared to venture that a pharmaceutical manufacturing building and research laboratory of pleasing character and of the same cubic feet of space could be built probably for one-third of the outlay necessary to construct the buildings in accordance with the Swiss designs . . ."

On his position and that of his Swiss colleagues in our plant, I tried to be as tactful as possible. "Due to the considerable influx of aliens into our organization we will have to be particularly careful so as to avoid the conclusion that we are now more or less under Swiss domination . . . In these war days, every alien's tongue must be bridled so as to avoid trouble. Above all, in my opinion, they must stop finding fault with our laws and customs and refrain from making disparaging comparisons of American methods versus European . . . We have the right of free speech in the U.S.A., and as a native-born citizen I can rail against laws and important political figures without fear. An alien cannot do so without getting into trouble."

On the most serious problem of all, our own personal business relations, I was blunt:

"It was my thought that you would act in a strictly advisory capacity during your stay in Nutley, and that your advice would concern, in the main, questions of policy of a character which were dealt with during the past years by correspondence and our occasional conferences . . . A number of our executives are utterly bewildered; they don't know whether to take orders from me or from you . . . I hate to see those who have worked beside me treated with a growing disdain and subjected to continual criticism and accusations of incompetency . . . To me, happiness in an organization means much more than perfect regimentation. It is my belief that it is impossible to have success without happiness . . . In my honest and carefully formed opinion, it is absolutely unwise from even a purely business viewpoint for you to assume actual managerial or executive control in Nutley in any fashion."

Barell apparently communicated the pain of his wounds to his management committee in Basle, for soon he proposed their solution to the problem: form a Nutley management committee composed of three Swiss and two American executives.

"I will not agree to such a committee," I told him. "I have been running this business since 1920 and I intend to keep on running it." Instead, I formed a general policy committee consisting of Barell, one of his Swiss associates, Nelson Peterson, and myself, but I gave the committee no executive authority.

Through the rest of that year and the next, we maintained a shaky rapprochment under which I managed the company like a beekeeper handling his hives; our production flowed as smoothly and as pure as honey, but I had to keep swatting the annoying Swiss who kept buzzing about, trying to sting me. Even a master beekeeper must occasionally ask himself if life is long enough to endure such hectoring annoyances every day. In 1944, as I approached my sixtieth birthday, I began to ask myself that question. I had contributed more to Roche than any other executive in its history; it had been fulfilling, often exhilarating work, but now it was not. I was in the peak of physical condition, and life still stretched open before me, full of unknown challenges. Why should I waste it on such annoyances?

● *Chapter Fifteen*

● There is a solacing observation in a couplet from Shakespeare's *King John* that applies to my increasingly uncomfortable position at Roche in 1944: "When Fortune means to men most good, she looks upon them with a threatening eye." I must confess that I found it hard to see what good possibly could come from my increasingly bitter relationship with Barell except, perhaps, total relief in the form of a final break with the company to which I had devoted thirty-four years of my life. The thought of that possibility after so many years of growth and progress was deeply distressing, but I was determined not to let it become an obsession with me. I was far too busy with vital wartime activities outside of the company to let self-pity or a morbid preoccupation with my management problems get in the way of what had to be done.

Among other urgent public tasks, I was on the Penicillin Advisory Committee of the War Production Board, helping to supervise the voluntary efforts of the American pharmaceutical industry to mass produce the miracle drug that Dr. Alexander Fleming discovered. The story of how Dr. Fleming found penicillin in a mold that had covered over and ruined an unrelated experiment is too well known to warrant retelling. But few today recall the desperation with which we worked during World War II to produce the powerful antibiotic in quantities that would help to save the hundreds of thousands of sick, wounded, and dying left in the wake of the war. All of the pharmaceutical houses pitched in to help in the unparalleled crash program. The best scientists of each company immediately went to work under the Advisory Committee's direction to find new and faster methods of fermentation. In the meantime, as much of the drug as possible had to be made. Each company proceeded with a tedious and crude production technique that was hardly more sophisticated than the accidental method by which Dr. Fleming produced his first fortuitous speck of the drug. No matter how wearisome the method, we had to begin producing as much penicillin as possible as quickly as possible in order to save battlefield lives.

The production facility that we established at Roche-Nutley typically reflected the difficulties that all the pharmaceutical houses faced. First we had to develop a germ-proof production laboratory in order to avoid corrupting the fermentation process with alien bacteria. Developing, building, and testing the lab consumed many precious weeks. Next we set up rows of sterilized milk bottles, the best containers available, and filled them with fermenting corn liquor. After days of patient waiting, a crust of mold formed on the surface of each bottle. We skimmed it off by hand. Finally, we processed it through a centrifuge apparatus that was very similar to a cream separator. It separated the penicillin from the culture in which it grew. Ironically, our very first batch of penicillin from the Nutley Laboratory never made it to the battlefield at all. One of our own chemists, vital to the overall project, suffered an infection and was near death. We rushed the first units of the drug to his bedside and saved his life.

Lederle became the biggest producer of the drug when it built the machinery and germ-proof quarters necessary to handle *one million* milk bottles. It was no wonder that the dairy companies had trouble finding containers during the war! All of this became obsolete, as even Lederle knew it would, when Pfizer made the breakthrough to mass production. Pfizer chemists developed a germ-free deep culture fermentation process in 15,000-gallon vats, just one of which produced more penicillin than all of the milk bottles in Nutley.

I met Dr. Fleming — by then Sir Alexander Fleming — in 1945, the year he won the Nobel Prize for his discovery, when he came to America to thank us for our help in solving the problem of mass production. In the course of his visit, I organized a drive for funds to finance his scientific work at St. Mary's Hospital in the Paddington section of London. He was overjoyed to receive the donation and later sent me a note to "convey to you my heartfelt thanks. The welfare of the laboratory here is very dear to me and your gift will make it possible for me to do things which would otherwise have been impossible. I sincerely hope that in the future our researches here will be as fruitful as they have been in the past . . . " I never learned whether his further research efforts bore the fruit that he hoped, nor did it matter. It was enough for him to give us this one momentous discovery that has since saved tens of millions of lives.

Another of my major war activities, the most important of all as it turned out, was the supervision of War Bond sales, first in Essex County, New Jersey, then in the entire state. I suppose I could have given the effort only token support, as I had seen some other business leaders do. They were content to let paid staff from the Treasury Department, or other volunteers, do the brunt of the work and only lent their names and occasionally their "illustrious" presence to the activity. But it is not in me to take on a responsibility and do half a job. I went after War Bond sales just as I would go after business sales, with a plan, an organization, and a hard-driving campaign. The experience served as an educational prelude to another public effort that I undertook a few years later, an effort that was to become the most important job that I ever did in my life.

When the War Bond drive began, I organized my campaign as I would a successful sales promotion drive. I first brought together a group of fifteen dedicated and important volunteers, all of them great salesmen, and called it the "million-dollar committee." Under the committee was a staff of sixteen paid office workers and 300 volunteers scattered throughout the state. Not long after we got organized, a young executive of the Prudential Insurance Company who lived in Montclair came to me with one of the best ideas of World War II. He wondered if the Treasury Department could arrange to sell bonds to industrial employees through payroll deductions. I immediately took the idea to Washington, in his name, and the most fruitful form of national public financing ever — payroll savings bonds — was born.

Throughout the war, I worked two or three afternoons and evenings a week on special War Bond appeals and fund-raising programs. Often I would gather special groups of wealthy men whom I knew could afford to buy more bonds than they were getting, give them a few drinks or dinner, which I paid for myself, then get down to business. "All right," I would announce, "today we are going to buy tanks for the army. They cost $260,000 apiece. How many are you going to take?" I would point to one of the well-heeled guests. "How many will you take?" I would point to another. The psychology was slightly hard-nosed, and I knew it. No one wants to appear to be a piker to the man at the table next to him. But as a result, bond sales quickly pyramided.

By the end of the war, we had sold more than seven *billion* dollars worth of War Bonds in Essex County alone, a national record, I think.

At the same time, I served on several other wartime pharmaceutical committees, which drew me to Washington almost weekly. The result was that, for a time at least, my abrasive conflicts with Barell and his colleagues were held to a minimum. I was simply too busy to pay much attention to them. But at the same time, Barell's opportunities to undercut me were broadened considerably by my hurried trips to Washington and my concentration on Bond sales.

The end of the Barell crisis finally came in September 1944.

● *Chapter Sixteen*

● What power I retained over Barell in 1944 stemmed mainly from his fear of the U.S. government becoming so irritated with his obtrusiveness that the Alien Property Commission would carry out its warning to him. But after D-Day, as Allied victory followed victory and the Germans fell back toward their homeland, Barell gained confidence. There was no longer even a remote possibility that the Nazis would invade Switzerland. As that threat waned, so did the threat that the U.S. might seize Roche assets as the property of an enemy-occupied country. As soon as the Swiss recognized that for them, at least, the war was over, they moved to regain the control that they had surrendered to me for their own protection in 1940. By this time, not surprisingly, the company had split completely into two factions: an American one for Bobst, and a Swiss one for Barell. Since the Barell faction included the Roche board of directors, which was completely out of my reach in Basle, the outcome of any prolonged battle was inevitable.

As the year 1944 wore on, Barell became more difficult and intransigent than ever, as if trying to provoke a final showdown. I soon discovered why. He had received a letter from the vice chairman of the Roche board in Basle ordering him to regain control of the company, on the false assumption that he had managed to supersede Barell in authority. "If you do not," the letter stated, "you will not be reelected president of F. Hoffmann-La

Roche International Company." Barell began interrupting me at meetings, sometimes to make ludicrous motions or to announce, grandly, "I am the president of Hoffmann-La Roche, of Basle, Switzerland, owner of everything."

"You're not the president of this company," I would reply as calmly as I could. "I'm presiding here and I don't want you to interrupt me." Still, he persisted. He was under pressure, and this kind of harassment seemed to be the only means he knew of responding to it.

I could readily understand why the board in Basle was worried and had given its order to Barell to regain control. They were in an awkward position, no longer able to control even their own shares in the company, and obviously fearful that my ultimate intention was to transfer the company's headquarters permanently from Basle to Nutley. In normal times, I am confident that I would have been able to sit down with them in Basle and reassure them that this was not my intention at all. But because of the war I could not even reach Switzerland; thus, in isolation they reacted quite naturally to their fears. After all, I had millions of dollars of their money entrusted to me in America, likewise a couple of million which Barell had sent to me of his money, and technically, at least, I owned 87 percent of their company. When added to the resentment that I knew the Swiss executives of the company felt towards Nutley, and the bitterness that had been generated in Barell's running feud with me, I can understand the quandary the Swiss board was in.

In addition to all of this, the Swiss had become increasingly resentful of my income. I was drawing $100,000 a year in straight salary and was entitled to 5 percent of Nutley's net profits before taxes, which entitled me to an income of 3 or 4 times the size of Barell's or any other executive of the parent company.

But the money was the least important thing on my mind. I was simply sick, tired, and disgusted — I don't know of a better way to phrase it — of Emil Barell. I held out as long as I could, for the sake of all that we had built at Nutley and all of the now two-thousand-odd people who worked there, but finally my exasperation grew too great to contain.

On an otherwise beautiful September day I called Barell into my office. The time had come. I gave him hell in terms so strong that most of them do not bear repeating. "The thing that's bothering you, Dr. Barell," I said, "is that you are not happy sitting in that chair you occupy. You want to sit in this chair, behind my desk. Well, you're not big enough to fill it."

"Shhh," he whispered, "my secretary will hear you."

"I don't care who hears me. If it weren't for the war, I would take you to Switzerland and lick you good. But I can't get there. Rather than put up with you any longer, I am through. Life is too short to live with you. I'm going to quit."

I never felt such relief in my life.

After my words had settled in with Barell, I gave him the second barrel.

"I am resigning, but you are going to give me a contract before I leave. In the first year, 1945, you're going to pay me $150,000 for advice."

"But I don't want advice," he protested.

"You're going to take it whether you want it or not."

"What else do you want?" he asked.

"I'm going to sell back to you my 5 percent of Roche-Nutley at three times what I paid for it in 1938.

Again he protested, but I stood firm. Today, 5 percent of Roche-Nutley probably would be worth more than one-quarter-billion dollars if the company traded its stock, but since it still is wholly owned by Roche-Basle, there are no public shares excepting international, not available in the United States on the American exchange.

"What about your 1 percent of Hoffmann-La Roche?" he asked.

"What do you offer?" I asked him.

"A quarter of a million dollars."

"That's not enough. I'll keep it. But I'm not through with you yet. In our contract, you are going to agree to pay me $5,000 a month for advice until I am seventy years old."

"I will be fired if I do that."

"I don't give a damn if you are fired," I said. "That's what

I think of you."

Barell decided to go to his lawyers in an effort to break me in my demands. I, in turn, went to Cravath, Swaine and Moore and engaged the services of the late and powerful legal figure, Hoyte Moore. At a meeting of both Barell and myself, with our lawyers and other representatives, Roche finally yielded to every single demand that I made.

Barell signed my contract and that was the end. I was almost sixty years old. I was unemployed. But for the first time since I brought Barell to America, I felt free.

As I conclude this reminiscence of my years with Hoffmann-La Roche, I must emphasize that the business methods, ethics, and morality of Roche-Nutley remained on the highest plane throughout the years of my own management and, so far as I know, throughout the years of my successors to this very day. My problems with the company were primarily caused By Emil Barell, and I was glad to have them ended.

● *Chapter Seventeen*

● I left Hoffmann-La Roche with a sense of joy to have ended, at last, the tensions generated by the Swiss, but with a deep sadness, too, over loyalty betrayed. I had given the company what I then thought to be the better part of my life, not knowing that I had a still better business life to come, and it hurt deeply to see it reach such a wrenching conclusion. When the word went out in the industry that I was quitting, several pharmaceutical leaders, among them my old friend, Gustavus A. Pfieffer of the Warner Company, immediately asked me to join them. But I was not ready to leap so quickly into a new career. Even before I made arrangements for my final departure from Roche Park, the prospect of devoting more time to War Bond work, along with a period of relaxation, reading, and contemplation, looked good to me.

First, however, I wanted to take care of those who were closest to me in the company: Nelson Peterson, Mae Murray, and my son, Walton. Miss Murray, a brilliant and intensely loyal person, had joined me in our old Cliff Street headquarters not long after she completed secretarial school in 1921. She was the daughter of the Irish riding master to the wealthy family of the president of the Swift Packing Company in Pride's Crossing, Massachusetts. Since she had been with the company long enough to qualify for an annuity under the pension program that I had instituted, she was not at all reluctant to retire from Roche and go on working for me in a private capacity.

Walton had developed extremely well as a pharmaceutical executive in the fifteen years that he had been with Roche. He was managing the Roche-Organon Company and turning a profit of about a half-million dollars a year at the time of my resignation. But his position became untenable within a few months of my departure. Barell made no secret of his belief that if Walton stayed on he would become some kind of "secret agent" for me. I tried to solve the problem by buying Roche-Organon outright from Barell, who had never liked Van Zwanenberg or his Dutch Organon Company and had transferred that dislike to Roche-Organon. But Barell refused to consider my offer. Soon after Barell's refusal to accept my million-dollar offer for Roche-Organon, Walton resigned. I had feared that the loss would be hard for him. He was upset in his personal life after an unhappy marriage in which he fathered two daughters. His antidote, as is often the unfortunate case, was a second unhappy marriage. Still, he did not let these personal and business blows knock him down. With my help he started an independent pharmaceutical agency of his own and swung out of Roche-Organon and into his new business with high spirits.

Nelson Peterson had been closer to me than any individual in my entire business career, a quiet, good companion who became the perfect executive and mastered every detail of our business. Since our first meeting, many years before at Harper's Ferry, his trust in me and mine in him had been unbounded. I had recognized then that he had a first-rate mind and my confidence had been rewarded. I recall once during the 1930s going to his house to call on him when he was too ill to come to work. In a room that I passed through on the way to his bedside, I paused for a moment to scan his bookshelves and marvelled at the breadth and depth of his reading. I remarked on his books as I sat down beside his bed.

"Why, Mr. Bobst," he admonished me, "don't you remember what is on those shelves? They hold the twenty-five books that you recommended to me when we first met. I've read and reread them many times."

Nelson asked me what he should do in view of my resignation. If I planned to take another job, he wanted to go with me. "Stay with Roche," I cautioned him. "Barell and his friends will have to rely on you. They have no choice. You are the only person who understands the business and can run it." Nelson later was made the president of Roche-Nutley. He lives in comfortable retirement now, not far from my home in Spring Lake, New Jersey, and we get together occasionally to wax sentimental about the good old days.

For myself, I was in no hurry to rush into anything. My only remaining link to Roche was a $10,000 pension, my separation contract, and the 1 percent of its stock that I had bought in 1922 for $24,000. For a time I held on to the stock, taking understandable pleasure in the knowledge that my continued stake in the company annoyed Barell. But after a few years I sold it through a Swiss bank to one of Fritz Hoffmann's heirs, at a satisfactory price.

Some of the job offers that came to me were intriguing, even though I was not particularly interested in them. Four large pharmaceutical houses and two chemical manufacturers sounded me out about accepting their presidencies. The chairman and principal stockholder of one major company asked me to come on at any salary I named as a "consultant," with the plan of taking over the presidency of his company within a year. The chairman had hardly communicated the offer when his incumbent president called and asked me to meet with him urgently in his hotel suite. Since I knew him rather well, I went to see him. He did not know that I was not interested in taking his job, and I did not immediately tell him. He threw off his pride and explained to me frankly that he knew I had been offered the job as "consultant." He said he also knew it meant that if I took the post, his days as president were numbered. He pleaded with me not to accept. When finally I assured him that I had no interest in the offer, he reacted as if he had been reprieved from a death sentence, an illustration of how uncertain some men wear the corporate crown.

Another rather bizarre offer came to me through Morris Fishbein. Morris had been approached for advice by Lewis Rosenstiel, the head of the Schenley Corporation, who wanted to branch out into pharmaceuticals, particularly the production of penicillin. As a distiller, Schenley had wide experience in fermentation, necessary for penicillin manufacture, and already had bought a former distillery for conversion. Rosenstiel wanted to set up his new pharmaceutical business as a quasi-independent company and had asked Morris for his recommendations concerning a president. Morris told him to get in touch with me, but to be prepared to pay dearly for my services. "I'll get him," Morris reports Rosenstiel told him, "I'll pay whatever it takes."

Rosenstiel arranged to meet with me on a Sunday morning and explained his plans.

"What are you going to call this company?" I asked him.

"I'm going to call it the Schenley Pharmaceutical Company."

"Why call it Schenley?"

"Well, frankly, because I want to be known as being in the pharmaceutical business rather than just the liquor business," he said.

"And you would expect the doctors of this country to favor the Schenley Pharmaceutical Company in preference to Eli Lilly, Upjohn, Abbott, Parke, Davis, and other highly-respected companies? Don't you see that the name itself would condemn the company? People would not credit it with being of value — neither the physicians nor the public."

"Look, I'll tell you what," he said, "if you take the job I'll give you a one-fourth interest in the company."

"I would not consider taking the presidency of a company named Schenley," I said. My objection was not that Rosenstiel was in the liquor business, but simply that I did not believe liquor and pharmaceuticals could mix successfully under the same corporate name. It would make about as much sense as trying to market Hoffmann-La Roche or Parke, Davis bourbon! As it turned out, the Schenley industries did try drugs and antibiotic manufacture briefly, but soon dropped out of the field.

The most persistent of my suitors, though, was "Mr. G.A.,"

as I had always called him — Gustavaus A. Pfeiffer, of the William R. Warner Company. G.A.'s brother Henry, with whom I had spent so many hours in my early years as a Roche salesman, had died in 1938. Henry's widow and G.A. owned the company outright but they were not doing so well. They were personally very wealthy, and the business was still an active one, but it was drifting slowly downhill under the faltering hands of its old-fashioned, seventy-two-year-old leader.

Actually, G.A. had begun to pursue me in 1942, at a time when I still thought my problems with Barell and his Swiss colleagues were only transitory. When he asked me then to take on the presidency of Warner, I told him, "Mr. G.A., I have the biggest job anyone ever had in our industry. There will never be another one like it. I cannot leave to go with you." James Adams, who became president of Standard Brands, told me that G.A. offered him the job next, but when Adams responded with a sizable list of executives who would have to be fired first, G.A. withdrew the offer.

Sometime after I left Roche, G.A. came to me again with a proposal: "Elmer, the Alien Property Custodian is going to sell Schering and Company pretty soon. (Schering had been taken as enemy property during the war.) I have the inside track with someone in Washington to buy it. If you take the presidency of Schering and then merge it with William R. Warner and take the presidency of both, it would give us a big business, and you love a big business."

I turned the idea down after warning him against the danger of counting on any "inside track in Washington," a foolish basis upon which to make any hard business plans. During the early days of the war I had been exposed to an "inside track" and I didn't want any more of it. A Washington lawyer, well-known throughout the country as one of Franklin Roosevelt's most intimate advisers, called me one day and asked me to meet him in the Oak Room of the Plaza Hotel in New York for lunch. I hardly knew the man and was quite surprised by his air of camaraderie on the telephone. In view of his prominence, however, I met him for lunch. He explained to me, quite expansively, that he

had convinced the president that I should be placed in charge
of the American interests of Sterling Products Company, which
had an important general affiliation with I.G. Farben, seized as
enemy property. The lawyer was an accomplished wheeler-dealer
and he laid it on thick, emphasizing his power to induce the
president to hand over Sterling Products Company to me. The
only condition suggested was that his brother, who worked for
Sterling Products Company, be given a substantial promotion
within the company; and at the end of the war — and the FDR
administration — the lawyer himself would like to explore the
idea of taking over all of China as his own territory for the company. President Roosevelt, he said, need never know of these two
"minor" conditions. (I think President Roosevelt *did* know of
these two "minor" conditions.) I was appalled and said so, but
I thanked him for lunch.

G. A. Pfeiffer dropped the idea of getting Schering on an
"inside track," but he continued to work on me to join Warner,
and I continued to resist him. After my resignation from Roche,
he came to me with an energetic plea. "I will have to sell the
business if I can't get someone to run it," he said. I declined.
Next he handed me a study of the company, which he had ordered. "The man in charge of our ethical and professional division made this review," he said. "Please read it and tell me what
you think." The study was worthless, but it did reflect the condition of the company, which like Roche in 1920 was oversupplied
with wartime goods and undersupplied with fresh ideas and energy. Finally, Mr. G.A. pleaded with me simply to become his
adviser. "Will you come and spend a month or two months in
the business and evaluate it for me? Standard Brands may want
to buy it from us." I agreed to talk to Jim Adams of Standard
Brands, but I turned down Mr. G. A.'s plea to investigate the
Warner Company from the inside. It would only have wasted
his money and the time of both of us.

It was awkward for me to continue turning Mr. Pfeiffer
down, because I loved him almost as much as a favorite uncle.
He and his brother had been good to me in my early days in
Philadelphia, and we had retained our close friendship over the

years. He was a fiercely independent man, and a lovably eccentric one in many ways. His dining habits were, perhaps, his most peculiar. I had become accustomed to his and Henry's rather strange notions of diet when they first introduced me to rice and prune lunches in Philadelphia. But I never got used to Mr. G. A.'s daily ritual with the waiter at his New York club. Whether dining there alone or with friends, he would carefully cut his single lamb chop or filet of sole straight down the middle and present half of it to the waiter with the words, "Here, this is your tip." But in most other respects he was generous to a fault. He was a trustee and benefactor of the American Foundation for the Blind, and a major contributor to many other charitable causes. He gave one of the dozen or so houses on his large estate near Easton, Connecticut, to Helen Keller, to live there until she died. One of the chief duties of his secretary was to act as his daily agent in buying and sending presents to his many friends and relatives. He possessed a literate and challenging mind, and I enjoyed being with him. But with the shape his company was in, it obviously required major surgery if it were to be revived. Even if I had felt like taking the job at that time, I did not believe that I could do it if Mr. G.A. remained in control, which he had every intention of doing. So, hard as it was to rebuff him, I turned him down time after time.

I tried to refuse a non-paying job, too, at the time. Thank heavens that I did not. It turned out to be the most important and satisfying work of my life.

I was devoting almost full time to War Bond work in 1945 when Governor Walter Edge, of New Jersey, and Eric Johnson, the czar of the motion picture industry, came to see me on behalf of the American Cancer Society. They wanted me to take charge of the Society's fund-raising drive in New Jersey. I had known both of them for years, and I knew that they were persuasive men, but the thought of adding another public responsibility to my War Bond work and my War Production Board activities in Washington was not appealing. I was determined to resist them.

"I am deeply interested in cancer and have learned a great deal about it during my career," I told them. "Like most of us,

I have had relatives who died of the disease. The American Cancer Society is a splendid organization that needs help. I know that. But I'm still completely concerned with Savings Bond work. I have sixteen paid people and 300 volunteers to look after. I simply cannot take on more work."

They refused to take my "no" for an answer. Reluctantly, I gave in and took on the job. Once into it, however, I was determined to give it all that I could, just as I had been when I assumed the War Bond effort. If I had wanted only to maintain, or slightly improve, the society's fund-raising record in New Jersey, I could have accomplished that goal with a few phone calls. The organization had never raised more than $30,000 in the state in any single year. It had been run like a small mom and pop business, content to putter along with limited results. Thinking back over my experiences in promoting bond sales, I decided to apply the same philosophy to the Cancer Society program: run it like a business with a well-planned "sales" campaign. I rented several rooms in an office building in Newark, brought a public relations man out of retirement to help me, hired a woman assistant to help Mae Murray, and we got under way.

My first step was to enlist the support of the strong team that had volunteered to help with the bond sales, because I knew them and I knew their capabilities. Without letting them know the reason, I invited all of my county bond chairmen and some other people of importance — about thirty in all — to join me for cocktails and dinner at a club. We enjoyed a convivial evening and a good dinner before I got up to reveal the purpose of the meeting. I explained, then, that I was about to undertake a mission — a spiritual crusade to save human lives, and I wanted them to go on the crusade with me. Then I introduced a distinguished guest, Dr. Clarence C. Little, whom few of them knew. Dr. Little, a top biologist and geneticist and director of the Jackson Memorial Laboratory in Detroit, had been scientific director and the leading force in the Cancer Society since 1929. As an individual and a scientist, he was a great man, but as an organizer and fund-raiser his talents and his goals were limited by a natural scientific diffidence that left him reluctant to employ modern business techniques. Still, he made a deep impression on my guests as he explained the need for funds to sponsor cancer research and outlined the hope for progress in combating the disease. At the end of the evening, all but two of my bond volunteers, including nineteen of the county chairmen, agreed to join the crusade. I told them that we would soon be feeding them material and advice for a major fund-raising campaign, and that I would volunteer to join them and pay for the cocktails any time they could gather a crowd of potential workers or donors together.

Before the end of that campaign, we had collected $300,000, far more than the society had ever received from any state since it was founded. The year before, total contributions throughout the entire country had been only $600,000. It was not surprising that the leaders of the National Cancer Society's headquarters began to take notice, even before our first campaign receipts were in. The most important of them and the leading layman in the Cancer Society was Albert Lasker, the humanitarian, philanthropist, and advertising genius who built the Lord and Thomas Advertising Agency. With his equally dedicated wife, Mary, Lasker had been working intently on national medical and health causes. They had entered the ranks of interested laymen behind the Cancer Society in 1943 and had been trying to prod its top scientists and physicians ever since to push harder for funds so that the organization could sponsor urgent research. At the time, there was so little money that none of it went to research. Even the National Cancer Society Institute of the National Institutes of Health, which the Society was instrumental in creating under the U.S. Public Health Service, spent only $559,000 in 1945, and most of it went for patient care rather than research. The entire federal medical research program in all areas in the early forties was only $2 million, far less than the research budget of even a medium-sized pharmaceutical company.

I had known Al Lasker for some years and I had visited him in his palatial home north of Chicago, where he also maintained one of the finest eighteen-hole golf courses in the country. I considered him to be almost in a true sense the father of modern advertising techniques. But I had not yet met Mary, whom I found to be an extremely attractive lady of great charm and grace. Apparently, they sensed that they had found a like-minded colleague in the fund-raising New Jersey chairman. I not only wanted more money for research but was willing to raise it. They invited me to speak about my techniques before a luncheon of the forty most important New York Cancer Society workers at the Waldorf. Afterwards, Albert Lasker asked me to join the national board of the Cancer Society. Within a few weeks — I think it was in June, 1945, while I was still running the New Jersey fund-raising effort — I was elected chairman of the executive committee, succeeding Emerson Foote, another great advertising leader, in the top administrative and policy position.

It took only two executive committee meetings in the society's one-room office in the Empire State Building to make me a total believer in the Laskers' cause. The society was being run by the scientists and physicians with a kind of polite sufferance of its lay leaders. As I told a reporter from *Time* magazine, they were "fine people who weren't particularly qualified to carry on a business of that character." That such was the case was immediately apparent when I saw how the "business" was being run from New York. The doctors didn't understand fund-raising or promotion, or even money. The major effort of the society, and most of its administrative funds, went into the organization and support of 30,000 dedicated volunteers called the "Women's Field Army," under the direction of a female "commander" in New York headquarters. The ladies rang doorbells every year, collecting cancer funds a dollar at a time. The society's treasurer, a Harvard man, kept the organization's accounts with a lead pencil. Albert Lasker had tried to overcome this inertia, but was exhausted from the effort and was almost ready to conclude that it was fruitless. Thus, it was like music to his ears when I volunteered to try to clean house and reorganize the entire society.

I decided that the first priority was to move aside the scientists and physicians who were in administrative control of the organization. They were good men, but they were not experienced leaders, and they were not getting results. I wanted majority control to be in the hands of qualified lay leaders. The physician members could form a scientific committee to make recommendations about scientific matters and advise the executive committee.

Second, we needed a great deal more money than we were getting. I wanted to establish an immediate goal of boosting our receipts tenfold in the coming year.

Third, the society needed to define its objectives, which at that time were hardly more clear than that the group was opposed to cancer. Our objectives, as I saw them, were to find the causes and cures of cancer through research: to educate the public on the early detection of cancer and the fact that early diagnosis and treatment could save one-third of the disease's victims; and to expand the society's equipment and service program for hospitals and the medical profession.

To accomplish these priorities, the society's constitution and bylaws had to be rewritten; and in order to effect such a sweeping revolution, there had to be a showdown. Since the society's present leadership under Dr. Little was well-entrenched and satisfied with the job it had been doing, I knew that there would be a fight. So I quietly lobbied among the organization's executive committee before the crucial board meeting. As a result, almost all of the members of the committee were present at the board meeting when the showdown came.

Naturally I had informed Dr. Little of my intention to call for a total change in the structure and leadership of the society. His first order of business at the meeting therefore was to defend the record of his administration and throw cold water on my plans for the future. "We must remember, gentlemen, that the chairman of the executive committee is just a pharmacist, and that the extent of his medical experience and knowledge is limited," he began.

I liked and respected Dr. Little as a scientist, but his personally disparaging remarks made me angry. Still, I held my tongue until he was finished, then I took the floor.

"I regret very much, gentlemen, that I am unable to speak to you with the same eloquence Dr. Little has demonstrated," I said. "He gathered his knowledge from Harvard, and I have had no formal education beyond high school. I only attended the university of the world. It's true that I'm just a simple pharmacist. So you'll have to excuse me." I paused.

"It so happens, however, that I'll match my knowledge in *materia medica* and 'therapeutics with any one in this room who is willing to meet me. I've read a great deal. I have a library of 300 medical books. I've been writing on medical subjects for twenty-four years, and I've gone through most of the disciplines of medicine. To be perfectly frank, I think I know nearly as much about cancer as any of you here.

"But the question is not how much I know about cancer. It's how the society is to be run to best achieve its major goals. And I am convinced that this society, from the time it was organized thirty-two years ago, has not done its job. It has been a failure. The only reason I am giving my time and effort is the knowledge that we are going to make something of it. To do that, we are going to have to put the balance of control in the hands of laymen.

"Now, Dr. Little, going back to your remarks about me; I would like to conclude by saying that this society is too small to have both you and me in it. I intend to stay."

I won the vote, not on eloquence, but because I had taken the trouble to make my case privately to each committee member before the meeting, something Dr. Little apparently neglected to do. My legacy, which perhaps I could blame more on my four-year battle with Barell than on the fight for control of the Cancer Society, was a duodenal ulcer which I had to begin nursing back to health after the executive committee meeting struggle. The conflict had been even harder on Albert Lasker, who was so exhausted from the squabbling of the society's doctors that he had to bow out of active participation in order to conserve strength for his other volunteer activities. I appointed Mary to his place on the committee, and she became one of the most noted of all cancer fighters. With her help, I took control of the society. I wanted to move fast, as I always had, to accomplish the goals I had set.

My first step was to get Jim Adams of Standard Brands on

the executive committee. I wanted him there as my second in command. Jim was a cool leader, a diplomat, and, as a former executive of the Benton and Bowles Advertising Agency, a promotion expert. He also understood medical research not only from his involvement with pharmaceuticals at Standard Brands, but as a leader in President's Roosevelt's Warm Springs polio foundation, as a member of the Tom Spies nutrition committee, and as committee member of the War Production Board team that spurred the development of atabrine as a substitute for quinine. I also drew other top people for the committee, among them General William J. (Wild Bill) Donovan, head of the wartime O. S. S., General John Reed Kilpatrick, the president of the Madison Square Garden corporation, Henry Von Elm, chairman of Manufacturers Trust, Howard Pew, the Philadelphia oil man, and Ralph Reed, president of American Express.

We moved rapidly to tighten and improve our paid staff organization and enhanced their career opportunities with a generous pension and insurance plan. We disbanded the cumbersome and expensive "Women's Army" and trained our best people in more sophisticated fund-raising techniques: special gift solicitations among wealthy potential donors; high-intensity community-wide fund campaigns; letter and card campaigns; arresting public service advertisements; fund-raising contests; special appeals to civic organizations, and so forth. I personally wrote a policy and guidance manual, setting up new rules and regulations for the society and its workers. Henceforth, each state organization would retain 60 percent of the money it raised to contribute to such local needs as better hospital facilities, radiological treatment equipment, and transportation of cancer patients. With our 40 percent share from each of the states, the national headquarters would spend 25% of the 40% on carefully selected cancer research projects and the rest on public education, promotion of fund-raising campaigns, and administrative costs.

The task of education was perhaps the most urgent then, because cancer still was and is perhaps the most frightening word in medicine, almost unmentionable in private conversation. As a result, public ignorance of the disease and its symptoms was abysmal. We began churning out educational material, using every medium, including radio commercials. At one point, *Time* magazine took note of our efforts in a story that began, "Not so long ago, people used to be reticent about mentioning the dread word cancer. But last week a citizen had only to twist a dial to hear it discussed at the top of radio's voice."

The first educational priority was to find a way to get people to act immediately as soon as cancer symptoms appeared. Four of us from the society were discussing this problem at lunch one day, tossing ideas back and forth. I began taking notes on the back of a menu, hoping they would help to clarify what we were talking about. When I looked at the menu after lunch, I found that my notes, in rough form, listed and explained the seven most common symptoms of cancer. We polished the rough menu manuscript and immediately began promoting "The Seven Danger Signals," which became probably the best-known educational campaign ever undertaken by a charitable organization.

The job of educating the medical profession was just as important, and it had been long neglected. Little research was being done on cancer at that time, and little was taught about it in the medical schools. There were no chairs in cancer, and what instruction medical students got usually came to them only as an incidental part of their studies in surgery and internal medicine. When I took the position of chairman of the executive committee of the Cancer Society, the best statistics available indicated that there was only one life saved out of five cancer cases and some 300,000 deaths were being recorded annually.

The "Seven Danger Signals" unfortunately were as new to many physicians as they were to potential patients. At the same time, surgery had made remarkable strides, thanks in large part to marked improvements in anesthesiology which permitted much longer and more complex operations to be performed. Prior to these advances, an operation of two or three hours duration left the patient in grave danger of dying from surgical shock. Given more time and steadily advancing technique, surgeons could do much more for cancer by 1945 than they could before the war. These advances, along with improvements in radiology such as cobalt treatment, profoundly influenced the treatment of cancer, and it was vital that all physicians learn about them.

I gave the volunteer effort as much of my time as an ordinary executive gives to a paying job. If I were not in the office every day, I was out making speeches from coast to coast, generating "sales" enthusiasm among Cancer Society volunteers or making pleas to special groups for funds. The opening of my customary speech to such groups may have been somewhat macabre, but it was effective. I would stand silently for twenty seconds or so after being introduced, then begin to count aloud:

"One . . . two . . . three . . . four . . . five," and I would point a finger, just as I had pointed when we were buying bonds to pay for army tanks. Then I would count and point again. "If you are wondering what this means, I can tell you. One in five of us here — every fifth person in this audience — will die of cancer." I used every promotional technique I could conceive to get people to open their pocketbooks. But I spoke from the heart after that opening, not from statistics. At the close of my talks, I would say something like, "The causes and cures of cancer still remain a mystery. This mystery as far as the medical profession and the scientists are concerned is locked up in an impregnable vault. There is, however, a golden key which some day will unlock the vault and thus put an end to the mystery. Each one of you carries a golden key in your pocket. In solving the mystery of cancer, you must consider the golden key as an emblem of the money you are willing to contribute to get the door of the vault open."

Happily for our embryonic program, the golden keys began pouring in. By the end of the campaign that we started after reorganizing the society in 1945, we had collected $5 million. As we made our plans for another drive, I saw no reason why we could not top that record by at least a third, if not a half. I was totally absorbed in the cancer effort, dedicated with all my heart to what I knew would be a task of many years to find the causes and develop the cures for this awful disease. Nothing was more important to me than to play my role as well as I knew how in that noble effort.

It was at the height of my involvement that the dread disease struck the person who was more dear to me than any other in my life.

● *Chapter Eighteen*

● As I read back over these pages I am not surprised to find that I have concentrated most of this story of my life on my public careers, neglecting to make a record of the private intimacies of my home and family. My reason is perhaps old-fashioned in this age of embarrassingly confessional literature, but I stand by it. While elements of a man's private life — his upbringing, his early hardships, the *tenor* of his relations with wife, child, close friends, his *feelings* about things — have a bearing on his character and personality and therefore are relevant to his career, most of his private life does not. The many shared intimacies with parents, wife, child, and close friends that are not relevant should be kept, I believe, where they live best, in memory. The danger, I suppose, is that one may come away from an account such as this with the impression that the subject had no warm and intimate private life at all. That most assuredly was not the case; but it is gratifying to me to add that almost all of my truly private memories are happy ones.

Ethel and I maintained a genuinely loving and close relationship together, and with our son, even after he gently broke the umbilical of parental ties and went out to make his own life. We loved, cared for, and, in the face of their broken home, tried our best to help our two granddaughters. I saw my brother and sisters often, shared their troubles when they permitted me to, and they shared mine. I had many close friends both within and outside of my business and public life, and such secrets and insights as we shared remain as dear, and as secure, with me as mine did with them.

But dearest of all to me was my mother, the gentle, sweet person who put me here and with her love, wisdom, and courage taught me to seize life and live it confidently. After my father's death in 1924, I probably spent more time with my mother than is the case with most grown sons, visiting her in Philadelphia or having her frequently at our home in Montclair. Our relationship remained far closer than that of mother and dutiful son living out their lives with periodic letters and occasional visits. Although we lived eighty miles apart, we remained spiritually together always. She was a vigorous and active woman throughout her years, engrossed with church work in Philadelphia, busily knitting or embroidering even when in the midst of committee meetings or conversation. I still use the linens that she embroidered for me fifty years ago, and antimacassars that she made are in daily use on some of my furniture. When I touch these things of hers, it is almost as if she is still here in fact, as she is in my memory.

At the height of my Cancer Society activity in the fall of 1945, I went down to Philadelphia, as I often did, to take Mother out to dinner, to the theater, and home to her apartment for a long talk. Such evenings were our favorite times together. She was in her eighty-third year and, as always, in good spirits, but I could see during dinner that something was bothering her. Her appetite was good and she said that she felt no pain, but she placed a hand on her abdomen and said, "I feel a great heaviness in here." Her doctor, she said, called it a "ballooned" gall bladder. The diagnosis seemed odd to me. Such a condition, if it occurs at all, usually occurs earlier in life.

When we got to her apartment, I said, "Mother, let me examine you." I pressed gently below her right rib cage and felt a lump. Without alarming her, I said, "I think this is something you ought to have taken care of." But my knowledge of cancer and its danger signals was enough to leave me reasonably certain that she was seriously ill. I arranged to have her admitted to the Episcopal Hospital, under the care of an excellent surgeon to whom I described my suspicion about her condition. He was skeptical of my diagnosis. I remained in Philadelphia with her all of that week, watching with anguish as she began dramatically to weaken. "Why don't you operate?" I asked the surgeon.

"Mr. Bobst, we want to get your mother into better shape before we do anything," he said.

I had been observing Mother's weakening condition closely. "She's getting worse each day, not stronger," I said. "I want you to operate at once."

"Do you demand that?"

"Yes," I said. "I believe it is her only chance."

The doctor still was not convinced that she had cancer.

Mother was prepared for surgery. I kissed her, I feared, for the last time, then went out and walked the streets, deeply troubled. When I returned, she was just being brought up to her room. The surgeon was with her.

"One whole lobe of the liver is cancer," he sighed. That meant that there was no hope; she was near the end of the final stage. Mother died thirty-six hours later without regaining consciousness.

Most of her closest friends had passed before her, so the funeral was a small one, in her apartment. The family gathered there again, after burying her beside my father on the quiet hill overlooking the Schuylkill River. It was a tragic reunion for Harry, my three sisters, and me, and a deeply emotional one. In the midst of it, the telephone rang. It was Gustavus Pfeiffer. Someone had told him that I was at my mother's apartment in Philadelphia but had not told him why I was there. He did not know that Mother had died, nor did he wait for me to tell him.

"I've got bad news," he said, when I answered the phone. "My executives have learned that I've been dealing with Standard Brands. They say that unless I call off the negotiations at once, they're going to walk out, all of them together. What am I going to do?"

I was in an emotional state, grieved by my mother's death

and burial. Perhaps I mixed my love for her with my fondness for Mr. G.A.; in any case, I had an instinctive urge to relieve his anxiety. Without even pausing to think about it, I replied,

"Tell them to go to hell. Let them walk out, and I'll walk in."

● *Chapter Nineteen*

● There was an inescapable feeling of déjà vu as I walked for the first time as president through the imposing doors of the old Altman store at 18th Street and Sixth Avenue in New York. For thirty years now, since Henry and G.A. Pfeiffer had first asked my advice about moving, this huge old building had been the headquarters of the William R. Warner Company. Although Warner was far larger and better known than all of Hoffmann-La Roche had been in 1920, when I first took over the old offices on Cliff Street, there were sufficient parallels to account for my feeling that I had been through this experience before. Warner was a company in trouble, staggering to adapt to a highly competitive peacetime situation after the comparatively profitable war years. And it was carrying on its shelves such a heavy burden of unsaleable goods that they threatened to carry the company under. The comparison with Roche in 1920 was inescapable; only the amounts of money involved were greater, the stakes far higher.

Mr. G.A. had made a colossal mistake in the business, one that did not fully come to light until I had Price-Waterhouse, the accounting firm, make a complete audit of our operations immediately after I took control. During the war years, Warner had sold goods under a standard contract that permitted customers to return unsold merchandise for full credit. We were being swamped with millions of dollars worth of returns. Some of it was obsolete stuff, products that were no longer manufactured or marketed. Some was below-standard merchandise, such as lipsticks that had been produced under rigid wartime controls but had since been superseded by better-quality post-war products. Some of it consisted of a vast amount of post-war overproduction. The size of the inventory constituted a far heavier albatross than I had encountered at Roche after World War I. But the most staggering thing about it was an error in cost-accounting and in judgment on Mr. G.A.'s part which had left him totally misinformed about his profits and losses. When the returned goods had been entered in inventory, they had not been recorded as routine liabilities, nor even at their realistic value, if they had any value at all. Instead they had been entered in the inventory as assets at their wholesale value, thus falsely inflating Warner assets and obscuring substantial losses.

When I talked to Mr. G.A. after my mother's funeral, he stated that he was earning a profit of about $1,500,000 on sales of $29 million. I was skeptical, but on the basis of his figures he sincerely believed what he said. Actually, after the Price-Waterhouse study revealed the unfortunate cost-accounting error in the inventory, I found that Warner was showing a loss of $1.5 Million a year instead of that amount of gain and Mr. Pfeiffer did not even know it. Thus I was presented a company in deeper trouble than I knew, as I had been a generation before with Roche. The differences were that both the company and its problems was far larger, and I was no longer the ambitious young salesman out of Philadelphia, but a thirty-four-year veteran of the pharmaceutical industry just a day past my sixty-first birthday. But I felt good about it, especially after settling a few important matters with Mr. G.A. I made it clear from the first that I not only would be president and chief executive officer, but that G.A. would bow out of active management altogether.

"I want you to buy whatever you want of my stock," he told me that first meeting. "I own all the stock except some non-voting shares that are owned by my sister-in-law, Anna, and they don't amount to much. You can have my shares at book value."

"Mr. G.A., I'm going to have a tough job rebuilding your company, if you will permit me to say so. It's badly run down. I'll take a chance and buy 27,000 shares, but I want to pay something over their book value, because I don't want the revenue people coming after me with the charge that I got them as compensation.

"Now Mr. G.A., for your sake and for my sake and for the good of the company, I want you to put the rest of your stock and the stock I purchase into a voting trust — one in which you will not be a trustee. You become forgetful, and I have a very tough job ahead of me, so *please* do what I ask."

"I'll take an office outside," he protested. "I won't bother you at all. I'll leave you alone. You'll run it."

"You don't need to take an outside office," I said. "I'm going to run it. You'll have three voting trustees. I'm going to make your wife one of them." Mr. G.A. wasn't entirely happy to surrender his total power in the company, but in the end he accepted the situation gracefully and agreed to the trust. I paid something over a million dollars for my shares of stock and limited my salary to $75,000 a year, which, incidentally, I have never exceeded to this day. Preserving the company was the only thing that mattered to me. If I saved the company and made it grow, my financial reward would come from the stock. If I failed, the size of my salary would not make much difference. When Henry's widow, Anna, died just a few weeks later, her non-voting shares became available and I decided to offer them for sale to the employees, so they, too, could gain an equity stake in the company. It was a clear indication of how shaky most of them felt about the future of Warner when, out of 1,600 employees, only a few sought to buy the shares. There was ample reason for their fears.

In addition to the inventory problem, the company was weak in management, marketing, and research, Mr. G.A. had a number of unproductive relatives on the payroll, as Jim Adams had noted several years earlier, but that was one of the least of our problems. There has been such a Topsy quality to the growth of the company that by 1946 it was crisscrossed with conflicting lines of authority and disorganization. If one traced the lines out on a management chart, the result would have looked like a spaghetti factory after an explosion. With their philosophy of "It's cheaper to buy goodwill than to create it," the Pfeiffers had bought more than fifty companies, plus a bewildering assortment of patents and trademarks. The most successful of these purchases had been of the Richard Hudnut company, the cosmetics firm. But Mr. G.A.'s attempts to integrate all of his purchases under one roof had created chaos, with only a few cases of talent in the ranks. One of these bright spots resulted from the purchase, in 1930, of the Schering and Glatz Company, the firm whose president, Dr. Edgar Sampson, took on my friend and old boss Charlie Cameron, Sr., back in the twenties. When Warner bought Schering and Glatz, they kept only two of the company's old employees. One of them was Charlie Cameron, and I found him still working for Warner when I took over. He ran a part of the promotion department that handled correspondence from physicians. It had been almost twenty years since I helped him get the job, and now he was seventy years old, five years past retirement age. One of my first acts at Warner was to ask him to come up to my office.

"Charlie, what are they paying you?" I asked him.

"Doctor, I'm getting the same from Mr. Pfeiffer that I got when I was made Dr. Sampson's assistant, $5,200 a year. But I'm not saying anything, because I'm past the age. I'm working hard and nobody's telling me to quit." He mentioned his wife, Ella, and added, "I have to keep on working."

"Charlie, I think that's a shame. From now on you'll receive $7,500 a year. And every day for the next week I want you to come in here and see me, and I want you to tell me everything you know about this business and about every one of the executives here."

Dr. Sampson and the Pfeiffer brothers had never realized Charlie Cameron's full potential; I suppose because he was a quiet, self-effacing man who did not push himself forward. But he was a brilliant fellow, and the help and information he gave me during my first week at Warner was invaluable. It was just a few days before Christmas, the time when the employees traditionally received a very small bonus check and a box of candy. I handed Charlie his candy along with an envelope that I asked him to open when he got home. His bonus, well-earned, was $2,500. The next day he looked five years younger and attacked his job with as much zest as the youngest man in the company. Charlie continued to work for Warner until he had a stroke about four years later. He died not long after that, leaving his wife, Ella, who is ninety as I write this today.

Their son, Charles Cameron, Jr., shared his father's brilliance. I had followed his progress through Hahnemann Medical College and his early career as a surgeon specializing in cancer. After his residency at Philadelphia General Hospital, he had worked and studied for four years on a Rockefeller Fellowship at New York Memorial Hospital, the greatest cancer hospital in the world. During the war he had spent four years as a Navy surgeon, part of it in charge of the cancer section of Brooklyn Naval Hospital. Not long after I moved into my new office at the Warner Company, young Dr. Cameron got out of the Navy and came to see me. He was feeling ambivalent about his future.

"Shall I continue in surgery, or should I use my talents and knowledge in other directions?" he asked me.

It just so happened that Dr. Cameron's question was fortuitous. It came shortly after Dr. Little, reacting to our irreconcilable clash in the National Cancer Society, had resigned as scientific director of the society. I already had asked Dr. Alton Ochsner, one of history's great surgeons and chairman of the department of surgery at Tulane University, to accept the post. As a member of the board of the society he had attended the showdown meeting and supported my plans for reorganization. Although he said he was "flattered and pleased" by the offer, he was far too busy to accept it. So I was looking for a cancer specialist when Dr. Cameron came to see me.

I suggested to him that if he was considering a broader future than the practice of surgery, I knew of two avenues open to him. One, which would please me and probably his father as well, was a post as assistant to the medical director of the Warner Company. The other, which would please me far more, was the medical and scientific directorship of the American Cancer Society. He elected to take the latter and, as a result, presided over the greatest ten-year period of growth in the society's history and was instrumental in establishing its most fruitful research programs. In 1956 he published *The Truth About Cancer,* which I consider the best layman's guide to cancer ever written. Dr. Cameron left the society to become president of Hahnemann Medical College and Hospital and has created there some of the finest research programs and facilities anywhere. One of the facilities is a sixteen-story clinical laboratory, the largest in the world, which I had a hand in funding. I am both proud and grateful that it bears my name, The Elmer Holmes Bobst Laboratory for Clinicial Research. Whenever I visit Dr. Cameron there, I cannot escape a feeling of true humility; the marvelous new laboratory is only a stone's throw from an old rooming house at 15th and Race Streets where Mahlon Yoder and I lived in near poverty at the beginning of this century. It was from this $3.50 a week room that I started out each morning through a terrible winter to walk to the stables of the U.S. Express Company in order to get my team harnessed and backed onto the platform by six in the morning.

● *Chapter Twenty*

● A pharmaceutical industry executive who watched the sagging fortunes of the William R. Warner Company in the early years once characterized the organization with these words: "Warner collected the most mixed-up assortment of patent medicines you ever saw, some of them country fair stuff. They would buy almost anything. Any company that was for sale, they'd buy it." The result was that there was no clear focus to the Warner business. We had many good products, but many weak ones, too. Among the good products where a few ethical specialities — Gelusil, Anusol Suppositories, and Agoral, all of which are promoted solely to the medical profession — not to the public — but there was no real strength in the ethical division. Our proprietary medicines were led on the marketplace by Sloan's Liniment, which had been strong for seventy years. In toiletries and cosmetics, where we got most of our sales, Warner had good products in the Hudnut and Du Barry lines, but it also carried unprofitable operations that included the Richard Hudnut Beauty Salon on Fifth Avenue, the Du Barry Success School, and the Du Barry Home Success Course.

We also had two monstrous and utterly inappropriate manufacturing plants. The old Altman store — actually a cluster of five- and six-story buildings that had been constructed for busy

Manhattan retailing — and a large plant in St. Louis, where the Pfeiffer brothers got their start in the pharmaceutical business.

My first moves were to begin culling dead wood from the managerial ranks, while simultaneously clearing the inventory, reorganizing from chaos into four clear-cut operating divisions, and generating new products to strengthen our sales. I suppose I would be rated low by the Harvard and Wharton business schools for my approach to the task, but I could see no alternative but to take it all on my own shoulders and function alone with no top executive assistance. Although I brought in Walton as a sales and promotion executive and hired other first-rate people to handle specific jobs such as research and production, I shouldered all administrative and managerial functions myself. I had always been a management "loner" anyway and, except for Nelson Peterson, never did have a close executive vice president to share the load, so it was nothing new to me. It only meant that I had to work many days from early morning to well past the dinner hours. I was used to that. Fortunately, I still had Mae Murray by my side. An executive secretary such as Miss Murray is invaluable to any man trying to run a complex organization, for by deftly managing his office, learning his business almost as well as he knows it himself, and anticipating his needs, she permits him to pack twice as much work into a busy day.

The difficult job of attracting top people to join the faltering Warner Company in specialist roles was made somewhat easier for me when several of my former scientists at Roche resigned their jobs in order to join me in this new business crusade. One of them was Dr. Ulrich Solmssen, a University of Zurich graduate whom I had brought to Roche years before on the recommendation of the head of that famous institution, the Nobel prizewinner Dr. Paul Karrer. He began as a top research chemist at Roche, and later became expert in chemical manufacturing. At Warner, I asked him to dig into our laboratories and make sense out of what under Mr. G.A. had become a sort of chemical nightmare. Warner people had for years been mixing chemicals for the company's products like cooks putting together great dishes according to remembered recipes: the products were fine, but the formulae for them often reposited only in the heads of the mixers. Dr. Solmssen spent months developing complete records of the formulae and the modus operandi for mixing them. In addition, he instituted a control code from which we could determine the lot number and time of production of each product. All of these steps not only were invaluable, but were essential to reliable and efficient production, and their absence when I took over Warner was one of the worst of the company's failings.

The most nagging item, for quite a long time, however, was our stock of dead inventory. Under the old Pfeiffer contracts, these products were being returned for credit in an onrushing stream so that the shelves refilled as fast as I could empty them. During 1946, $2-million worth of goods was returned; during 1947, $4-million worth came in. In addition to out-of-date cosmetics, much of the oversupply consisted of standard non-specialty pharmaceuticals, "me-too" pills that Warner had begun producing simply because other houses made similar products, and elixirs, syrups, and tinctures for pharmacists that Warner for some strange reason had been selling below cost. I got rid of what I could at fire-sale prices, took us out of the "me-too" and elixir business, and gave about a half-million dollars worth of what was left to Greece, then suffering from a Communist-led rebellion.

Our cosmetic business, probably the company's strongest division before I took over, was faltering under the shock of war's end. Cosmetic companies had vastly overproduced in order to fill empty store shelves when wartime controls ended. As a result, we were caught with a surplus of unwanted goods and no clear notion of what to do next to recover from the blow. One major problem that I discovered immediately was that the business was dominated by what I call "cosmetic cooks" who created products solely on the basis of sight, smell, and feel. They either knew nothing about the real physiological and chemical needs of skin and hair, or they ignored them. I hired a top cosmetic chemist to build our products on the basis of high health and hygienic standards, and took over every phase of the management of the division myself. Soon we began marketing vastlt improved products and once again began to lead in the field that Hudnut for many years before the war had dominated.

Among our most successful products was the Warner-Hudnut Home Permanent, which I frankly "bought" by purchasing Raymond Laboratories and hiring the owner, Ray Lee, who was the genius of the home permanent field. Lee had invented what became the Toni Home Permanent and had sold it to Harris Bros. of Minneapolis at a very large profit. Harris later sold it to the Gilette Company at a price about twenty-five times what they paid for it. I talked him into joining forces with Warner, and soon we had his new home permanent as well as another of his developments, the Warner-Hudnut Rinse.

Warner had never given its products the strong, selective advertising I thought they deserved, so I moved as quickly as possible to correct that deficiency by spending heavily on radio, which was then the most popular medium in America, newspapers, magazines, and even the fledgling new medium, television. Out greatest effort went into a news and gossip show that is all but forgotten today but was the most popular thing on radio for two decades. It opened every Sunday night with a familiar, raspy, stacatto voice saying "Good evening Mr. and Mrs. America and all the ships at sea . . . let's go to press . . ." Walter Winchell. Sales of the products that we advertised on his radio show boomed.

I also did what I could to improve our work surroundings by clearing an entire floor where our surplus products and old machinery had been stacked. I remodeled it, including a home-like, panelled office for myself, the decor of which I adapted from rooms that I had studied at the Metropolitan Museum. I installed a cafeteria where employees could buy low-cost, company-subsidized meals, and began the truly impossible task of sprucing up all areas of the department-store-turned-factory building. "I want everybody to sort of feel a little pang of regret at the end of each day when he leaves this place," I told the employees when we gathered for a company-wide meeting in late 1946. "I want each of you to feel that you do enjoy your work and that you do like your environment."

Unfortunately, no matter how much cosmetic repair we devoted to the old building, it was bound to be a losing battle. The place was infested with mice and open to city grime and dirt, as the old Roche headquarters on Cliff Street had been. It was a half-block-long firetrap enclosing 450,000 square feet of utterly inappropriate space for a pharmaceutical and cosmetics firm. Even its fourteen antique elevators were a liability: if a crew took a heavy load to the upper floors in one elevator, the thirteen other operators had to wait for the mission to be accomplished before they could start up or down; there wasn't enough power in the system to run all of them at once. I had realized one dream of overcoming similarly unsafe and unsanitary conditions at Roche in 1928; now I began to dream of another beautiful home for medicine in lovely surroundings. I also began to dream of making Warner a world leader in ethical pharmaceuticals, as I had done for Roche, and I was determined to realize that dream, too.

There were innumerable problems that had to be coped with first, however, and one of the most important was employee morale. The company during my first year was obviously in trouble and equally obviously was going through radical and quick changes the outcome of which, to many, seemed uncertain. Even more damaging were the company's salary and fringe benefit policies, which not only were below standard for the industry, but were filled with inequities. Management in the past had too often been generous with a favored few and penurious with the rest. The employees, naturally, resented it, and their resentment showed in their work and their attitudes toward the company. Pilferage and absenteeism had become major problems. The quickest cure for such inequity is justice and generosity, so I began quietly and equitably to raise wage scales and drew up plans for a new Christmas bonus schedule and a radically improved insurance and pension plan. I announced these plans to an understandably rapt audience at the company-wide meeting in 1946. Christmas bonuses, henceforth, would be revised upward on a graduated scale that would give a month's salary to those with five or more years of service to the company. Vacations, too, would be increased to three weeks (which was then considered an extraordinarily long period of leisure) for ten-year veterans. Company-paid insurance policies would henceforth be the rule of the day. And the pension plan was being boosted to the point where a retiree could get up to 80 percent of his average salary, for life. I concluded my announcements with this homily:

"I am having a lot of fun running this business. I can quit tomorrow; I have no obligation to anyone, except the obligation of my promise to Mr. G. A. Pfeiffer to run this business for five years — beyond that, nothing. But I am not going to quit. I am here because I love to work and I love to build. I am going to work alongside of you, with every bit of energy I possess, to drive this business on and on to higher levels, to safeguard it and you, as far as I can, against depressions, against the hard times that may come.

"I am working, I repeat, because I love to work, but in doing so I want to have around me men who love to work, too, and workers who will cooperate. I want our workshop to have a happy atmosphere. We want you to feel at all times that your employer is fair, and we want to feel, in turn, that you are fair. If we can both share that feeling of faith in each other, then our work will indeed become a pleasure and our business will thrive in full measure as time goes marching on."

The employee welfare program was an immediate success, as I knew it would be. A fair offer begets a fair return, confidence begets confidence, and success begets success. Attitudes improved, production improved, and most crucial of all, sales and profits began to increase. By 1948 we had moved from a loss position after a devastating downhill slide, into a profit position. Worldwide sales, about a third of them from our fourteen branches and eighty-five agencies overseas, rose to $41.7 million, an increase of 60 percent over 1945. By 1950, we reached $48.75 million in sales. On the ethical side, where we had been weak, we were undergoing clinical tests of a dozen new products for use in, among other areas, the hormone field, and in treating menopausal conditions, bronchial asthma, and peptic ulcer. By 1951, our sales climbed to $53.6 million and our net profit to $3.3

million. The company was at what I like to consider the "'takeoff' point, the spot on the uneven runway of business growth where enough speed and momentum has been established to begin climbing rapidly away from the bonds that held us down.

One of the bonds was the company's name, which evoked little recognition among consumers. To those who knew it, the name smacked of an old-fashioned enterprise, although William R. Warner, from whom the Pfeiffers bought the old Philadelphia concern, was the most advanced and modern pharmacist and pharmaceutical manufacturer of his day. He invented the sugar-coated pill and built a fortune on it. But cosmetics had become our main sales line, and the name Warner was an anachronism in that field of Rubinsteins, Ponds, Du Barrys, and Hudnuts. I changed the company name to Warner-Hudnut, and almost instantly we began to receive better brand-name recognition.

Although it may seem paradoxical, I also began subtly trimming our interests in the cosmetic business. Some industry observers thought that I was shifting emphasis away from cosmetics simply because of my acknowledged deep emotional and philosophical attachment to the pharmaceutical business. But that was not the only reason. Cosmetics, particularly the high-volume powders, creams, lipsticks, lotions, and nail polishes that women use and replace constantly, are so intensely competitive that profit margins are extremely low. It takes armies of demonstrators and salespeople to sell them. By the end of a year, the small profits of a few percent or less seem hardly worth the massive effort. I decided to concentrate on the specialty cosmetics that offer a fair return for the man-hours and capital invested and dropped much of the rest. Among other things, I closed the Du Barry Success School and dropped the Home Success Course, both losing propositions from the start.

At the same time, I saw that it was time literally to capitalize on our success by making a public issue of the firm's stock. The proceeds from the sale of about 800,000 of the 1,500,000 newly authorized common shares were used to retire Gustavus Pfeiffer's preferred shares and thus bring our preferred and common stock shares into balance. Because of their heavy prior claim on the company's assets, the large number of preferred shares in the Pfeiffer portfolio had made our common stock relatively unattractive.

It was then that my two dreams for Warner began to coalesce. I had been looking, ever since I took over the company, for a small but strong ethical drug manufacturer with which to merge, in order to strengthen our specialty business. Among other companies that I had quietly investigated was the Chilcott Pharmaceutical Company, once called the Maltine Company, of Morris Plains, New Jersey. Chilcott had just introduced a new ethical product called Peritrate, a nitrate similar in action to nitroglycerin, which is the classic treatment for angina pectoris. Like nitroglycerine, Peritrate dilated the coronary vessels of the heart, thus permitting more blood to flow to the oxygen-starved heart muscle of angina victims. It was very effective. I was impressed by the drug, but more impressed by the lackluster promotion the Chilcott company was giving it. They didn't seem to realize what a valuable product they had and were not marketing it as they should.

One Sunday morning in 1951, I drove out to Chilcott's twenty-acre plant and laboratory in Morris Plains, not far from the Morristown site where George Washington and his army spent their first bitter winter, a far tougher ordeal than the celebrated winter at Valley Forge. I wandered around the area like a tourist, without telling anyone who I was or why I was there. Chilcott did not know that it was being surveyed by the president of Warner-Hudnut. As I walked around the spacious, well-landscaped grounds of the progressive, small company, I could not help but think of our own outmoded factory building in St. Louis and the unsuitable white elephant we occupied in New York. I had wanted for several years to close down the St. Louis plant, because it was losing about a half million dollars a year. But we had kept it going mainly to please Mr. G.A., who had a sentimental attachment to it. It was there that he and his two brothers had begun in the late 1800s, and although the third brother, Paul, retired and went into farming, Henry and G.A. always retained their deep sentimental attachment to it. By this time in 1951, however,

Mr. G.A. had lost his interest in the management of the St. Louis plant, so it was time for change. As for our New York building, the sooner I got rid of it and moved the company to the country, the better.

That night as I thought over what I had seen of the Chilcott facilities and what I knew of their solid pharmaceutical products and the unrealized potential of Peritrate, I decided to take the step. On Monday morning I asked Miss Murray to get James C. Chilcott on the telephone. Jim Chilcott was the company's largest stockholder, with an equity of about $750,000, and ran it in a firm and enlightened way. He had built its sales to about $3.3 million a year and generated sufficient profit to invest in a modern research facility at Morris Plains, which he called Chilcott Laboratories, Inc.

"Jim, how about having lunch with me tomorrow?" I inquired.

"I'm getting ready to go fishing, Elmer," he said, "is there anything special?"

"Yes, there's something quite special."

"What is it?"

"I'd like to buy your business."

"Well . . ." he paused. "The business is not for sale. But I'll have lunch with you."

I knew Jim Chilcott, and I knew that if he was really opposed to selling his business, he would never cancel a fishing trip for a pointless lunch date. He was interested. Within three months his business was a part of Warner-Hudnut, purchased on an exchange of stock worth about $4.5 million. I was then chairman of the board as well as chief executive of the company, and I invited Jim to join the board as vice chairman, which he did. He served happily and conscientiously for fifteen years thereafter. That was the way I liked it, the way I have always approached mergers and the acquisition of other companies. I have never forced my way into any company through pressure or a proxy fight and never intruded where Warner wasn't wanted, but only when both parties found the merger advantageous and were happy with it. That is not to say that I will not scramble to gain an advantage for my company, or use all of the honest sales techniques that I know in order to convince the other party of the wisdom of joining forces; but I will not engage in a damaging public battle to gain control of someone who cannot see the advantage of lining up with me.

While making the deal with Chilcott, I managed to keep two of my goals in the dark. One was the great expansion I had in mind for the Morris Plains operations. I intended to close down St. Louis, phase out New York as quickly as possible, and move the Warner Company. To facilitate this, I quietly bought options on eighty acres of land surrounding the Chilcott plant. When the original property owners ultimately learned that I intended to move my company there, they protested that they had let the options go at too low a price, but I simply told them, "We gave you the price you asked; it was fair." My second goal was to get behind Peritrate and promote it to the leading place in the market that it deserved. I did as I have done so often with ethical products in my career: trained our detail men in the best techniques of arresting the attention of doctors, and sat down to write my "Dear Doctor" letters and other advertising and promotional pieces. I had been writing this kind of material on my quiet Sunday afternoons for more than thirty years, and I saw no reason to stop or to turn the job over to a subordinate. My letters still drew a greater response than any other direct mailings to doctors by any company; somehow, no one else seemed to be able to get the hang of it and duplicate their success. There was no magic to it, really; just a simple, relaxed style in a conversational format that I believed conveyed the sincerity which I actually felt. I did all of the promotional writing on Peritrate for the first three years after taking over Chilcott. As a result, it not only became, but remains today, one of the largest-selling ethical items in our repertoire of prescription pharmaceuticals.

It was a busy and productive time for Warner-Hudnut and for me. We successfully shifted our operations to a new, air-conditioned, $2-million production-research-administration complex at Morris Plains, merged our product lines as well as our research laboratories with those of Chilcott, and didn't drop a stitch in the process. But it was not so busy that it monopolized all of my time. I continued to have an active collection of second lives, in politics, in civic affairs, and in play. Although I did not know it, life also held for me both tragedy and love.

The author, left, with the then U.S. Secretary of the Treasury John W. Snyder aboard Alisa IV *at Spring Lake, N.J., in the summer of 1952.*

● *Chapter Twenty-One*

● I never agreed with Henry Adams observation that "politics is, at bottom, a struggle not of men but of forces." I suppose I am Aristotelian in believing that man is a political animal by nature and that the public welfare depends upon the political actions of individual men. I would no sooner turn away and let natural forces mold a political cause in which I believed than I would turn away from a bountiful table and let starvation take its course. To my mind, the more citizens who feel that way, the stronger is democracy and the more effective, government. I am a natural-born reformer and a life-long Republican — although many of my friends would not agree, I think the two go together. From the vantage point of eighty-seven years, I can see that I was right to get involved and not to turn away from politics, because however small it may have been I know that my efforts have had an effect at both the local and the national level, and it would be false modesty indeed to claim that I have not been pleased by it.

Among the rewards of getting involved, as I have been ever since the Judge Pennypacker campaign in Philadelphia early in this century, is the simple pleasure of meeting and learning from great men. I have known, at least casually and in one case intimately, every president since Teddy Roosevelt. Most of the truly great senators and members of Congress of both parties since

World War I have been among my friends. I would hate to be put to making a list of the great ones. Because it would be small and many of my less distinguished political friends would be offended. I have worked for many men whom I admired, all the way from the Philadelphia wards to the White House, and I know whereof I speak when I say that men and not just anonymous "forces" shape our political destiny.

But, however partisan I have been, I believe the most rewarding of my political activities were non-partisan ones performed, as a result of my work in the American Cancer Society, on behalf of American health care generally. My involvement with the Cancer Society brought me into contact with a small group of active people — someone called them "benevolent plotters" — who set out during and after World War II to revolutionize American medical education, research, and health care. They included Albert and Mary Lasker, Dr. Alton Ochsner, Dr. Michael DeBakey, Emerson Foote, Dr. Frank Adair, Anna Rosenberg, my old friend Jim Adams, and a number of other well-known and not-so-well-known people who were willing to devote time and energy to this noble cause. All of them did not agree all of the time, but all were united in one purpose: to stimulate federal support of medical research and education. To accomplish this required the ear of Congress, and to gain that ear required enormous voluntary expenditures of time and energy, cultivating senators and congressmen, educating them and creating forceful advocates for medical progress. Each of us willingly testified before congressional committees whenever the chance arose, or called on members of Congress, to proselytize for greatly expanded appropriations and responsibilities for the National Institutes of Health. Federal spending in medical research during the early forties was about $2 million a year, enough to sustain only a handful of important projects.

As Jim Adams once described our work, "The heart of the program was always to have at least one advocate in the House and in the Senate — someone who would be so knowledgeable that other members would seek him out for information and opinion on all matters involving medicine." We worked hard on a succession of these advocates. We cultivated, trained, and educated them. It required enormous patience and many hours of time. Mary Lasker, for example, went to Washington seventeen times in one year to testify or to proselytize. Albert Lasker used to advise us to be patient and cautioned us never to fight publicly with anyone, especially if he was in government, no matter how much of an impediment he might be. He would say, "You can't call that son of a bitch a son of a bitch. He may end up some day as chairman of a health committee."

This was a never-ending job, because after we had made our advocate into a real believer and true expert, he would die, or retire, or lose an election, and we would have to start all over again. We lost two in one year. Those members of Congress performed a service for their colleagues and their country. The best of them, I think, were John E. Fogarty of Rhode Island, a bricklayer without college training, twenty-six years in the house, to whom everyone turned for advice on bills pertaining to health and medical research; Lister Hill of Alabama; Claude Pepper of Florida; Warren Magnuson of Washington; Harley Kilgore of West Virginia; Charles A. Wolverton of New Jersey, a member of fifteen Congresses; Dan Flood of Pennsylvania, and Harold T. Burton of Ohio.

The results of this loosely-coordinated group effort to influence policy and legislation in Washington were spectacular — almost too spectacular at first. I remember once that Jim Adams and I had to rush to Washington to head off a $48-million appropriation for the National Cancer Institute. We wanted the institute to have the money, but it was not ready yet to administer it, and the grant, applied too early, would have led to chaos, which, in turn, would have disillusioned Congress. In time, however, NIH grew to include the Institute of Arthritis and Metabolic Diseases, and several others with appropriations for research of hundreds of millions of dollars. Federal assistance to medical education grew apace, as did medical aid to communities through the great Hill-Burton hospital act. The effects of our activities, which were often frustrating, annoying, sometimes downright maddening, were two explosive decades of medical discovery and progress from the fifties to the seventies, achievements which have only laid the groundwork for greater medical progress to come.

I did not put aside my partisan goals entirely, though, despite that consuming non-partisan effort. My activities on behalf of Republican candidates, in fact, always have been vigorous. One of the most engaging of these candidates was Wendell Willkie, the tall, stocky, outspoken Wall Street lawyer from Indiana who opposed Franklin Roosevelt in 1940. I had known Willkie through business contacts before he entered politics and liked him immensely, because he not only had a first-rate mind but the sincerity that was written on his face was genuine. I worked on his finance committee and contributed a substantial sum to his presidential campaign, unfortunately to no avail. (I doubt if anyone could have beaten FDR on the eve of World War II.) We remained good friends, however, and I saw him frequently. Following his globe-circling trip, I stopped in his office one day and found him busily correcting the pages of a book manuscript. "Wendell, how do you find time to write?" I asked him. "I get up at four-thirty in the morning and spend two to three hours on it every day," he said. Some time later I stopped by his office again, and he held up the first copy of *One World,* which he had just received from the publisher. As he held his literary creation in his hands, he said, "Elmer, I am going to give you one of the first copies; in fact, the copy I hold in my hand." He then said he had had a surprise that morning: "The publisher of the book called me up and told me that he already has orders for 25,000 copies!" "My goodness, I did not think that the book would ever have that number of people who wanted to buy it." It became a best-seller running over two million volumes in its first year and was a fine book, except that Willkie was much too sanguine about Stalin. He never recognized the Soviet dictator as a wicked man. Sadly, he died at age fifty in 1944, otherwise I think he might have made another run for it and become president. He wrote to me from his hospital bed just a few days before he died. "Dear Elmer," his letter said, "I expect to get out of here within a few days for my throat trouble has almost vanished. In the current issue of *Colliers,* I wrote an article that had to do with what I believe will become a conflict between the whites and blacks. Please read it and tell me what you think of it." I put his last letter between leaves of his book, *One World,* and it is still there today.

I also was active in both of Tom Dewey's campaigns for the presidency, as well as his gubernatorial campaigns in New York, and we became very close friends. Our friendship, as it turned out, played a part in General Dwight D. Eisenhower's choice of a political career.

I had met Ike for the first time in 1949, when he was the head of Columbia University. Bernard Baruch, who had become a close friend of mine, asked me to participate in a series of seminars at Columbia. I sat between Bernie and Ike at two seminars and formed a rather clear impression of the future president: he was an impatient man, constantly shifting his legs to and fro or tapping his feet, and when he wasn't bordering on irritation, he appeared to be bored. His temper flared at the least provocation. But he had an enormous strength of personality and a quick mind, which outweighed his apparently mercurial temper. There was talk then in both parties of running him for president, and Ike was holding it off by declining to say whether he cared for either, or for the challenge of running. At the time that I met him, I don't think it really mattered to him whether he was a Republican or a Democrat, but I got the definite feeling that he had a natural leaning toward the Republicans, and I was convinced that he would gain the White House if he ran.

At that time, Tom Dewey was completing his second term as governor of New York. He already had told me, privately, that he did not plan to run for a third term. He had been in public life since his racket-busting days in the thirties, and he felt that it was time he stepped down and began to work at building some financial resources for his family.

Not long after Tom confided his plans to me, I invited a group of army generals whom I knew for a short cruise on my motor yacht, *Alisa IV,* a beautiful, eighty-seven-foot, mahogany-hulled boat that I loved. I named it after my mother and father:

Al for Alice and *isa* for Isaac. It was the fourth in a succession of five increasingly comfortable and commodious *Alisas* to which I fled whenever I had the chance. Among the half-dozen officers along on the cruise was Edwin Clark, a close friend and former aide-de-camp to General Eisenhower.

In the course of the evening, I mentioned to General Clark that Govenor Dewey had decided against running for a third term. "It's too bad," I remarked, "because if Eisenhower decides to run for president on the Republican ticket, he will have trouble carrying New York without Tom Dewey's help from Albany. I think it is high time for General Eisenhower to say yes or no as far as running is concerned, don't you?"

Clark thought over what I had said, then replied, "Elmer, if I tell you by tomorrow evening whether Ike will run or not, and if the answer is yes, will you carry the message to Governor Dewey?"

Of course I will."

"And will you try to have the Governor change his mind and run for a third term?"

"Yes, I will."

The next day Clark got through to Eisenhower, who was fishing for trout in Colorado. True to his word, he called me that night.

"Elmer, I've talked with Ike," he said slowly. "The answer is . . . yes, he will run."

The next morning I met with Tom Dewey at his headquarters in the Roosevelt Hotel. I knew that he might be hard to handle, so I sidled up to the proposition slowly. After a few pleasantries, I told him that I had just received definite word from one of Ike's closest friends that he had decided to run as a Republican, and that I was authorized to carry the word to him.

"And what does that mean as far as I am concerned?" he asked.

"It means that for patriotic reasons you will have to run for a third term and win, so that Ike can be certain of carrying New York state."

Tom reacted as if I had given him a hotfoot. His face went red and he let me have it.

"It's all right for you — well-fixed financially — to tell me what I have to do for patriotic reasons. I'm supposed to forget my own financial responsibilities to my wife and kids, just to be a patriot?"

It took all the sales persuasion I could muster to answer him. In the end, of course, he did run for a third term and was elected, handily carrying the state with him in Ike's column. Naturally, I did everything I could to help his campaign, financially and otherwise.

One of my board members at Warner-Hudnut was even more active in Republican politics than I was. He was Guy George Gabrielson, who was the party chairman in 1952. He also was a solid supporter of Senator Robert Taft, and he liked to needle me, because he knew I was supporting Ike. Just before he left for the crucial Republican National Convention in Chicago, he gibed at me by saying, "Elmer, it's in the bag for Taft."

"Gab, I'm not sure of that," I said. "Tom Dewey and Herb Brownell will be out there." To my mind, Tom and Herb were two of the most astute politicians this country has ever produced.

The convention turned into a free-for-all between the Taft and Ike forces, with a critical fight over the seating of contested Southern delegates. There were charges that Taft's managers had "stolen" Southern delegates, including the important Texas delegation, from Ike, and there was a full day's delay in the convention before the Eisenhower forces under Brownell and Dewey won the dispute. When Dewey delivered New York's delegates ninety-two to four for Ike, the Taft forces were licked, and they knew it. I met Gabrielson a week later and chided him, "Gab, you'll recall that I told you Dewey and Brownell would be there." He groaned and said, "Don't remind me. They kept yelling 'Stop thief.' 'Stop thief,' and while they were doing it they stole my Texas delegation and won for Eisenhower."

I liked Senator Taft as much as Gabrielson did, but I did not think that he could win the presidency, and I was confident that Ike could. I first met Taft through my friendly relationship with Gabrielson, and we saw one another a number of times at the home of New Jersey Senator Alexander Smith, in Princeton where Taft stayed when he made speeches at the university. I considered him to be one of the ablest American statesmen and surely the leader of the U.S. Senate during his term of service.

After the Convention, I was in the thick of the campaign, helping to raise funds for Ike and assisting with some of the campaign planning. It was exhilarating work, until the end of October, 1952. I had been at a day-long planning session at Tom Dewey's house and went home in the early evening, mildly feverish and suffering from a chest cold. My granddaughters, Anne and Stephanie, were staying with Ethel and me at the time and they were anxious to have me take them out to play "trick or treat" in our Montclair neighborhood. It was Halloween. I asked Ethel to take them and went to bed. The next morning I felt much improved and decided to drive a load of canned goods and other provisions down to Bay Head, New Jersey, where *Alisa IV* was moored. Her captain and crew were making preparations to take her to Florida, where she would be available to me for winter cruising. I was in the boat yard when someone rushed up and summoned me to the telephone. The caller was a close friend of mine in Montclair.

"Please don't get too much alarmed, Elmer. Ethel has had a coronary attack and I'm sure you will want to come home right away."

● *Chapter Twenty-Two*

● I have never driven faster than the eighty-five to ninety miles an hour that I raced from Bay Head to Montclair. When I entered the large living room of our house, Ethel was lying on a love seat, weak, frightened, and in ·pain. The doctor was there, but she had refused to leave for the hospital until I got home. We took her immediately to the hospital in West Orange. After talking with the doctors there, I sat beside her bed and explained to her what had happened.

"You've had only a slight heart attack," I said. "Don't worry about it. People who suffer this kind of attack usually recover in a few weeks and live normally for many years. Everything is in hand. We have it under control and you'll be all right. You may have to stay here for a couple of weeks and rest, but I'll come to see you several times a day. Please try to relax now. It's over and you will be all right."

I continued to reassure her, to restore her confidence along with her health, during the three weeks that she was hospitalized. Every morning I arrived before going to work. Every afternoon I returned, then went home for dinner, then returned to her room again. She began to make a good recovery, and I brought her home. For a time her progress was rapid. She regained her strength and felt like her old self again. But then she began to have fleeting angina pains. Both the doctors and I reassured her, but I suspected that the impairment from her coronary attack was greater than we had thought at first. By February, I was deeply troubled about her condition, but I hid my anxiety from her lest it set off a new and damaging train of worry.

Every February for some years we had invited one or two couples to join us on *Alisa IV* for a cruise of a few weeks to the islands — Cuba, the Virgins, often the Bahamas. Both Ethel and I looked forward to the occasion with as much enthusiasm as children feel about Christmas. But this year I was reluctant to subject Ethel to the sometimes breathless activity of a boat at sea. Yet she was very anxious to go and I could not forbid it without alarming her, which probably would have been even more damaging. I resolved to take it easy on this cruise and keep to calm seas for Ethel's sake.

We met our guests and the boat at Miami, then motored quietly down to the Angler's Club in the Keys, where we had good friends. One of them was Alton Jones, the head of Cities Service and Ike's close friend, who was killed some years later in a commercial airplane crash. We arranged to join him and his wife, Nettie, for cocktails the next evening, but on the morning of his party I changed our plans. The weather was beautiful and the sea was flat calm. We had planned to go to Cat Cay in the Bahamas the next day; but the Gulf Stream can kick up in a hurry and become as rough as the North Sea; I decided we should take advantage of the good weather while we had it and leave for Cat Cay at once.

"Captain, we can cross the stream now without disturbing Mrs. Bobst. Let's get ready to go." I made our apologies to Alton Jones, and we got under way.

"Pete" Jones, as his friends called him, and I became acquainted when both of us lived in Forest Hills, Long Island, back in 1920, and this friendship endured through the years. After his tragic death, there was a strange epilogue to our friendship. I was searching for an apartment in New York, and my real-estate adviser shoved me one, which I loved immediately, at One Sutton Place South on the East River. When I asked whose apartment it was, I was told that it belonged to Mrs. Alton Jones, Pete's widow. I bought the apartment and still love it.

It was a lovely, relaxed crossing, and all of us, including Ethel, felt good enough to go to a lively beach party that night at the famous Cat Cay Club, of which I am a member. It is located on a small Bahamian island about twelve or fourteen miles south of the Isle of Bimini. Two days later we set out for Nassau, again taking advantage of calm, beautiful weather. From Cat Cay we crossed the Bahamian flats and passed over the tongue of the Atlantic, one of the deepest and sometimes roughest parts of the ocean. It was smooth as glass, and we enjoyed the trip, wrapped in blankets on the bow and singing sentimental songs.

The next day was Saturday, and Ethel felt so good that she insisted on inviting fourteen guests to a party at the Bahamian Club. I got a table on short notice, which was hard to do, but saw that we returned to the boat early so that she would not become overtired. She slept well that night, but on Sunday morning she complained of a shortness of breath. I carried her up the stairway from the cabin to the deck where she could get some air, and had her lean forward in a chair. Then I asked her to swallow little sips of brandy between breaths. Within fifteen minutes she was feeling better. A doctor came and gave her an injection to calm her nerves. He thought she would be fine.

Monday morning she felt almost normal again, and on Tuesday she felt even better. One of our guests had been to the Nassau straw market and had bought some bizarre hats, which were an occasion for much merriment. Ethel went to bed calm and happy. But at around 2 A.M. we were awakened by the raucous sounds of a noisy drunk on the pier to which *Alisa* was tied. I put on my slippers and went up on deck, furious that Ethel had been awakened. In scathing terms I told the drunk that unless he had sense enough to leave the pier at once I would throw him into the ocean. I was sixty-eight years old and he was young and large, but I could have tossed him over easily, and I was so angry that I would have done it without a qualm. He sobered enough to walk quietly away.

"Oh, Elmer, you spoke terribly to that man," Ethel said when I returned to our cabin below decks.

"He deserved it," I said. "I meant exactly what I said."

"Well, he certainly woke me up. I think I'd better take a sleeping pill."

Ethel took the pill and lay quietly. I hoped she was falling asleep again. But in less than half an hour she began gasping for breath as she had on Sunday morning. Her physician, who called on Sunday, had left me a vial of demerol. He said that if she had a recurrence of what seemingly was cardiac asthma, to give her an injection of the demerol. Without alarming her in the least. I quickly sterilized the hypodermic syringe and gave her a deep intramuscular injection, like the one she had from the doctor on Sunday. Between her gasps, she managed to say, "It's not working." Hurriedly, I awakened one of our guests and asked her to stay with Ethel while I broke out an oxygen tank that we had stowed aboard. I rushed the tank to Ethel's bedside. I had barely opened the valve to let her breathe, when she died.

Walton, then working in London, flew to Nassau to join me in our common grief. We chartered an airplane to fly Ethel home for burial beside my mother and father on the hillside overlooking the Schuylkill. Curiously, this mournful flight to Philadelphia was the first time that I had ever ridden in an airplane.

● *Chapter Twenty-Three*

● A philosopher once wrote that "old age is an island surrounded by death." That is an unnecessarily grim way to look upon one's advancing years, but there is obvious truth in the observation. The more blessed with years one becomes, the more often one grieves for loved ones and friends. None of the closest friends of my early youth, save Erla Buch, survives. Few friends from my first days in pharmaceuticals and medicine still live. Of my nearest relatives born in the last century, Mother, Father, Harry and Katie are gone; Mildred (Mrs. Mildred Biles), widow, mother, and grandmother at seventy-five lives in Fort Lauderdale, Florida, and Dorothy (Mrs. Dorothy Kelley), also widowed and now seventy-three, lives in Philadelphia. Howard Story, Mahlon Yoder, Bernard Gimbel, Bernie Baruch, and many, many more have passed on.

This inevitable and hard fact of life stings, but a wise man arranges his life in such a way that the accelerating toll among those he loves does not make of him a morbid island of nostalgic isolation. In age, as in youth, I remain a gregarious person, and I make new friends today as readily as I made them seventy or eighty years ago. My criteria for new friendships are perhaps a bit more demanding now than they were, but not much more so. I have always been somewhat selective, choosing my friends among men and women of accomplishment. They are the most interesting; they "wear" the longest because their minds are active and their characters strong; and I can learn the most from them. It does not matter to me, as I hope it does not matter to them, if my companions on my twice-weekly eighteen holes in golf (I shoot in the nineties, having regressed with failing eyesight from a twelve-stroke handicap at age seventy-five), or at a new Broadway show, or at the opera, or at a robust, late-hours party are my contemporaries or are half my age, I enjoy them all. So, while the ranks of my oldest friends thin with the onrushing years, the ranks of my friends at large remain full. For this I am grateful.

Perhaps the strongest, certainly the most propitious, friendship of my life is that of a young man from California whom I came to know well just a few months after Ethel died in 1953. As a widower living alone, I had resisted the natural temptation to withdraw from life in sadness, but, rather, had intensified my activities; hard work and a full schedule are the most solacing and the healthiest companions of grief. Among my many other activities was the chairmanship of the United States Savings Bonds program in New Jersey, as well as the honorary chairmanship of the national Savings Bonds committee. I had carried on this work since World War II and meant to keep on with it as long as I could. Each year, in order to stimulate bond purchases through payroll savings plans, I invited 200 of the state's leading industrialists to a dinner at the Spring Lake Golf and Country Club, of which I was the president. Since I had to attract many of the guests from the far corners of the state to Spring Lake, on the Atlantic coast due south of New York, I always arranged to have a prominent speaker whom they were anxious to hear.

In 1953, my speaker was to be an old friend, Secretary of the Treasury George Humphrey, but his office called shortly before the date of the dinner, to say that he was ill. I was crestfallen and told the secretary's office so, because I had to have an important speaker. They suggested the newly-elected vice president of the United States, and I leaped at the idea. He was a better choice than the treasury secretary, and in many ways even better than President Eisenhower himself.

I had met Vice President Richard Nixon during the campaign, and I had followed his career as a congressman and senator with interest, but I had never had the chance to get to know him. He had evoked my strong sympathies and great admiration during the campaign, when he courageously laid bare his life on national television in order to put to rest scurrilous rumors concerning perfectly legitimate contributions that he had received as a senator. On the night that he made what became known as his "Checkers" speech—after his daughters' pet puppy—I remember turning to Ethel with a tear in my eye and telling her, "Dear, we have just witnessed one of the most courageous and intelligent political acts of our lifetimes." Eisenhower had been vacillating over the frightened urgings of some of his advisers to drop Senator Nixon as a running mate because of the rumors. To my mind, William Rogers, later President Nixon's secretary of state, became the hero of the day when he convinced the young Californian that he should go on television and assert the integrity of his action in plain terms, straight from the heart. Millions of Americans reacted to the talk as I did. As a result, Eisenhower reaffirmed his confidence in the vice president-to-be.

Not surprisingly, the vice president drew a packed house to my bonds dinner. Everyone there had seen him on television, and a few had shaken his hand during the campaign, but all of the Eastern industrialists whom I invited to the dinner were anxious to take a closer look at this rising young political leader from the West. As chairman, I introduced him to individual guests during the cocktail hour and sat beside him at the head table during dinner. Normally, head-table conversation at such affairs is rather desultory. The chairman rarely knows his featured speaker well enough to engage in deep conversation, so the two generally have to settle for small talk, or feel around for a neutral subject about which neither of them cares very much.

Vice President Nixon was different. The intent face, with outthrust chin, that had always seemed so deeply assertive and serious in photographs and on television was relaxed and quick to smile and laugh. There was no uneasiness about him and no diffidence; he thoughtfully asked questions about me, my business, and my thoughts on national and world affairs. From his animated expression, I could see that he was absorbing and weighing my answers as if he genuinely cared about them, not merely lending a polite ear as politicians often do when they must endure public functions among strangers. He was just as quick to reply to my questions, to volunteer his opinions and his feelings, and to explain his deep faith in the American ideals of justice, peace and progress. We became so engrossed in our conversation that I even dallied a little over dessert in order to listen to his ideas before he rose to make his formal speech.

When the address was completed, we talked some more. Throughout the evening I naturally had addressed him formally, and sometime after dinner I began a remark to him with the customary phrase, "Mr. Vice President . . ." He quietly interrupted me.

"My name is Dick and your name is Elmer. Let's cut out the Mr. Vice President," he smiled shyly. From that moment we were friends.

Some say that I filled the place of his father, whom he loved deeply. When our friendship ripened, both Dick and Pat welcomed me as if I had become a member of their family, but I have never thought of my role with them as a fatherly one. I doubt if they have, either. Perhaps Julie and Tricia defined my position better. They began calling me "Uncle Elmer" when they were little girls, and they still do today. With Dick I think that it was friendship alone that he sought from me, and I from him, not a father-son relationship. But there is no doubt that both of us have felt a strong kind of familial tie that far transcends political friendship or even a strong ordinary friendship. I like to think of it as a bond of brotherhood, even though we are separated by almost thirty years in age and a continent's width in background and upbringing.

By the purest coincidence, not long after his speech at my dinner, a political friend of the vice president offered him the use of a house near my Spring Lake home for a part of the summer. I arranged honorary memberships for him in the Golf

Club and the Bath and Tennis Club, of which I was chairman, and managed to play golf with him, relax with him or at least visit with him every day for four weeks. It was during this period that the friendship we formed at the bond dinner grew close. One reason that it did, I think, was that I made no demands on him; I had no political axes to grind, no favors to ask, no wish to share his limelight. "There is nothing that you have that I want, except your friendship," I told him not long after we first met; and I meant it then just as firmly as I mean it now, almost nineteen years later. He and Pat responded in kind by inviting me to Washington often to share family weekends or holiday dinners at Thanksgiving and Christmas time. I knew that our friendship had become truly a family affair when they asked me to come to a reception they gave in honor of Queen Elizabeth of England and the Duke of Edinburgh in 1957. When he introduced me to the queen, Dick said, "Your Highness, Elmer Bobst is family to us." Pat then introduced me to Prince Philip with the words, "He's part of our family, and he has similar interests to yours, a wonderful yacht and fishing boat."

During his years in and out of office I have tried to provide both a retreat and a sympathetic ear for Dick. He learned early in our friendship that I had no taste for preening myself in the light of his prominence, and as a result he relaxed in my presence without worrying that I might repeat his words in public. He also knew from the start that I would tell him exactly what was on my mind, without pulling punches, so he could use me as a backboard for his ideas without fear that I would react to them like a sycophant. In consequence, most of our talks have been serious, illuminating, and private. There have been both light and serious moments, however, which I do not believe he would mind my sharing.

Dick probably was the hardest-working vice president in our history, a man who took completely seriously his role as the president's understudy. He had very little time for relaxation and play during the Eisenhower administration and took far less, in fact, than the president did. But on occasion, he liked to slip quietly up to Spring Lake on the spur of the moment to play golf with

me. Whenever he did this, I would drop whatever plans I had
in order to spend the day with him. One of these visits brought
another close Nixon friend into my circle of acquaintances. It
was rather late one evening in 1955 when the telephone of my
Spring Lake home rang. I had been reading the local newspaper,
which was filled with stories about a Billy Graham religious crusade then taking place in Ocean Grove, New Jersey, a famous
Methodist retreat just a few miles from Spring Lake. I answered
the telephone, and an animated voice inquired, "Is this Mr.
Bobst?"

"Yes," I replied, "it is."

"I'm Billy Graham."

I have a number of friends who like to pull my leg, and
I thought this was one of them. "The hell you are," I said.

"I really am Billy Graham," he repeated.

"The hell you are." He couldn't fool me.

"Mr. Bobst, I really am. I'm calling for Vice President Nixon.
He asked me to arrange with you for the three of us to play
golf at your club tomorrow."

With that, he convinced me. We met the next day. Dick
was accompanied by his Secret Service escort, and the Reverend
Graham by two of his associates, who followed us around the
golf course. As I recall, Dick hit some beautiful long shots, although his approaches were spotty, and Billy Graham played
a strong game, but I won with an eighty-three, which was not
bad for a seventy-year-old. After putting out on the eighteenth
hole, Dick and I started for the locker room to shower and change
clothes before lunch. The great evangelist said that he planned
to change at his hotel in Ocean Grove, but he would join us
for lunch. Meanwhile, he would wait for us with the Secret Service men and his associates in the dining room. As we dressed,
Dick and I each had a gin and tonic, but decided to forego a
second one rather than keep Dr. Graham waiting in the dining
room. I missed my customary second drink, however, so when
we got to the large round table at which Billy Graham, his friends,
and the Secret Service men were sitting, I called out to the maitre
d'. I did not want to embarrass Dr. Graham, who I assumed

correctly was a teetotaler, so I said to the maitre d', "Lou, I seem to be dehydrated. Will you kindly bring me a nice-sized glass of tonic water?" Lou had served me for enough years to know that I never drink tonic water without gin in it, so he smiled understandingly and started toward the bar. Without blinking an eye, Dick Nixon looked at me, then at the maitre d', and quickly interjected, "Lou, would you mind bringing me some tonic, too?"

When time permitted on other occasions, Dick and Pat cruised with me on *Alisa V*, an extremely comfortable ocean-going motor yacht a little over a 100 feet with which I replaced *Alisa IV*. Seeing him often under these circumstances, sometimes with other people, sometimes alone, I probably had a better chance to observe him than most of his other friends. It is a truism among yachtsmen and sailors to note that a few days in close company, on a boat at sea will bring out the real character of any man; there is no more certain way to see beneath a man's exterior. As I saw more and more of him thus, I became more and more impressed with his integrity and brilliance. Although he can talk directly and at length on virtually any subject that is raised, because he has studied long and hard, he tends toward taciturnity in private, preferring to listen and learn rather than monopolize center stage. A certain basic shyness has something to do with it, but I think that his legal training is more the cause; he has the instincts of a good judge, listening to all shades of opinion and holding an open mind until the facts are in. When he listens, he seems to be saying, "Let me have the facts. I want them in full, plus and minus, pro and con. I want to know why you have this opinion, and don't hesitate to tell me. Are you basing your conclusion on prejudice, or have you really made an impartial, realistic decision that this is the proper course to pursue?" Then he retires to make up his mind in solitude.

Like all great men, he frequently asks his friends for their opinions on matters of importance to him, and in the spirit of friendship I often have volunteered my opinions to him, even when he has not asked for them. I offered what I suppose was one of the more noteworthy of my voluntary expressions just before he left for Moscow to open the U.S. trade exhibit in 1959.

Dick and Pat had invited me down to Washington for dinner two nights before he was to leave for the Soviet Union, and as I rode toward the capital on the train I began ruminating over my views of the Russians. I jotted these down on the pages of a lined, yellow note pad, then folded the several pages of notes and tucked them into my pocket.

It was a festive evening with just a few of us on hand: Dick's longtime executive secretary Rosemary Woods, one of the most brilliant women in government, who also is one of the most astute political analysts of either party; Bob Finch and his lovely wife, who are perhaps the closest of Dick's California friends, and I. After dinner, Dick and I went into the small study where he kept his political mementos. We had chatted for only a few minutes when I remembered the ideas that I had jotted down during the train ride. I mentioned them to him, and he said, "Let me have your notes."

"My handwriting is not so good," I said, "I don't think you would be able to read it."

"Well, then you read what you have written to me."

I read aloud from the yellow sheets of paper, paused near the end, then gave special emphasis to the final lines.

"You are going to Russia in a couple of days ostensibly for the purpose of opening an exhibit in Moscow." I had written. "But that should not be your primary purpose. Your primary purpose should be to stick your fist under Kruschev's nose and become president of the United States."

Whether Soviet Premier Kruschev's subsequent foolish behavior in the famous Moscow debate was purely fortuitous or whether Dick remembered my words of advice when he stood up to the Russian leader and faced him down, I never learned, nor did I ever ask my friend. Although many men don't acknowledge it, I believe there is an unwritten rule that should be observed by the friends of presidents: Let them receive what you have written or told them and leave it at that; it is unseemly to try to discover afterwards whether you have guided or influenced them, and your efforts to do so not only weaken your friendship, but make it less likely that they will listen to your advice again.

When Dick won the Republican nomination for president in 1960, I naturally joined his campaign team and used all of the talents I could muster as a fund-raiser. I not only believed that he should be president of the United States, but that if he won the office he would enter the White House as the best-prepared president in our history. His conscientious attention to learning the job under Ike was such that he knew it better than any man before him, and he proved it more than once when Ike was ill with his coronary attacks. During the second episode, when Eisenhower was out of commission for weeks, Dick quietly took over without fanfare or publicity and smoothly ran the government until the president returned.

Not surprisingly, I was not particularly fond of the Kennedys, although I thought John Kennedy the most engaging of all of them. But I was naturally opposed to Kennedy when he ran for president, and not alone because he was running against my best friend. I never believed that his record as a congressman and senator qualified him for the presidency, and I still do not believe that he was prepared for the office or that he managed it well. But he was a charming person. I met him for cocktails on two occasions before the election. At the second meeting, he smiled disarmingly and said to me, "Mr. Bobst, I know that you have a good friend in Washington," referring of course, to Vice President Nixon.

"Yes, Senator, I do," I said, "but my attitude is, 'Let the best man win.' "

Unfortunately, Kennedy won. But he did it by a margin of only a few thousand votes, and there were enough dubious election practices in Mayor Daley's Chicago, Texas, Missouri, and South Carolina to have made a recount necessary if Nixon had asked for one. Without those highly questionable votes, Kennedy would have lost. I was with Pat and Dick after the returns were in and watched the two of them at this time of his most crushing defeat. Typically, he was calm and quiet, but Pat's Irish blood was boiling. She knew, as did we all, that a recount would show political chicanery in some of the dubious districts that had gone for Kennedy — the questions that were raised then were later documented in at least some of the Chicago voting precincts. Some of Dick's advisers urged him to ask for a recount and an investigation.

"I will do nothing," He calmly replied. "I will not give this nation's enemies an opportunity to downgrade democracy and to say that our elections were fraudulent. I will not make a single move." He stuck adamantly to that position, in the face of urging by many advisers. Thus the best man, in my view, lost.

The day before Kennedy's inauguration, Dick telephoned me.

"Elmer, tomorrow is going to be one of the most trying days in my life and Pat's," he said. He would, of course, have to sit on the inauguration platform and pretend amiability while his opponent was sworn in as president. "We want to get away from Washington, and we want to get away from people when it is over. Would it be possible for you to have your yacht in Nassau the day after the inauguration?"

"Dick, I appreciate your feelings fully," I said. "I'll call my captain immediately and tell him to have both *Alisa V* and my fishing boat *Alisita* at the Lyford Cay Club."

After they had put in all the necessary appearances in Washington, the Nixons and their old friends Mr. and Mrs. Roger E. Johnston from Whittier, California, and Bebe Rebozo joined me in Nassau. We set out the next morning for Eleuthera Island on *Alisa V*. To his great credit, Dick was relaxed and affable, never showing the depression that he must have felt. At Eleuthera, he, Pat and their Whittier friends occupied a beach house that had been offered to them by another friend, and I anchored nearby so that I could sleep on my boat while spending my days with them. Every day for a week, we talked of the future. It was a time of serious reorientation for the former vice president after so many years in Washington, and he was uncertain about the best direction to take. Pat was anxious to return to California, and he leaned toward her view, but I earnestly tried to convince him that he should take up the practice of law in the East. I felt that whatever he chose to do must provide sufficient income to take care of his family for the future, while still assuring him a respectable vantage point from which to rebuild his political strength. I doubted if he could manage that in California, and said so. Someone mentioned the possibility of his entering the California governor's race. I spoke strongly against it and Dick said he did not like the idea, either. I told him he had nothing to gain by it and everything to lose. He promised me that he would not run. But he did decide to return to California.

The aftermath of the 1960 election must have been the unhappiest time of the Nixons' lives, but I have to confess that I sailed through it on a cloud of private joy. For while Dick's political fortunes and his future were among the most important things in my life that year, they were not *the* most important. My business was active and booming. And I was deeply in love with a beautiful woman, and I had never been happier in my life.

The author at the helm of Alisa V.

● *Chapter Twenty-Three*

● Love has inspired more art and more nonsense than any of the feelings or activities of man. Among the most foolish notions, doubtless inspired by anguished young poets, is that perfect love is the exclusive province of youth, a golden fruit that is never quite the same after its first early ripening. Believe me, this finest, most exhilarating and infinitely rewarding emotion, this focused collection of feelings, chemistry, humane challenge, mutuality and intellectual surrender that we call love, is more durable than some of the young poets, engulfed in its first wave, think it is. From my vantage point far from the shore, I look back at young love and see timid swimmers, just entering the water, not strong enough to breast out where the surf breaks. I rode to the crest of the highest wave of all when I was seventy-five years old, and I am still on it today, more inspired, refreshed, excited, and fulfilled by love than ever in my life. It came about through a chance meeting that I wanted, actually, to avoid, a meeting that left me almost speechless.

Paradoxically, it was my interest in speech — speech disorders, to be precise — that brought the meeting about. I had been interested in speech disorders, particularly those caused by oral and facial deformities, for many years. One of my closest friends, Dr. Herbert K. Cooper of Lancaster, Pennsylvania, revolutionized the treatment of cleft palates and other speech-

disabling conditions, and I had not only followed but had supported his research and therapeutic programs at the famous Lancaster Cleft Palate Clinic. I had known Herbie Cooper since he
was a young man. He came from a town near Lititz and for
a time he squired around my youngest sister, Dorothy. He was
more than a little chagrined on the first occasion to find me following their horse-drawn buggy, just to assure myself that his
intentions where honorable. After that beginning, I watched the
development of his career. Herbie became an orthodontist, practiced in Lititz for about six years, then moved to Lancaster and
began work on developing a plastic oral device that dramatically
improved the speech, breathing, and swallowing of cleft palate
victims. A selfless and totally dedicated man, Herbie literally impoverished himself to support the clinic, which he founded in
1938. By the early 1950s, the clinic was so deeply in debt that Herbie
was almost desperate. I made a contribution and arranged for
a grant of funds from the Gustavus and Louise Pfeiffer Foundation, of which I had been named president after Mr. G.A.'s death
in 1953. Later introduced Herbie to Morris Fishbein and William
L. Laurence, science editor of the New York *Times,* at an AMA
meeting in Atlantic City. Laurence, who did the first story on
the atomic bomb, after visiting, with Morris Fishbein, Cardinal
Spellman, myself, and Herbie's scientific display at the Exposition
Hall, was so favorably impressed that he did the first story on
the front page of the New York *Times,* and as a result, several
other publications, including the *Saturday Evening Post,* were
prompted to visit the clinic in Lancaster and published four or
five pages of pictures and the story of Herbie's accomplishments.
The publicity brought official AMA recognition of his work —
a hard thing for doctors to grant to a dentist — and formal support from the state of Pennsylvania. It also opened the door for
both private contributions and federal research grants, so that
the clinic not only survived but expanded its efforts in both treatment and research.

Many of my friends knew of Herbie's work because of my
interest in it. One of them was Stanton Griffis, the investment
banker and diplomat, who had served for some years as chairman

of the National Hospital for Speech Disorders. It was only natural then that when Griffis decided to retire from some of his volunteer work, he would call upon me. Because of my interest in Herbie's research efforts, I took on the chairmanship of the American Hospital for Speech Disorders, and because of that, I had the chance encounter that changed my life. So, while this may seem a roundabout way to tell a love story, all of it is relevant. Had I not grown interested in Herbie Cooper the day that I followed his buggy when he carried my sister off on a ride in the country, then perhaps I never would have developed my interest in speech disorders, nor accepted the hospital chairmanship when Griffis retired. And if I had not gone as chairman to a fund-raising tea for the hospital on April 7, 1960, I might today still be a lonely widower. But on that day another circle of seemingly unrelated events that sometimes form a comforting halo around one's future was closing.

One of the members of my board of directors at the hospital was Mary Doane, wife of Richard C. Doane, the president of International Paper Company. She was a woman of achievement, an active professional who wrote a syndicated column under her maiden name, Mary Goodfellow, but she devoted a great deal of her time to such voluntary organizations as the Hospital for Speech Disorders. In the spring of 1960, she suggested that she give a tea at her townhouse in Manhattan for a group of wealthy women. "You might stop over in the latter part of the afternoon to meet them and sort of help me to get them interested in making contributions," she said to me. I agreed to drop by with Dr. Lynwood Heaver, the hospital medical director. The meeting was successful. Afterwards, Dr. Heaver and I lingered to chat with Mary.

"Where's Dick?" I asked.

"He's in Boston."

Then, speaking to Mary, I said, "Would you like me to take you out somewhere for dinner?"

"Yes, I want you to take me to the "21 Club," she said.
"All right, let's get going."

"I have to stop in at a cocktail party first, at the Manhattan House."

"Well, Mary, you go ahead in your car and I'll go home. I'm not going to any cocktail party tonight."

"But I'll only be fifteen minutes," she pleaded. "I have to go. I promised a fascinating and charming lady from Lebanon that I'd be there. She's the hostess. I'm writing an article about her."

"All right, but not a minute more. We'll go in my car. If you stay longer than twenty-five minutes you can walk home, because I'll leave you."

Mary, Dr. Heaver, and I arrived at Manhattan House on 66th Street to find a quiet party of about thirty people in a tastefully furnished apartment. The hostess, to whom Mary introduced me, was petite, fashionable and strikingly beautiful. I actually caught my breath when she turned her soft oval face up to look thoughtfully at me, then broke into a warm smile that radiated welcome. Her name, Mary said, was Miss Mamdouha As-Sayid, but its pronunciation escaped me completely as she held out a delicate, well-shaped hand in greeting.

"How do you do?" I said. "I'm the uninvited guest."

"I am *very* pleased that you have come," she replied politely, then introduced us to some of her guests. There were several ambassadors and some medical men from the Middle East, including one doctor whom I knew. Most of the doctors were taking graduate courses in American medical schools. Our beautiful hostess, I learned, was an unmarried public health specialist, already distinguished in the Middle East, who was the first and youngest Lebanese woman ever to become a delegate to the United Nations. The guests were interesting people, too, and I found myself talking with them long past the deadline I had given to Mary Doane. But most interesting of all was the all-too-brief, completely absorbing five minutes that I spent talking with the hostess. I was so absorbed in her, I'm afraid, that I could not remember what we talked about or even where we were. But I could not erase the vivid image of her from my mind.

In time, Mary Doane and I said goodnight to the hostess,

parted with Dr. Heaver, and went on to dinner, after which my chauffeur took me home to Montclair. The next day, a Friday, I went on to my summer place at Spring Lake and had a busy weekend of golf and parties. But the lovely Lebanese delegate to the United Nations remained fixed in my mind as I had seen her on Thursday evening.

Sunday nights are my quiet evenings at home. I have always liked to relax then in order to be fresh on Monday morning. On this particular Sunday I ate a light dinner, selected a book to read, and started up the stairs to my bedroom. As I approached my room, alone as I had been for more than seven years, a deep feeling of loneliness, almost as palpable as an isolation chamber, enveloped me. Here I was with two large houses, a sizable yacht, a fishing boat, fine cars, an interesting art collection, and every material blessing a man could want, plus more than enough business and public activity to keep me more than occupied, yet the only people in my house who were truly happy were the servants. I couldn't blame them. They were working for a widower who was rarely home, and they had my property and its benefits pretty much to themselves.

The feeling stayed with me after I crawled into bed. It was impossible to concentrate on my book. Instead, my mind kept turning back to the cocktail party on Thursday, and the lovely woman who gave it. She was beautiful and extremely intelligent. The thought that she was probably forty years my junior never crossed my mind. I had to see her again.

Throughout my life I have striven to make my dreams and hopes come true, and I have discovered that the best way to achieve that is to act on my decisions as soon as I make them. The trouble was that I could remember neither the lady's name nor where she lived. I picked up the telephone beside my bed and dialed Mary Doane's townhouse in New York. A servant answered the phone and told me that she was on her way to Canada and could not be reached. Frustrated, I turned back to my book, but still I could not concentrate. I hate to be thwarted. Again I reached for the phone, this time to call my chauffeur, George Courts, who was in Montclair.

"George, on Thursday evening after I left Mrs. Doane's home you drove us somewhere on the East Side. Do you remember where?" I asked him.

"Mr. Bobst, you were in the Manhattan House." He even remembered the apartment number we had visited.

"Do you remember the name?" I asked.

"No, sir, I don't know all the names of your friends."

I called the Manhattan House switchboard and tried to explain my plight. "I do not know the name of this person," I said. "She is from Lebanon and she is a delegate to the United Nations."

"I'm sorry, sir, but we do not give out that information," said the operator.

Next, I called the United Nations, but the answer was the same: "We never give out the names and addresses of any of the delegates."

By now, I was completely absorbed in the quest. I called the chief operator of the New York Telephone Company, but she wouldn't help me either. Feeling completely balked, I tried to read a few more pages of my book. Then suddenly I recalled Dr. Heaver. Perhaps he remembered our hostess's name. I telephoned the hospital to get his home address so I could look up his number. "Dr. Heaver lives in the penthouse of the hospital," the operator said.

"What is his telephone number, please?"

"He has an unlisted number and I'm not allowed to give out that information."

"Operator, this is an emergency!" I honestly felt as if it were. "I am chairman of the hospital and I must talk with our medical director." She left the phone to consult with her supervisor, then returned to give me Dr. Heaver's number. I called immediately, and Dr. Heaver's wife answered.

"This is Mr. Bobst. May I speak with Dr. Heaver?"

"I'm sorry, Mr. Bobst, but he's in Connecticut at a medical meeting."

"Can you get in touch with him?"

"Yes, I can."

"Well, he was with me at a cocktail party in the Manhattan House last Thursday evening. It is very important that I get the name of the young lady who gave the party. Will you please call and ask him? I'll call back in fifteen minutes."

A quarter of an hour later I telephoned Mrs. Heaver, who said, "The name is Miss Mamdouha As-Sayid." Mrs. Heaver also had looked up Miss As-Sayid's telephone number for me. I dialed the number immediately, even though it was close to midnight. There was no answer. I called again in fifteen minutes. Still no answer. Finally, at 12:30 A.M., she answered.

"This call is coming from the uninvited guest at your cocktail party last Thursday," I told her. "If you do not think it too presumptuous, I would like very much to take you to dinner on Tuesday night at the Colony in New York."

There was a moment's pause, I suppose while she reflected on the odd behavior of an American of such slight acquaintance who would call in the middle of the night to make a date. "I am very sorry, I have an engagement Tuesday night," she replied firmly.

"Being a good bit older than you are, and having had a great deal more experience in life, I have learned that there is no engagement so important that it cannot be broken if there is sufficient urgency to break it, and I can tell you that I'll greatly appreciate it if you break this one."

"I won't be able to do that," she said, even more firmly.

"Well, I shall call you tomorrow morning and ask you again."

On Monday morning I reached her again. "Have you succeeded in breaking that engagement?" I asked.

"No, I have not, and I don't think that I shall," she said.

"Well, I am sure that you should. And I'm certain that if you want to break it, you can. It is very important to me that you do. I will call you up again tonight."

That night when I called, she said "No" again.

"Well, tomorrow's Tuesday and I'm going to ask you again. I don't like to beg for anything, but I continue to urge you, if you have an engagement, to change it. You will favor me highly by having dinner with me at the Colony. I'll have my chauffeur call for you at your apartment."

When I called on Tuesday morning, her resistance had broken down. With feigned exasperation, she said, "You're so persistent that I guess I will have to give in and change my engagement."

She was as beautiful as I remembered her, and as calm and cheerfully welcoming. As we dined at the Colony, I found her conversation and her presence even more absorbing than I remembered. After that first dinner together, I called her every day and monopolized her free time, at least two or three evenings a week. I was in love; I knew it; and I loved it.

She told me about her childhood in Tripoli, the ancient, second-largest city of Lebanon; about her father, an importer of English woolens, and about her mother, her brother, and her five sisters. Her family lineage was ancient and honorable. She had attended an American college for girls and then graduated with a degree in sociology from the American University in Beirut, the leading school of the Middle East. From there she went to the University of Birmingham in England for two years of graduate work in sociology and public health, then attended lectures at the Sorbonne in Paris. For a short time she worked for *Radio Diffusion Francaise* in Paris and for the Voice of America in Washington; then she took a World Health Organization fellowship at the University of California in Berkeley, where she received her third university degree, this one a master's in public health. When she was twenty-six, the World Health Organization sent her to Libya as a public health consultant. She found there a society just beginning to emerge into the contemporary world. Women, still veiled by custom, had no share in public life, and there was not even a training school for nurses. With the support of the government, she picked out a select group of young women and within two years had a nursing school started. Next, at the request of the Ministry of Public Health she developed a complete public health program for all of Libya. Although the king, who has since been deposed, asked her to stay on to help his country, her own nation beckoned. In 1959, the premier of Lebanon appointed her to the United Nations as the youngest delegate and the first Arab woman so honored. Her given name, Mamdouha, was propitious. It means, "To be praised." But her pet name, by which she is known to her friends and to me, is "Dodo."

I recognized, of course, that falling in love with Dodo raised problems for both of us. She was thirty-four when I met her, less than half my age. As a devout Moslem, there also was a religious difference for Dodo to consider. It was not so profound a difference to me. Although raised in the Lutheran faith, I tried to embrace the best elements of all religious philosophies as I grew older, and I am stoutly convinced that where religious orthodoxy holds people apart, it is wrong. Neither of us agonized for long over these two problems, however, and the longer we knew one another, the less formidable they seemed. We simply became two happy people, no matter the disparity of age and of birthplace.

During the election campaign of 1960, I took her to Washington, knowing that Dick Nixon was campaigning in the mid-west, but hoping that Pat was home. She was. We visited her for an entire afternoon that was so pleasant and relaxing that we forgot we had left a taxicab with its meter running outside the Nixons' home. Pat was drawn immediately to Dodo, and I was glad to have her approval. It was a busy and wonderful platonic year for us. Near the end of it, we went cruising on my yacht in the Florida Keys with Leah Ray and David "Sonny" Werblin and Robert Sarnoff of RCA as chaperones. On April 7th, the first anniversary of our meeting, the Werblins gave a party for us at a restaurant on Islemorada. A number of our friends, including Bob Sarnoff, who sits with me on the board of Franklin and Marshall College, were there. During the champagne toasting after dinner, I was called upon to mark the occasion with a little speech. Blithely I rose and promptly put both feet in my mouth.

"This day marks the first anniversary of my meeting with Dodo," I began. "I'm very proud of having met her and of having become her friend. During that time, I've made it possible for her to meet almost all of my good friends, including Richard and Pat Nixon. And I want to say this, that in meeting each

Mamdouha (Dodo) Bobst, wearing the diamond tiara that her husband gave her in 1966. It was designed originally for Queen Geraldine of Albania.

one, never once did she say anything or do anything that embarrassed me."

Well, the words tripped out and I meant them as a tribute, but I suppose it would be a rare woman who would not react to them as Dodo did. She took my remarks as an insult and furiously asked me, "Why should I do anything that would embarrass you? I don't like that remark at all!" It broke up the party, and for a time afterwards it looked as if our relationship had ended at exactly one year.

When we returned to the boat, Dodo said, "Good night!" very curtly, and headed toward the stateroom that she shared with Leah Ray Werblin.

"I'd like to talk with you," I called after her.

"I don't want to talk with you!"

"You are my guest on my boat, and I think that I have the right to tell you that I have something to say to you," my voice was steady and firm. "I want you to listen to it. It's very important."

"Well, what do you have to say?" She was still seething.

"I want you to marry me."

"There you go again with another mistake!" Her quick reaction made my heart sink. Then she uplifted it. "Why don't you say that *you* want to marry *me?*"

"Well," I said, as we both broke into joyous smiles, "have it any way you want."

We were married on April 22, 1961, and the only unhappy note was that the servants looked pretty glum over the prospect of surrendering the freedom and independence that they had enjoyed under their mostly absent bachelor employer.

The author speaking at the dedication in 1967 of the Elmer Holmes Bobst Institute of Clinical Research at Hahnemann Medical College in Philadelphia.

● *Chapter Twenty-Five*

● At about the time that I first met Richard Nixon, I was carefully forming plans for a vast expansion of Warner-Hudnut. We had completely rebuilt from the shambles in which I had found the company in 1946 and were growing rapidly in sales, which had reached more than $60 million, and profits, about $4.2 million. The company had more than four thousand employees, half of them in our American plants and the rest in our fifteen plants and offices abroad. But still, management was pretty much of a one-man show. I was operating as I had for years, supervising promotion, marketing, production, research, and administration with the help of senior executives, but with no close executive alter-ego at the top to whom I could delegate my authority. Although I liked hard work and lots of it, the heavy responsibilities of one-man executivemanship were becoming somewhat onerous to me, for several reasons. I wanted and needed more time for the Cancer Society, for lobbying on behalf of health causes in Washington, for my duties as a board member of Franklin and Marshall College and of the University of Pennsylvania, for my Savings Bonds work, and for a dozen other voluntary jobs in both private and industry associations, not to mention my political activities. I took all of these responsibilities too seriously to pass them off with mere token support. Together with my consuming responsibilities at Warner-Hudnut, they were wearing: Reason enough to begin looking for a high-level executive helper.

But there was a more important reason than any of these. I was seventy years old in 1954. Although I was in excellent health and as vigorous as I had been in my forties, I faced an inexorable chronological fact: No matter how young I felt, I was becoming old, and my remaining time as a fully active businessman was at best unpredictable. If I were to be suddenly disabled, or to die, the company would be left with a lot of first rate sub-chiefs, but there was no one who could move smoothly into my office and run it. Too many of our plans, our marketing techniques, and our business and administrative methods reposed in my brain alone.

I had tried for a time during the late forties to find a good executive vice president whom I could train to succeed me, but the result had been disappointing. My friend Ferd Eberstadt told me, "The trouble with you, Elmer, is that you are looking for an Elmer Bobst, and there's only one of them." I retained an executive "head-hunting" firm to help in the search for likely candidates. The one they found and urged on me most energetically turned out to be only marginally capable. I learned later that his chief qualification was that he was an old schoolmate of the "head-hunter" who recruited him. The experience soured me on that kind of executive search, and on such consulting firms. Although highly specialized consultants often can be useful, sometimes invaluable in business, I think that too often they fit the characterization given by a San Francisco advertising man named Howard Gossage. He said that "A consultant is someone who borrows your watch and tells you what time it is." Sometimes they can't even do that. Mr. G.A. once had a prominent consulting firm do an exhaustive study of the old Warner Company and was tickled to death when they told him that his company was extraordinarily well-organized, growing by leaps and bounds, and certain to go on to phenominal success. The report came in just at the time that Warner began to collapse in shambles on poor Mr. G.A.'s shoulders.

In 1953, I began scouting for a senior executive on my own,

and the most likely candidate that I found turned out to be a distinguished guest at the bonds dinner at which Richard Nixon first called me Elmer. He was Alfred E. Driscoll, then fifty, nearing the end of his second term as governor of New Jersey. I had met him many times and liked him personally. He was an outstanding lawyer and one of the best governors New Jersey ever had. He conceived the idea and carried out the development of the New Jersey Turnpike, which became the model for the national Interestate Highway program, and he acquired the land and built a major portion of the Garden State Parkway. When his term ended in 1954, he left the state with a surplus of $50 million in its treasury, an extraordinary achievement for a popular politician. Although he had no pharmaceutical experience, he was obviously a man of strength, personality, and executive leadership ability. When he left the governor's mansion in Princeton, he accepted the presidency of Warner-Hudnut. I became chairman of the board and chief executive officer.

To strengthen our international operations, which were growing almost as rapidly as our domestic activities, I chose a skilled Belgian-American international lawyer with considerable experience in pharmaceutical marketing, Paul van Der Stricht, and eventually he became president of our International Division, then doing about $12 million annually in sales, but destined to grow under his leadership to more than $200 million.

In the same time period, the death of Gustavus A. Pfeiffer in August, 1953, left us with an urgent need to do something about the 558,441 shares of common stock that Mr. G.A. had owned. His holdings comprised roughly 45 percent of the company's stock, and it was unhealthy both for the company's future and for the Pfeiffer estate to leave it in the hands of his trustees, of whom I was one. In June, 1954, my old friend Ferd Eberstadt of the financial firm bearing his name, and Jim Adams, by then a partner in Lazard Freres, joined together to buy the Pfeiffer shares for the purpose of redistributing them widely in the market in order to avoid company domination by any single outside interest.

All of this was mere prelude, however, to the best move

the Warner Company ever made. For a long time I had been shopping around, as I had in the case of Chilcott, looking for a pharmaceutical company of quality whose best virtues would compensate for our weaknesses, and whose weak points would be strengthened by our strong ones, in other words, a perfect candidate for merger. I thought that I had found such a candidate in the Bristol Myers company of New York, and had been negotiating with Lee Bristol of that firm. We were tentatively agreed to a merger that would have created a single large company much stronger than our two companies separately; putting them together under a single management would have had synergistic effect. Unfortunately, the Bristol sons, while attracted by the financial benefits of merger, was reluctant to lose the company and its identifying family name in the process. Amicably, but disappointedly, I agreed to end the negotiations.

However, one of Gustavus Pfeiffer's last requests led me to a far more beneficial deal just a week later. It was in October, 1954. I had to attend a meeting of the American Foundation for Pharmaceutical Education at the Biltmore Hotel in New York, because Mr. G.A. had left the foundation $900,000 in his will. I was looking toward the doorway of the meeting room when Edward T. T. Williams, president of the Lambert Company of St. Louis, arrived late. As I looked at Ed Williams, whom I had known for years, I had one of those flash inspirations like the kind that cartoonists caricature with a light bulb glowing over the head of a character shouting, "Eureka." I scribbled a note on my personal card: "Ed: I must leave this meeting in fifteen minutes to go to another meeting. Will you be kind enough to meet me at the door? Elmer." I passed the note across to Ed Williams.

He met me in the corridor outside of the meeting room. "What's on your mind, Elmer?" he asked.

"Marriage," I said.

"I'm already happily married. You know that," Williams laughed.

"I don't mean that kind of marriage. I was thinking of your

company and mine. If you're interested, drop by and have lunch with me tomorrow."

Williams said he would talk with his company's major owner, Gerard Lambert, and get in touch with me. A few days later he dropped by for a long, private chat. Lambert was interested. The next step was for Al Driscoll and me to interest our own board of directors, which was more crucial than, perhaps, it sounds. Although I was the largest individual stockholder in the company and thus had a powerful voice, I did not, for the moment at least, represent the most powerful stockholder voice on the board. Ferd Eberstadt and Jim Adams did. The merger proposal came just at the time when they held Mr. G.A.'s 45 percent of the common stock, before they had begun placing it on the market, so their acceptance of the proposed merger was essential. Driscoll and I assembled our board for dinner at the Links Club in New York and convinced them that the merger made sense. Warner-Hudnut, with its full line from cosmetics to ethical drugs, had no products that were in competition with Lambert, with its drugs, Pro-Phy-Lac-Tic toothbrushes and famous Listerine oral antiseptic. Lambert's distribution system in drugstores and the fast-growing supermarkets complemented rather than competed with ours. Since we were not in competition, there were no grounds for anti-trust objections by the government. It was a perfect marriage, and the board approved with enthusiasm.

But some of my colleagues in the industry scoffed at what they thought was my foolhardiness. Lambert's drug products and its plastic and toothbrush business were of marginal value to me. Listerine, the company's most successful product, was such an old standby that industry observers were beginning to dismiss it as of little consequence. It was developed by a physician seventy or eighty years before and came into the hands of Gerard Lambert's father, who recognized its remarkable antiseptic qualities and built a company around it. When he acquired the formula for the then still-unnamed product, the elder Lambert had a bold and ingenious idea for its introduction and promotion. Staking every penny that he had on the trip, he went to London to try to arrange for a test of the product's bacteria-killing qualities by the famous Lord Lister, the father of sterile surgery. Unable to arrange an appointment with the illustrious surgeon, Lambert spent his last dollars on a coach-and-four with driver and footman and went to Lord Lister's London townhouse. The lord's butler, assuming Lambert to be a gentleman of fine quality, never questioned whether he had an appointment, but ushered him directly into the great surgeon's presence. Lambert convinced Lord Lister, by showing him previous experimental data, that he should test the new sterile antiseptic, and the surgeon agreed. Lord Lister was so impressed with the results of his experiments that he agreed to let Lambert name the product after him: Listerine.

And Listerine is what I was after in the Lambert merger. Although it's total sales at that time were only about $15 million a year, I had no doubt that with the proper marketing and promotion I could multiply that many times over.

The negotiations, intricate and complex in detail, could be boiled down to the simple question of which of us wanted the merger the most, Warner or Lambert? It soon developed that Warner did. But there was a further complicating factor involving personalities. Gerard Lambert's adviser and negotiator was Sidney James Weinberg of Goldman Sachs, a brilliant financial specialist who often was called the "director's director" because he was sought by so many boards. Mine was Ferd Eberstadt, an old friend and long-time adviser. The trouble was that Ferd and Weinberg had served unharmoniously together on the War Production Board in 1942 and 1943, and ever since had refused to speak to one another. Jim Adams stepped into the breach of silence between the two and got them to sit down together. But Weinberg drove a hard bargain.

Lambert's 1954 sales were $34 million. Ours were $63 million. Their net earnings were $2 million, compared to our $4.2 million. Lambert earned $2.71 per share in 1954, versus our $3.04. Lambert's stock was selling at 23 and ours at 29. Nevertheless, Weinberg insisted on a straight share-for-share exchange of stock in the merger, which would have left me paying a six-dollar-a-share premium. Actually, I wanted the merger so badly that I was prepared to pay the premium, but by the time we actually settled on terms, there was only a three-dollar spread between our stocks, both of which had risen, so the premium was just half what I had expected to have to spend. By March, 1955, we were one company, the Warner-Lambert Pharmaceutical Company of Morris Plains, New Jersey. I remained chairman and chief executive officer of the company. Jim Chilcott remained vice chairman. Al Driscoll remained president. It was then that I decided to change the name of our firm to Warner-Lambert.

Among the most beneficial results of the merger was that Ed Williams came on as chairman of the executive committee. Ed was an old and brilliant hand in the business. He had been an industrial engineer, then established himself in the 1920s as a consulting specialist in the management of pharmaceutical companies, and then became the president of Becton Dickinson & Co., widely known manufacturers of medical instruments. After his wide-ranging experience in the drug industry, he became president of Lambert in 1948, and he was still as sharp and energetic as ever, particularly as a quick-thinking trouble-shooter. I was enormously comforted to have him there as a backstop to Al Driscoll, who, following a life in law and public service, still had a lot to learn about pharmaceuticals. As a further bonus to management, Ed Williams, Sidney Weinberg, and Gerard Lambert joined our board of directors. From a $63-million company in 1954, we suddenly became a company with $103 million in sales and $6.8 million in net earnings by 1955. That is when I began to dream of driving Warner-Lambert sales beyond the billion-dollar mark.

Listerine, the product that the industry thought had seen its best days, became one of the greatest sources of growth toward that dream. Its sales, by 1957, had been projected as $16 million, an advance from $15 million just three years before, but not healthy enough to suit me. I was waiting for an opportunity to give it a boost that would be spectacular. That chance came with the great flu epidemic of 1957. I had spent a pleasant evening on my yacht, berthed in the Hudson River, dining with Roy Larson, one of the founders of Time, Inc., one of his associates, and Al Driscoll. We talked about advertising in Time, Inc.'s magazines, *Life, Time, Fortune,* and *Sports Illustrated.* The next

morning, while riding to Morris Plains in my car, I happened
to think of *Life* in connection with a notice that I had received
from the Public Health Service, a warning of the approaching
Asian flu epidemic, which already had swept as far as Mexico,
California, and New Orleans. Since it was expected to be more
dangerous with a higher mortality than the customary flu epidemic, I decided that Warner-Lambert should play a part in alerting
the public. I wrote an editorial-style advertisement under the
heading, "A Timely Warning," describing how the epidemic was
approaching the U.S., and what preventive steps people should
take citing the do's and don't's: See their physicians for flu shots;
use common sense by avoiding sources of the infection, such as
crowds; and gargling twice a day with Listerine. Our advertising
agency scoffed at the ad, and so did some of my associates. Despite their skepticism, I bought three pages in three issues of
Life August, September, and October, the traditionally slack
months of advertising. I don't think any three magazine pages
in the history of advertising ever produced such prompt and gratifying results. Overnight, Listerine sales increased so rapidly that
we had to put two shifts on our production lines and even subcon-
tract production out to another bottler. Our year-end sales figure
was $26 million, $10 million more than we had projected. Since
then it has grown to an extent where it is probably the highest
selling proprietary in the United States.

Curiously, I found that I was enjoying the challenges of a
more complex management situation than I had been accustomed
to. In years past, when I ran the show alone, I was able to make
decisions, such as the one to move Roche to Nutley, without a
great deal of cajoling and negotiating among my distant associates
in the business. Now I had two close management associates —
Al Driscoll and Ed Williams — as well as a strong vice chairman
and board of directors to consider before every major move. And
I had a major move in mind at the time of the Lambert merger.
I wanted to concentrate the production of Listerine and some
other products in a single plant, preferably in a near-rural setting
where the labor supply would be honest, steady, and reliable.
I suppose another of the many circles of my life was beginning

to close on itself, because I couldn't erase Lititz, Pennsylvania, from my mind as the ideal place for a major pharmaceutical plant. For one thing, the honesty and devotion to hard work of the Pennsylvania Dutch is legendary, and after running plants in New York City, where a substantial number of my workers were ex-felons, and pilferage and laziness were the order of the day, I longed for the old-fashioned virtues that I knew still lived in my boyhood home. For another, the rolling countryside, surrounded by knobby mountains and Revolutionary War landmarks, is spectacular and clean — a perfect home for medicine. But while it was easy for me to be drawn back to Lititz for those and for sentimental reasons, I wasn't so sure about my associates. Al Driscoll, for example, was scurrying all over New Jersey, looking for a suitable plant site in the state over which he had presided as governor, an understandable expression of loyalty and pride. But as far as I was concerned, Lititz was the place. I didn't tell my associates what I was thinking, however. I decided on a subtle diplomatic strategy instead.

I have subscribed to the Lititz newspaper since 1902, which makes me, I suppose, its oldest continuous reader. One day the paper noted that Newton Buch's fine 150-acre farm on the edge of Lititz was for sale. I knew the property, far enough away from the center of Lititz so that a modern plant there would not alter the character of the historic town, yet close enough to be just a few minutes away. I called Herbie Cooper, who has a lovely summer lodge on a trout stream nearby, and asked him to speak to Nate Buch and tell him I would like to have an option on his farm. Furthermore, if and when I exercise the option, which I probably would, that what we probably would do with his acreage would be for the general benefit of Lititz. Herbie carried out my desires to the letter. Then I began to figure out how to sell the idea of Lititz to Driscoll and Williams. The plan wasn't hard to concoct. One Friday morning I casually asked Driscoll, "Al, have you ever met Dr. Cooper of the Cleft Palate Institute? I think you really should know him. He has invited us to come to visit him this weekend. He has a hideaway house in the Furnace Hills in Lancaster County. I think you'll get wonderful Pennsylvania Dutch food like you've never eaten before. I hope you can come."

Driscoll shook his head with regret. He was giving his annual cocktail party for the New Jersey press, a lingering relic of his political years, that very Friday night, at Washington's crossing on the Delaware River.

"Cocktail parties don't need to last too late," I mused. "Suppose I met you there with my car, and we'll drive to Herbie Cooper's place together. I'll pick you up at eight and we can make it in two hours." Al agreed to come.

Later in the day I caught up with Ed Williams, who had been hard to reach. "Ed, Al and I are spending the weekend in the Pennsylvania Dutch country as guests of Dr. Herbert Cooper. Would you like to join us? You'll have a good time and you'll get some food you've never eaten before. We're going to an old Moravian town called Lititz."

"It sounds interesting," said Williams, who made a hobby of studying American history. But he seemed doubtful.

"Lititz is very historical . . . its buildings and other associations. It's not far from the place where the first cannonballs were made for George Washington in the Cornwall Furnace."

"It's pretty late," Williams said. "I'd have to send someone home for my clothes."

"Well, do it right away. Send my chauffeur."

On the way to Lititz, I told them about Herbie Cooper's work on cleft palates and facial deformity. He had given his heart, early in his career, to people thus afflicted. "We spend millions of dollars straightening arms, legs, and backs, so a man can walk in and ask for a job," Herbie used to say. "But we do nothing for a person who can walk in all right, and who can work, but who can't ask for a job because he can't speak." He developed his prosthetic device to fill the disabling gap of cleft palate, then coordinated the talents of oral surgeons, prosthodontists, dental hygienists, pediatricians, plastic surgeons, psychiatrists, and other medical specialists who joined his clinic to correct speech, facial, and other deformities that made social and emotional cripples of otherwise healthy people.

Both Williams and Driscoll were overwhelmed by Herbie's hideaway, a beautiful one-story, three-bedroom ranch house partly cantilevered over rushing Hammer greek, a mountain stream that is so filled with fat speckled and rainbow trout that the water churns when you drop a piece of bread in it. Herbie and his wife, Merce, are probably the two best cooks in Lancaster County. They had a late supper ready for us: Lynn Haven oysters brought that day from the Maryland shore, steaks, home-baked bread, and shoo-fly pie. By midnight, Driscoll and Williams looked as if they never wanted to leave the place as they listened to the musical wash of the trout stream and breathed the pine-scented air.

After a breakfast of country sausage, biscuits, eggs, and sweet-rolls the next morning, a stranger dropped in. I knew who he was, because I had secretly arranged with Herbie to have him there. He was one of the leading real estate men of New Jersey. Several reporters and photographers from the Lititz and Lancaster papers followed behind him. I put on an act of sternly rebuking the real estate man for calling, then talked glowingly to the reporters about the virtues of the Pennsylvania Dutch and the beauties of the countryside, much to Driscoll's and Williams wonderment. Then we toured historical sites around the county, with Herbie, who is something of a local historical expert, as our guide. By carefully pre-arranged chance, we ended our tour at the old Buch farm. I guess Williams and Driscoll became a little suspicious when the real estate man, who had tagged along, remarked that the Buch farm would be wonderful for any company that wanted to build a plant there, provided it was acceptable to the community.

On Sunday, after a visit to the Moravian church at which Al Driscoll could not forebear from making a speech to the Sunday school, particularly due to my having offered to take Herbie's place in running the program of his large Bible class, we started back to Morris Plains. My two colleagues were so full of good food, good cheer, and good impressions of Lititz that each, as if it was his own original idea, suggested that we consider locating our new plant there. I said, "That's a pretty good idea. I feel fairly sure that we can get that Buch property at a favorable price." Neither of them knew that I already had an option on it.

We completed the Lititz plant by the summer of 1956 as part of a $10-million Warner-Lambert expansion program carried out without external financing, and celebrated the move of Listerine production and that of some of our New York Products with a gala entertainment provided by the stars of "Your Hit Parade," which Warner-Lambert sponsored on television. But after the stars of the show and my management colleagues had gone home, I stayed on in Lititz for a few days to join another celebration, the bi-centennial anniversary of the founding of the Moravian town. The ceremonies in Lititz Springs Park were touchingly nostalgic to me. They began with a carefully rehearsed pageant, recalling the old times there, beginning with the park's first use as an Indian camping ground, and recreating the annual Fourth of July celebration held there every year since 1775. When darkness falls on the fourth, the scene in the park is spectacular. Thousands of tallow candles are lighted almost simultaneously throughout the park, with the flames forming symbolic shapes that often are more breathtaking than elaborate fireworks displays. Many of the candles are rigged on waterwheels which form fantastic patterns of light and shadow on the glistening clear water of the stream that flows for an eighth of a mile through the park from the three hillside springs. As a boy, I used to get fifty cents for placing the candles in position for the annual display; then I would set up my bun and cake stand to sell sweets to the thousands who came to watch the show. In those days the park was a lush green sward, refreshingly clean. By this anniversary, however, it was showing the effects of more than two hundred years of constant use. When I was asked to address the 4,000 people who came to the celebration, I elected to direct their attention to this beloved park.

"I played in this park from the time I was six years old," I said. "I waded in the cold stream and enjoyed the shade and cool of its trees on hot summer days. As I grew up, I played football and baseball here on the town teams. The young ladies of my age sat on the benches by day and in the darkness of the evening.

"This park took the place, for me, of traveling to other parts of the country. To me it was like going to the mountains or to the seashore, places that I could not reach.

"I walked through this park today and what I saw disturbed me. It has not been kept up as well as it was in my boyhood. It looks down at the heels. I know that it will take both time and money to rehabilitate the park. Tonight I will pledge $150,000 for that purpose, if you fine citizens of this community will pledge your time, not only to bring it back to what it was, but to make it an even better park."

The next day, Herbie Cooper and I were strolling through the park when we came to a dilapidated old building close to its edge. When I was a boy it had been a cigar factory. Now it looked as if it were not good for anything. I asked Herbie whether it was in use any more. "Not as a cigar factory," he said. "It's being used now for a recreation center." I was so shocked that the town had only this crumbling old structure for "recreation" that I decided to do something about it, too. Eighteen months later, the park had been spruced up so that it appeared, again, as it had when I was a boy. In one corner of it stood a tastefully-designed modern brick recreation center containing music and art rooms, playrooms, and a large auditorium. It was named in honor of a man, dearer to my heart than any, who had served the Lititz community devotedly for 13 years: the Reverend Isaac Walton Bobst.

Lititz prospered from the addition of Warner-Lambert, which became its largest single employer, and my company prospered from the location of its new plant in Lititz. The kind of internal corporate growth which the new plant represented had increased our assets manyfold since the days of near collapse in 1946. So had several other judicious acquisitions and mergers. One of our more noteworthy acquisitions of that period was the Emerson Drug Company of Baltimore, which manufactured Bromo Seltzer as well as the familiar blue bottles in which it is sold. Another was the Nepera Chemical Company. Although little known to consumers, Nepera was a leading producer of pharmaceutical specialties, fine chemicals, and intermediates for manufacturing pharmaceutical end products. I had viewed the company longingly for several years after Warner-Lambert began to take off in its growth, because Nepera's products and facilities would provide a strong backbone to the body of our manufacturing needs. The head of the company was William S. Lasdon, a handsome, aggressive pharmaceutical leader about eleven years my junior whom I had known for many years through industry associations. I had negotiated with him over a product distribution agreement years before when I was with Hoffmann-La Roche and when his pharmaceutical interests were still quite limited. Over the years I had watched the growth of his company and had been impressed by the conscientious way he ran it in the interests of other non-pharmaceutical members of his family who shared the ownership with him. In 1954, I began talking to him in a preliminary way about a possible merger. Our conversations continued for two years, culminating in a merger in 1956, shortly after we opened the new Lititz plant. Because of the exchange of stock involved in the merger, Bill Lasdon and his family became the largest group-stockholders in Warner-Lambert, and Bill joined our board to lend his considerable knowledge of pharmaceuticals to our management. He later succeeded Ed Williams as chairman of our executive committee.

During the same time period, I began to toy with the idea of another merger, one that was almost too good, in strictly financial terms, to be true. It would have created a giant, our stockholders would have benefited immensely, and I personally would have become considerably enriched by it. But despite these attractions, it troubled me from the start, when I first began talking of possible merger with the late Bowman Gray, president and principal stockholder of the R.J. Reynolds Tobacco Company. On the financial face of it, the merger was irresistible. Reynolds's worldwide sales in 1957 were slightly over a billion dollars, with net earnings of $50 million. Warner-Lambert sales in the same year were $151 million, with net profits of $14.3 million. Both of our stocks were selling at about the same price a share, and Gray was willing to merge on a share-for-share exchange that would have left us owning 25 percent, or about $220-million worth, of the new conglomerate. For Reynolds, the merger would have meant profitable diversification and access to our superb domestic and foreign distribution facilities. For us, it would have meant a huge capital advantage with more than ample resources for continued growth. But it also would have meant submerging Warner-Lambert as the junior member of a much larger company. And it would have put me, by association and direct financial benefit, into the tobacco business.

As honorary chairman of the American Cancer Society and chairman of its annual fund campaign, I was hardly in an appropriate position to become part-owner and beneficiary of the massive sales of a cigarette company. I had remained as deeply involved with the Cancer Society through the 1950s as I had been during the late forties. I recognized it for what it was: the most significant and humane work I had ever done in my life. And I devoted more of my free energies to it than to any single thing outside of my corporate responsibilities. During that first decade that I worked with the Cancer Society, Dr. Charles Cameron and I led a revolution that not only altered the society's course but immeasurably increased the funds available for research into the causes and cures of the dread disease. Dr. Cameron, with the advice of lay leaders in the society, brilliantly managed the research program. By 1955, we were raising more than $25 million annually for the society, as opposed to only $600,000 when I joined it. We also had taken three fundamental steps that affected the health and lives of millions of people around the world. I was justifiably proud of the role that I played in taking those steps.

The first great leap forward after the society's reorganization was our sponsorship of Dr. George Papanicolaou, who was working in the forties on what was later to become practically a household term, the "Pap Test" for cancer. I had known Dr. Papanicolaou for many years, having consulted with him frequently during my time at Roche when he was a professor of medicine at Cornell. He was concentrating, even then, on uterine malignancies. When I became involved with the Cancer Society, I directed some of

our research money to support his work. In 1948, he reported
his astonishing results to the society. He had devised a painless,
simple, routine test of the cervix and uterus that almost unfailing-
ly detected cancer cells long before they became apparent by the
presence of a tumor or by a careful physical examination. Dr. Papanicolaou's momentous discovery deserved urgent and widespread
publicity so that women throughout the world could begin bene-
fiting from it. Every day's delay in disseminating his results and
applying the test meant lives unnecessarily lost. Yet some of the
board members of the Cancer Society, mindful of the traditional
caution of the medical profession, felt that the Papanicolaou findings had not yet been exhaustively tested, no matter how conclusive they appeared to be, and that releasing them as I wanted
to do would be premature. Fortunately, Dr. Cameron, our scientific director, agreed with me. "The society must make this information immediately available and give it wide publicity," he insisted. So did Dr. Alton Ochsner, who probably had done more
cancer surgery than any member of the board. After a strenuous
and partly acrimonious argument, we won the conservative board
members over and made the announcement as soon as we could.
Since then, thanks largely to the Pap Test, deaths from uterine
cancer have decreased by about 50 percent and would fall still
more if all women religiously had the test every year.

We continued to support Dr. Papanicolaou after his great
discovery, when he turned to what Dr. Cameron believed was
a very promising research program on the detection of breast
cancer. At one point, I recall, two super-millionaire Greek shipping magnates tried to lure Dr. "Pap" to a new research laboratory on an island off Greece. He asked me what he should do
about the offer.

"If these gentlemen wanted to set you up in a new laboratory
in Geneva or anywhere else, I would advise you to accept the
offer. But their desire to have you on a Greek island looks to
me as if they are simply trying to use you to establish their own
importance in Greece. I'd turn it down."

Wisely, I think, he rejected the offer and instead accepted
the directorship of a new research institute at Miami University.

When he took the post at Miami he was hale and hearty, and extremely hopeful about the outcome of his research on breast cancer. Tragically, he died of a coronary attack not long after that, his work still not completed. Every year since then I have invited his widow to my home in Palm Beach to reminisce about this great man who made one of the most significant of all life-saving discoveries in the battle against cancer.

Another major step that we took in the Cancer Society grew out of a trip to Europe that I took in 1954. I visited eight European capitals for the purpose of talking about our cancer research programs and the progress that we had made in the American Cancer Society. I made public speeches, held press conferences, and talked to professional medical groups, all of which were intrigued by what we had been doing. No matter who was in the audience, one of the first questions, in every case, was "How do you raise money?" Europeans had not benefited from the tradition of public fund-raising that we enjoy in America. Equally important, however, was a distressing fact that became apparent to me as I talked with people interested in cancer abroad. There was not a two-way flow of information between us and Europe. They knew of cancer research programs that were unfamiliar to me, and many of our efforts were unfamiliar to them. When I got home, I broached the idea of starting a healthy two-way program of information and cooperation. One such effort — the Union Internationale Contre Le Cancer — had almost died aborning after three modest international cancer congresses in Paris. It was short of funds and operated with a small staff that had little effect. I suggested that we organize the fourth international congress on cancer in the United States, and assure its success by funding it from generous private sources. Dr. Cameron put the idea into action. The congress, finally held in St. Louis in 1957, was a complete success, and made international headlines when the U.S. government used the occasion to announce that it would make radioisotopes available for cancer research and treatment all over the world.

With the definite idea of creating an affiliation with cancer societies throughout the world, I proposed this step on my return from Europe after making quite a number of cancer speeches and noting an intense interest of those devoted to this wonderful cause. Our board of directors, however, for two years or more were not sufficiently interested to bring about the relationship I originally had in mind. But Mary Lasker, hand in hand with me in the thought of developing the worldwide affiliation with our American societies, decided to bring a reasonable number of cancer workers from varied countries in Europe to visit our American Cancer Society meeting in Detroit. We both put up $25,000 to defray expenses. Delegates from twenty-five countries spent ten days studying the Cancer Society's operations in work shops in New York, and a month in the field, studying the society's installations and visiting clinics. The foreign delegates were particularly impressed by our fund-raising techniques and carried the knowledge home with them to begin their own nation wide drives for cancer research funds. As a result of these and other efforts, the Cancer Society is now directly affiliated with 144 other societies in seventy-two countries, including some behind the Iron Curtain. The exchange of information on procedures, promotion, and research is free flowing, heavy, and beneficial to the victims of cancer everywhere.

The third and perhaps most significant step taken by the society had to do with tobacco. It grew out of my years-long habit of reading professional literature to keep abreast of developments in world medicine. One evening in the fall of 1950, I sat down with a copy of the British Medical Journal and came across an article entitled "Smoking and Carcinoma of the Lung," by Richard Doll, M.D. and A. Bradford Hill, Ph.D. The article recounted the results of a study conducted by the authors, one of them a member of the statistical research unit of the Medical Research Council and the other a professor of medical statistics at the London School of Hygiene and Tropical Medicine. They were looking for the cause or causes of a fifteen fold increase in the number of deaths in England attributed to lung cancer in the years 1922-1947. After examining case histories of 1,732 patients admitted to twenty London hospitals and conducting a statistical analysis, they drew a firm conclusion: There was a direct association between lung cancer and cigarette smoking, and heavy smokers ran a greater risk than light smokers. They also presented a graph showing the increase of lung cancer along with the increase of cigarette consumption in England.

I had read speculative reports in American medical literature that linked lung cancer to cigarette smoking, but none of them had presented so broad and convincing a statistical picture. In the late 1930s, Dr. Alton Ochsner and his protege, Dr. Michael E. DeBakey, published several reports on cancer victims whose lungs they had removed at Tulane Medical School in New Orleans. In each of these reports on lung cancer surgery, they theorized that cigarette smoking was an important causative factor. Dr. Ochsner had spoken out on the subject so often, in fact, that many medical men considered him a "nut" on the subject and disregarded his warnings despite his vast experience and acute observations as a thoracic surgeon.

I had been inclined for some time to believe Drs. Ochsner and DeBakey, even though they had no broad statistical proof of their theory. My own experience with cigarettes, while not so dismal as that of the cancer victims, had been damaging enough to make me realize that they were harmful. I remembered back to 1936, at a time when I was physically and intellectually on top of the world, building Hoffmann-La Roche. I enjoyed smoking, even though I knew cigarettes probably were not good for me. But when I began to have slight dizzy spells, I wondered if they were not far more harmful than I had supposed. At first I did not connect the spells with my smoking. I would lean down to tee up a ball on the golf course, and become dizzy when I stood up again. I recognized the condition as extra-systoles — a momentary interruption in the blood supply and lack of oxygen in the brain. It never caused me to faint, but it left me feeling weak. I visited several cardiologists, but the best any of them could offer was the gratuitous advice to "take six months off from work." One night I got dizzy on a dance floor. By now I realized that cigarettes, by cutting my oxygen supply, probably were the cause. The next evening, Ethel had a group of couples in for bridge and a buffet supper. As I played, I smoked, and the more I smoked the more convinced I became that cigarettes were causing my dizziness. About half-way through the evening I turned to a friend at my bridge table and said, "This is the last cigarette I'm ever going to smoke." He laughed as I drew on the cigarette. When it was about half burned, I stubbed it out in the ashtray. "Fini. Zu ende. No more," I said. Everyone laughed. But I never touched another cigarette or any form of tobacco since that night. If I had continued to smoke, I feel reasonably certain that I would not be alive today.

The British study that I read that night in 1950 was ignored by most medical people in the United States, because few of them wanted to believe it. But I felt that it was of vital importance. So did Dr. Cameron. After discussing it with him, we decided that it should be called to the attention of the American Cancer Society. Shortly after I first saw the article, I presided over a full meeting of the society's 450 delegates and board members in New York. Since many of the delegates were physicians and cancer researchers, I probably had the most sophisticated audience on cancer that could be gathered in one room. I opened one of our sessions with these remarks: "Now, my friends, I am going to call your attention to an article in the *British Medical Journal*. I don't have it with me, but I have practically memorized it and I would like to tell you what it says." I recounted the findings of the two British medical researchers and their conclusions concerning cigarettes and lung cancer. When I had finished, one of the delegates, a past president of the society, rose to object.

"I do not believe that it is appropriate for the chairman to bring such a subject before this body," he exclaimed. A delegate from Boston stood up to support him by saying, "I agree. This is neither the time nor the place for that subject." I knew both of them well, and both were heavy smokers.

"I do not agree with you at all," I retorted. "I want to tell you and everyone here that I have been traveling up and down this country and collecting money for one purpose: To find out through research the causative factors and possible cures of cancer in any form. The disease has been increasing just as much here as in England. There may or may not be a relationship between cigarette smoking and lung cancer, but there certainly are grounds for investigation. As chairman of this meeting, I intend to take action and appoint a committee that will develop ways and means of finding out. The American public has been generous to this society and has the right to know the truth."

A bitter argument from the floor ensued, but when Dr. Ochsner and several other respected people rose to support me, my action was reluctantly approved. Dr. Ochsner was the first man I appointed to the committee. With the approval of the board, we hired two well-qualified experts, Dr. C. Cuyler Hammond, a noted specialist in epidemiology and the analysis of epidemics, and Dr. Daniel Horn, a respected statistician. We enlisted 22,000 of our own trained volunteers to work in 400 counties in eleven states, each reporting on ten smokers and non-smokers, there being in all 100,000 each nonsmokers and smokers of a pack or more a day. There was a steady flow of reports from the volunteer reporters as the subjects under study became ill or died. By 1954, we had detailed records on more than 187,000 men, smokers and non-smokers, living and dead. Statistical analysis of the broad-scale study bore out everything the British researchers had said. There was not the slightest doubt that cigarette smoking, even down to six cigarettes a day, can produce lung cancer.

We released the first results of our study in June, 1954. Although the reactions of the tobacco industry, much of the public, and even many medical people ranged from outraged disbelief to quiet skepticism, we stuck by our guns and continued the study. As more reports came in and were evaluated, we refined the results to show that a person smoking one pack a day ran at least fourteen times more risk of lung cancer than the non-smoker, and that as the number of cigarettes consumed increased, so did the risk. Within a few years, we noted a statistical correlation between smoking and coronary heart disease, and a positive cause and effect relationship between smoking and emphysema. The denials and skepticism that our reports first raised have long been conclusively put to rest by further studies, all based on that first statistical research project that Dr. Cameron and I insisted the Cancer Society undertake in 1950.

As I look back over all that I have done in my life, there is nothing more rewarding to me than my Cancer Society experience. If I have performed a service to mankind, this is it. We are edging slowly but surely toward that time when we will bring this terrible disease under control. In the meantime, there are at least two million Americans alive today who have been cured of cancer, and the cure rate of cancer victims is up from one in five in 1945, to one-plus in three or nearly 40 percent compared with 20 percent in 1945. Hundreds of thousands more, it is hoped, will never contract the disease because they have been warned away from one of its most insidious causes: cigarettes.

For the sake of my stockholders and for the obvious benefit of Warner-Lambert, I proceeded with my negotiations with Bowman Gray and Reynolds Tobacco despite troubling misgivings. It was a kind of personal ethical dilemma that business, fortunately, does not often present: A distinct and unsurpassable gap between personal conviction and corporate responsibility. The dilemma had been starkly drawn for me before in my conflicts over narcotics with the Swiss. Now it confronted me again over tobacco. My own health played the decisive role in resolving the dilemma.

While negotiating with R. J. Reynolds concerning the proposed merger, I noticed a slight change in my bowel habits. Most people, particularly men in their seventies, assume such changes are a natural part of the aging process and do not think of them in connection with cancer. But I did. I conceived and put into effect the extensive publicity given to cancer's seven danger signals, and I recognized this as one of them. I knew that something was wrong. Several of our cancer experts in my company, and my private physician, disagreed with me. "It's just age, Mr. Bobst," They said. "Everyone has such changes when he begins to get on in years." I didn't believe them. Instead, I asked Miss Murray to telephone Dr. Isadore R. Ravdin at the University of Pennsylvania. Dr. Ravdin was one of the greatest surgeons this country has ever produced, an expert in cancer, and a former president of the American Cancer Society. I asked him to get me a room in his hospital and told him that I would come to

Alisa V, the author's last and largest yacht.

Philadelphia right away. Then, because of the merger negotiations, I cautioned Miss Murray not to mention my destination to anyone. "I don't want a soul to know that I've gone to a hospital."

Dr. Ravdin, a dynamic but diminutive man who had to stand on a stool to command his operating table, looked me over searchingly when I got to Philadelphia and asked, "Elmer, what are you here for?"

"I don't know, Doctor. You have to tell me." I did not explain what was worrying me, because I wanted him to examine me without preconceptions of any kind. During the next few days, I had a complete rundown by specialists in each field, then a complete gastro-intestinal X-ray examination.

"Elmer, he said, there's something here that shows up on the picture of the colon. I have to use a proctoscope to get a better look at it." Twice he employed proctoscopy, took specimens in the area of the seeming trouble, sent them to pathology. Both times the specimens were negative. Then he decided to be even more thorough and conduct a proctoscopic examination a few centimeters higher in the colon, taking a larger specimen. He found one. It was malignant.

I can see Dr. Ravdin now, sitting behind his desk smoking a cigarette despite his knowledge of its danger, explaining to me the possible course of my malignancy. There was definitely cancer there, but there was no way to tell from proctoscopic examination whether it was extremely limited or extensive, or whether there was any sign of metastasis. At my age, surgery was something to consider before undertaking. He could promise me nothing.

"The fact of the matter is that you won't know what you can do until you open me up," I said. "I don't want to take any chances with cancer, so please go ahead." The operation, under spinal anesthesia, lasted for about five hours, and Dr. Ravdin found a malignancy that certainly would have spread fatally if it had been left alone much longer. I was conscious through most of the operation and chatted with him and the anesthesiologist as they worked, finally asking, "Who is doing the hem-stitching," when they closed the incision. The operation turned out to be a complete success.

I had a rapid recovery and even began to resume my business activities while recuperating in the hospital. Dr. Ravdin, always smoking when I saw him, dropped in on me whenever he made his rounds and smiled his approval when he saw me working in bed. One evening after he had dropped by, I lay in bed contemplating the all-but-complete merger with R. J. Reynolds. Our negotiations already had been reported in the press, and *Fortune* magazine had published a brief item accepting final approval of the merger as a foregone conclusion. But as I lay in my hospital bed recovering from a cancer operation, it was far from a foregone conclusion with me. I had not yet resolved the dilemma. "The merger is certainly advantageous from a financial standpoint," I told myself. "It will increase our dividends substantially and also the price of the stock. It will strengthen our management. But how can I make such a deal with a clear conscience? I *know* without the slightest doubt that there is a relationship between cigarette smoking and lung cancer and emphysema." I shook my head. "Morally it's wrong," I said. I called out to my nurse. "Please bring me a telephone." She put the phone beside my head and I called Governor Driscoll. "Al, I've been doing a lot of thinking, lying here in bed. I don't want to go through with the Reynolds merger."

"Why? What's wrong now?" he asked in astonishment.

"What's wrong is that, from a moral standpoint, I don't believe I could live with it. I'm the one who started the Cancer Society research campaign against cigarettes because of lung cancer, and here we are about to get into the cigarette business. Al, I want you to call a special meeting of the board in my name and state to the members that I am definitely opposed to going any further with the merger. Then advise Bowman Gray in a very nice way to issue a statement, and we'll issue a statement that will not be derogatory to either concern, nor will it make any explanation of why the merger was dropped."

I have had no regrets about that eventful hospital experience, save one. Dr. Ravdin did not listen to my repeated admonitions that he stop the habit that he knew to be dangerous. He continued smoking heavily. Once he told me that he had managed to quit for a few months, but he started up again while attending a prize fight. A few years ago he suffered the all-too-common fate of heavy cigarette smokers: He had a coronary attack. While recovering from the heart condition, he suffered a severe stroke which marked the end of a great humanitarian and surgical career. He is still living, but his memory and brain activity have ended completely.

The death toll from cigarettes among men and women whom I have known in my lifetime has been as steady as a funeral drumbeat, and as tragic, for it has caught so many of them in the prime of life, when their contributions to the nation and to mankind were only beginning to be felt. One of them I recall most vividly was a man whom everyone in the United States recognized on sight as a brilliant radio and television journalist, a wise political and social analyst, and a confirmed chain smoker. He was Edward R. Murrow, who throughout his career smoked so much that a burning cigarette became his trademark. I remember once, not long after we began our cigarette-lung cancer studies in the Cancer Society, when he sat between Eleanor Roosevelt and me at a New York banquet. He arrived a little late, with a cigarette in his mouth, and he continued to smoke one after another throughout the dinner.

"Ed, you ought to quit. Really you ought to quit," I told him. "You are aware that our Cancer Society studies have established the relationship between cigarette smoking and lung cancer. We have been searching out the truth, and the results are absolutely convincing."

He never quit. A decade later, he died of lung cancer.

● *Chapter Twenty-Six*

● During the Eisenhower years, I spent a good deal of time in Washington with the Nixons, because they were like members of my own family. But I visited the White House only rarely, even though I knew President Eisenhower and liked him. One reason that I remained somewhat shy of the presidential mansion during many of those years was that I did not care for or trust Ike's highly efficient chief of staff, Sherman Adams. I felt that he had taken advantage of Ike's natural love of relaxation and diversion, urging the president to take it easy while he, Adams, took over the onerous details of the presidency. Ike hated details and what he called "staff work." Thus, he did not object to Adams's increasing assumption of presidential responsibilities. The result was that Adams took center stage in the White House and, it seemed to me, ran the government. The consequences. I think, were bad for Eisenhower because Adams managed to construct an almost impenetrable screen that isolated the president from opinions that he should have had. Adam's power in the White House made my friend Vice President Nixon's position very uncomfortable, to say the least, because the former New Hampshire governor tried to put obstacles in his path, too. Despite Ike's own desires to emphasize the importance of the vice presidency, Adams encouraged the view among his White House staff that the second-highest elective office in the nation was of little real consequence.

Had I been in Dick's position then, I know that my impulsive nature would have led me to raise hell regardless of who suffered embarrassment in the process. When Adams finally fell, it was like the cascade of ice from the shearing face of a glacier. Ike seemingly paid no attention to reports, widely circulated by the news media, about an alleged business favors relationship between Adams and a Boston industrialist named Bernard Goldfine. I was with Dick and Pat one evening during that brief period, riding home with them from a formal reception. Rumors about the Adams case had been on everyone's lips at the affair we had just left, but the vice president, quite properly, had displayed no reaction to them.

"Dick," I said in the privacy of the car, "Adams is either a fool or worse. Ike must get rid of him at once. If I were you I would go to the president tomorrow and tell him so." Pat nodded her agreement with my emotional outburst.

Dick smiled tolerantly at both of us. "The president knows his own mind," he said. "I'm not worried. And I'm not going to try to tell him what to do."

A few days later, Adams resigned, and Ike never again let any one reestablish the unprecedented base of power that he had held. In retrospect, I saw that Dick had been right to remain as calm as he had during the crisis and leave it to the president to resolve, because he was the only man who could do it.

After Adams left the White House, President Eisenhower did a great personal favor for me, one that since has proven of immeasurable benefit to the people of Korea. It involved a cause that has been close to my heart ever since I first became a pharmacist in Philadelphia. The most distressing of all developments to me as a professional pharmacist has been the increasing separation of the two most natural health allies, professional medicine and professional pharmacy. It had come about through a short-sightedness in both professions. Medical practitioners unfortunately have tended to be scornful of apothecaries, as Dr. Little scorned me during our final clash at the Cancer Society. Colleges of pharmacy, on the other hand, have been slow to recognize the real needs of physicians and have continued to educate their students as if training them to mix tonics and elixirs for turn-of-the-century general practitioners. The truth, as everyone who has ever watched a modern pharmacist at work knows, is that more than 95 percent of all prescription drugs nowadays are pre-packaged by pharmaceutical houses and have only to be counted or measured and dropped into a druggist's own prescription bottle, vial or package. In my early days, almost every prescription had to be made from materials by the pharmacist himself. The sophisticated developments of the pharmaceutical industry have freed the pharmacist from the need to mix elixirs, mortar his own powders, and measure the compounds of pills. By the same token, they have made the task of education in the dispensing of prescriptions drugs far less demanding than it used to be. Yet the colleges of pharmacy have gone on wasting valuable classroom time on irrelevant courses and outmoded techniques. At the same time, pharmacists have been forced by modern merchandising and economic conditions to become primarily marketing men and soda-fountain managers, rather than scientific professionals.

I have campaigned within the profession for many years to bring it up to date by drastically revising pharmacy curricula to train pharmacists as true health care professionals who not only can help physicians but can even take over, as para-medical technicians, some of their less demanding duties. I like to characterize my professional goal as "changing the greasy apron of the restaurant for the white coat of respectability." In my view, irrelevant and outdated courses such as botany should be thrown out of the curriculum and relevant scientific courses added. The result would be pharmacists trained in such things as laboratory research methods and objectives, who could handle at the corner drugstore the complex diagnostic bio-chemical tests that physicians now must send off to county, state, and federal labs. They would learn such subjects as cytology and pharmacology and graduate from a five-year course with such professional depth of knowledge that they could qualify for work as medical allies with duties ranging from skilled service behind a drug counter to highly specialized roles as pharmaceutical engineers, better qualified than present-day chemists for demanding research jobs in the drug industry. Then they might truly deserve the title of "doctor" that all of us, in the old days, once answered to informally.

During the mid-1930s, as a member of the board of trustees of the Rutgers College of pharmacy, I tried valiantly but vainly to turn my dream of a revised curriculum into a fact. All I gained from the process was the truth of an old educational saw: "It is easier to move tombstones than to change a college curriculum."

In the 1950s, I was approached by Columbia University to head a committee seeking $10 million for new buildings for the Columbia College of Pharmacy. Once burned by Rutgers, I told Columbia that I was too busy, *unless* they would couple the building program to a complete overhaul of their curriculum for pharmacy both in the classroom and the laboratory. I told them that I wanted to see true professional training that would produce knowledgeable scientists and medical technicians. I gave them what became known as the Bobst-Columbia Plan for Pharmaceutical Education, added $100,000 of my own money and arranged for a $500,000-grant from the Pfeiffer Foundation to start off the building program. A committee appointed by the board of trustees made a deep study of desirable curriculum changes. Their study was received with enthusiasm, but no action. Very little, including the building plans, materialized, although a few U.S. colleges of pharmacy picked up some of the better features of the Bobst-Columbia plan and put them to work.

Paradoxically, my ideas found full acceptance in a nation that did not even have a college of pharmacy, and that is what brought me to President Eisenhower, seeking his help. At the request of Dr. Howard Rusk, the great rehabilitation specialist and international medical statesman, I attended a dinner of the American Korean Foundation. President Syngman Rhee, on his last visit to the continental United States, was the honored guest. I chatted with the aging Korean president during the reception prior to the dinner, and he asked me what business I was in. When I told him, "Pharmaceutical manufacturing and medicine in general," he replied, "Unfortunately, we have no college of pharmacy in Korea."

"I have heard that," I said. "I understand that you are forced to import all of your medicines, mostly from Japan."

"That is true," he smiled ruefully, for the Koreans have a historic suspicion of the Japanese.

In a sudden burst of enthusiasm, I said, "I feel very strongly your need for a college of pharmacy, and I am going to see that you get one."

President Rhee looked at me with conviction and said, "Mr. Bobst, I will remember each word that you have spoken."

He did not forget, nor did I. I was toying with a novel plan to raise money for the project when Dr. Rusk called again and asked for my help in connection with the Rehabilitation Institutute, which he headed. I agreed, but asked for his help in return. I explained that I wanted to enlist President Eisenhower to assist me in persuading twenty-five leading pharmaceutical companies to donate the funds and supplies necessary to establish a college of pharmacy in Korea. To help capture Ike's interest, I wanted the sponsorship of Dr. Rusk's American Korean Foundation. He agreed. Together, we called on the president, who helpfully consented to invite my list of twenty-five pharmaceutical leaders to the White House for a luncheon. I could hardly have found a better place than the White House for a platform for educational fund-raising or a better host than President Eisenhower.

The invitations went out, and all twenty-five guests naturally appeared as if by command. At that time, the president had just been through some uncomfortable publicity which raised a storm among animal-lovers. He had asked the White House grounds keepers to do something about the squirrels that were ruining his golf putting green. When some of the squirels were exterminated, animal-lovers reacted with horror. Most of the guests at the luncheon thought the squirrel crisis something of a joke and assumed that the president did, too. I had seen his short temper in action years before at Columbia, however, so I cringed a little when one of the pharmaceutical leaders made a facetious remark aout the White House squirrels.

Ike's face flushed when he heard the remark. "Don't you talk to me about those damned squirrels," he growled, and turned away. He was genuinely angry.

The luncheon, however, was a noteworthy success. Dr. Rusk, the surgeon general and the president where the only non-pharmaceutical people present, so the audience was a sympathetic one and responded enthusiastically when I talked about the urgent need for a college of pharmacy in Korea. Dr. Rusk added a few helpful words, and by the time we left the White House the project was assured of enough support to get started. I later persuaded the Pfeiffer Foundation to put it over the top with a $200,000 contribution, then personally brought and paid the total expenses of five of Korea's leading chemists to the U.S. for an accelerated course in pharmacy so that they could become the nucleus of the new faculty. The result was the College of Pharmacy of Chungang University in Seoul, which now graduates 200 students a year out of a student body of 1,000. Equally satisfying to me is that they follow the Bobst-Columbia plan curriculum. As a result, the graduates are equipped to render para-medical services in remote areas of Korea that have no doctors. Interestingly, Australia, which like Korea suffers from a shortage of physicians, also has adopted the plan with beneficial results.

On another occasion I visited Ike in the White House on behalf of the Cancer Society. We had arranged for President Eisenhower to push a button that would trigger a small nuclear electrical impulse to light the Cancer Society's familiar "Sword of Hope" in Times Square in New York, thus symbolically linking radiology, cancer, and national commitment. Among the notables who attended the ceremony in Ike's oval office was the great lady athlete, Babe Didrikson Zaharias, who was fighting a courageous but tragically fatal battle against cancer. Like many Americans, especially golfers, I had been intrigued by Babe Zaharias's athletic prowess ever since she first gained fame as a track star and later as an amateur and then professional golfer, because she was better than many of the most accomplished male athletes of the day. She was so good, in fact, that uncomplimentary locker-room jokes used to pass concerning her true sexual identity. I remember once meeting her great baseball namesake, Babe Ruth, at a private fishing camp where we both were guests. He said that he had appeared with Babe Didrikson at a charity event in which the two were pitted against one another to see who could drive a golf ball the farthest. The great Yankee slugger told how both of them warmed up by hitting a few balls. Her drives matched his every time. At last he drove one 300 yards or more and turned to her in exasperation: "Babe," he said, "if you outdrive me on that one I'm going to knock you down and find out if you're really a girl."

Before going to Ike's office, I invited Babe Zaharias and a few others who were involved in the White House ceremony to come to my hotel suite for cocktails. They put their coats in the bedroom, and we had a pleasant hour of conversation before it was time to go. As we were getting ready to leave, Babe, who had been so ladylike that it was hard to think of her as an athlete, said, "Elmer, wait here just a minute. There's something I'm dying to show you," I waited, a little puzzled, while she went to the bedroom. In a moment she came out, wearing a luxurious white fur stole that her husband had given her. "Don't you just adore it?" she asked, spinning around like a fashion model. There was never any doubt in my mind, no matter what Babe Ruth may have thought, that Babe Didrikson Zaharias was a real lady.

But she could not escape her image as an athlete even in the White House. She watched as I presented President Eisenhower with a model of the Sword of Hope that was about the length and weight of a number one wood. He hefted it with a golfer's grip and swung it a few times. Then he handed it to Mrs. Zaharias, in her fashionable dress and lovely stole, with the words, "Here, Babe, show me how you swing."

One of Ike's shortcomings as a president, I believe, was that he never fully recognized the art of politics for what it is, the life blood of a constructive adversary system that keeps this nation alive by subjecting the party in power to continuous challenge. He was conditioned by his years as a military man to view "politics" as a distasteful subject, beneath the dignity of the commander-in-chief. While he carried many Republicans into office in the aura of his great personal charisma, he never really got into the political fray, but instead took an unfortunate pride in his role "above" partisan politics. Unhappily. I believe this resulted in the 1960 defeat of his own political protege, Richard Nixon. Had Ike been more vigorous and politically realistic during the 1960 campaign, there is no doubt in my mind that Nixon would have won enough additional votes to surmount the slim and dubious lead that Kennedy gained in the questionable precincts of Illinois, Texas, Missouri, and South Carolina. The history of the last disordered decade, to say nothing of that of the tragedy-struck Kennedy family, would have been far different.

President Nixon has never once expressed to me any bitterness over this fact, and I honestly believe that he does not feel any, although he surely must know that he would have realized the White House eight years sooner than he did if Ike had not remained so aloof from the real work of a political leader. As perhaps the most sophisticated political realist of his time, Nixon simply accepted President Eisenhower for what he was, a great national leader who suffered from some unhappy political shortcomings. Instead of brooding over these shortcomings, Nixon mustered his own great strengths and created, by the most patient and skillful political effort of modern times, a base of political leadership that was his alone, not merely the reflection of another leader's charisma. I am proud of the supporting role that I played in helping to make his final victory possible.

Along with others of his friends, I worried when Dick and Pat moved back to California after our post-inaugural trip to the Bahamas in 1961. I knew that he would face strong local party pressures there to regain the governorship from the Democrats, and I was certain that no matter what the outcome of such an event, it would do him no good toward the realization of his ultimate goal, the presidency. He had told me that he did not want to become involved in the California gubernatorial race, but the only way for a political leader such as Dick Nixon to stay out of a contest like that one would have been to stay away from the arena altogether. That is why I hoped that he would join a law firm in the East, because I feared the pressures to which he would be subjected in his home state. My fears were confirmed when he telephoned me in 1962. He told me that he felt forced by the pressures of important members of his party to take the step that he had not wanted to take: He was going to run for governor. It was a mistake.

The day after the election, when the returns were in and he had conceded his defeat, Richard Nixon lost his public composure for the first and only time since I have known him. He attacked the newsmen, who, he felt, had covered his campaign unfairly. To those of us who had closely followed Nixon's political career, his attack was totally justified. There was no doubt that he had been more unfairly, even destructively, treated by the press than any modern political leader.

The result of the California election and the unhappy publicity that followed in the wake of the press conference was that Nixon was unfairly tagged as a "loser" who would never regain his political strength. Most people thought that he had given up entirely on his political career and would not even try to make a recovery. I never believed that for a minute. He was simply too hard and tenacious a worker to give up. He had never done so before: not when he was young and worked tirelessly in his father's small grocery store: nor when he sold fruit from a stand outside the store in order to pay his tuition at Whittier: nor after any of the critical conflicts that he had faced during his life. Still, many of his former supporters characterized him as a "two-time loser," and the odds against his ever recovering from that damage appeared to be overwhelming. As far as I was concerned, they certainly would be overwhelming if he stayed in California. I urged him as persuasively as I knew how to consider pulling up stakes and relocating, because I feared that he would die on the vine politically if he remained. It was a difficult job of salesmanship for me. I suppose there is no harder task than that of convincing a man in public life that he should move away from the state that is his base, but I mustered all of my arguments and my sales ability to explain that California was no longer his base. Pat, too, was hard to convince. They had just built a beautiful house and she was loath to leave it. Julie and Tricia, however, were willing from the first. But Dick held off for a time, considering the consequences of such a drastic move. Apprehensively, I awaited his decision.

One day in the spring of 1963, while I was playing golf in Spring Lake, the caddy master drove out on the course to page me to the telephone. It was a long-distance call from California, he said, and the party wanted to talk with me as quickly as possible. I rode in on the caddy master's golf cart and picked up the phone. It was Dick Nixon. He had made his decision to move East. I was vastly relieved. Now, I knew, he could realistically begin rebuilding his political base while at the same time undertaking professional work that would provide for his family without detracting from his personal stature as a leader. What kind of work it would be, however, was an open question. His political ambition and his professional position would have to strike a delicate balance, one that would be suitable in the public eye, yet would provide him with a rather large income, because through his many years of public service he had never earned enough to build financial security for his family.

As soon as it became known that he was willing to leave California, a number of opportunities opened up to him, several of them leading jobs in industry, that would have paid him $100,000 or more. One rumor reached print that he would assume a $100,000-a-year post with Warner-Lambert. As it happened, I was presiding over our 1963 stock holders' meeting when Lewis Gilbert, the perennial gadfly of corporate annual meetings, rose to ask me if the rumor that Richard Nixon would join the company was true. I denied it unequivocally, whereupon Gilbert expressed concern over what would happen to the company when I was no longer able to preside over it. "At that time, Mr. Gilbert, I assume that you will still be annoying management at stockholder meetings," I said.

My denial of the Nixon/Warner-Lambert rumor was well-founded, because I not only had never suggested such a job to my friend the former vice president, but had strongly counseled him against accepting any position in industry. The companies that had offered him high-paying posts merely wanted to trade on his name. Moreover, I already had acted as the catalyst in an arrangement that provided Dick with the perfect professional position, the senior partnership of a major law firm.

For quite a number of years I had been a close friend of Matt Herold, nephew of G.A. Pfeiffer and the top senior partner of the New York law firm of Mudge, Stern, Baldwin and Todd. I also came to know John Alexander, Milton Rose, and Bob Guthrie, who, by 1963, after Matt's death, were the three senior partners. Milton Rose began handling my own legal affairs, and in time Warner-Lambert became one of the largest, if not the largest, of the firm's clients. It was natural that I thought first of their firm when I began thinking of a legal position that would be suitable for the former vice president.

One morning shortly after Dick's call to me from California, Milton Rose was sitting in my Manhattan office, a comfortable panelled room in a commodious complex of Warner-Lambert executive offices that we lease in the landmark Metropolitan Club mansion at 7 East 60th Street. We had just finished going over some corporate legal matter when I said to him, "Milton, you have a very good law firm and we have received excellent service. But it seems to me that you're pretty badly in need of new blood." Milton looked both surprised and disturbed, but before he could react verbally, I continued:

"I don't mean just younger blood. You need new blood at the top. Someone who can serve to bring the firm into the eyes of Wall Street and to the attention of industry throughout the country. Now, for instance, supposing you could get Richard Nixon to join the firm and head it. What would you think of that?"

Milton, who obviously had been perplexed over what I was leading up to, broke into a broad smile. "I would say 'yes,' right away, and I think I could get my other partners to say 'yes' by tomorrow." That was on Tuesday. By the next day the other two senior partners volunteered their enthusiastic approval of the idea. On Friday, Dick came East. Saturday, he and I made up a foursome with Alexander and Guthrie at the Baltusrol Golf Club in New Jersey. After an hour of conversation at the nineteenth hole, I felt the negotiations we had undertaken were completely and perfectly satisfactory to all concerned. Richard Nixon was now a senior partner of the newly-named law firm of Nixon, Mudge, Rose, Guthrie and Alexander.

At the time, I am sure that Dick considered his position in the firm as a long-term professional commitment, and not a political springboard. Neither he nor his new partners would have entertained any other arrangement. Nevertheless, I was certain that the Republican party — and a vast segment of the American people — would not allow this great statesman to remain out of the public eye very long. The call to duty would again come some day, and Richard Nixon would heed it. And, of course, he eventually did set forth on what all political observers, regardless of party, have acknowledged as the most remarkable political comeback in American history. Meanwhile, he earned his pay as a lawyer, handling cases, arguing before the U.S. Supreme Court, and travelling widely abroad for some of the firm's clients, a responsibility that incidentally enhanced his already deep knowledge of foreign affairs. But his most important legal role to Dodo and me had nothing to do with Nixon, Mudge, Rose, Guthrie and Alexander. It was strictly personal. He stood up as the formal sponsor of Mrs. Mamdouha As-Sayid Bobst when she became a citizen of the United States at the U.S. district clerk's office at Newark, New Jersey, on January 19, 1965. We were immensely proud: I to be her husband, she to become an American citizen, and both of us to have a man who we were confident would become president of the United States to be her sponsor.

Dodo's marriage to me and her new American citizenship, of course, ended her promising career as a delegate to the United Nations, although she still serves as an honorary adviser on sociology and health to the Lebanese delegation at the UN. But these radical changes in her life and citizenship have not lessened her love for her home country, nor her deep and compassionate interest in finding peaceful solutions to the problems of the Middle East. Since our marriage eleven years ago, we have visited the Middle East twelve times. Her mother, father, brother, and five sisters have become dear to me, as I hope I have to them. And

Dodo has continued, as an American citizen of Arab origin, her lifelong studies of Middle Eastern history and political affairs. It was against this background that I asked her to lend her knowledge to Richard Nixon during his 1960 campaign for the presidency. At my request, she wrote for him an incisive 6,000-word essay on the Arab world, in which she reviewed the history of the Middle East. Without vindictiveness and with compassion for both Arabs and Jews, she summarized her considerable knowledge of American policy in the Middle East and emphasized the need for "mutual understanding and respect."

As I have noted earlier, a wise presidential friend never asks if his or her advice has been heeded. In one area, however, I know that my deeply-felt advice about America's greatest problem in the 1960s, the war in Vietnam, was not followed. I have never remonstrated with him over this, because I know that a president sees our world problems in far more complex detail and shades of gray than a private citizen, but I still wish that he had been able to accomplish what I suggested to him during the 1968 campaign.

I naturally volunteered to do all that I could for his candidacy when he decided to seek the Republican nomination. I served as vice chairman of his campaign finance committee and, in addition to helping raise $1.3 million at one $1,000-a-plate dinner alone, contributed to the campaign myself. I also contributed advice which, welcome or not, I felt that I had to urge upon him. In private conversations, I suggested that he pledge to bring the war to an immediate end once elected. On June 18, 1968, I wrote to him that "I think we must develop a plan for withdrawal from Vietnam. We must stop this war because of the uselessness of having to keep on killing and maiming thousands of human beings who have the right to live. We will have to face up to the world and state that for reasons of humanity alone we wish to bring this godless war to an end without having to thrust further hundreds of thousands of Vietnamese into the earth. . . What I suggest, Dick, is that you should take another look at McCarthy's ideas and likewise the late Bobby Kennedy's various suggestions and proposals, together with ideas that have been expressed by other statesmen of the world, and then make a package of your own."

On August 24, I told a reporter who interviewed me that "In the eyes of the world, we have lost the war in Vietnam. We are viewed as a great country — one that brought an end to World War II by our might — but after losing thousands of Americans and spending upwards of $30 billion a year, we are unable to overcome North Vietnam, a sixth-rate nation. We certainly have the power to bring North Vietnam to its knees, and the world knows this. As a nation, we should take a valiant stand and announce that for humanity's sake we are going to end that war and withdraw our forces from Vietnam. The North and South Vietnamese are related by blood and culture, and they should be permitted to resolve their own differences without outside interference."

The president and I still are not in total agreement on this subject, three years later, and I can only conclude that from his difficult vantage point in the White House the problem of complete and rapid disengagement does not appear as straightforward as it has appeared to me. Actually, the president knows, for I have told him many times, that I am unalterably opposed to any attempts to settle our competition with Communism on the battlefield. I have opposed this kind of bloody confrontation all of my life. I believe the president has come to share my view as he works to bring the three great powers into an era of peaceful negotiation.

One of my father's favorite books was a life of Saint Paul written by a nineteenth-century author who described the crucifixion of Christ in terms more meaningful than any I have ever come across. He depicted Pontius Pilate as a Roman governor with deep feelings of responsibility to the law, trapped in a dilemma when Christ was brought before him. He was fully aware that Jesus had not committed any major atrocity against the law, and that in fact he could become an influence for peace and stability if he continued along his successful ministry. Yet the public clamor was, "Crucify him! Crucify him!" So Pilate went to the leader of the Great Sanhedrin, the Jewish legislative council, and laid his delemma before him. The leader was a wise man who hesitated thoughtfully before responding to the Roman governor, then said, "If this man is a false prophet, a faker, then in short time this fact will become known to everyone. He will walk the streets alone. Supposing, however, that he is the son of God, as he claims? Do you want to have on your head the fact that you gave the order to crucify the son of God?" Pilate, of course, bowed to the public will, and Christ was crucified.

The story is fanciful, I know, because there is no valid record of Pilate's activities as he made that fateful decision, but the dialogue in that biography of Paul made an indelible impression upon me and remained with me all of my life. What it taught me in relation to our own titanic struggle with Communism is this: if Communism is right and more helpful to the people in every sense than Democracy, then it will emerge supreme and nothing will stop it. If it is not right and cannot match the great human progress that Democracy has made for the people of America and many other nations, then it will come to its own end, eventually. I believe, in fact, that the end of Communism, the totalitarian version that we have rightfully feared, already is in sight. In order to resolve the instinctive human demand for decency and freedom, the Communist nations have had to make substantial concessions that have slightly narrowed the abysmal gap between our form of government and theirs. If this process

does not accelerate so that their people truly begin to enjoy freedom from oppression, then I believe they will rise up and rebel against the very cliques of bureaucrats who control them. If the process does accelerate, however, then Communism will eventually become simply another form of Democracy. There is no need to shed blood on a battlefield over what history inexorably will decide about the fate of Communism.

The 1960s began in loss and ended in victory for my friend Richard Nixon. For myself and my two pretty granddaughters, Mrs. Anne Highley of New York and Mrs. Stephanie Haynes of Montclair, the decade was marked by marriage and by deep personal loss. Their tragedy and mine came without warning.

Shortly after I had helped to get Dick established in New York, their father and my son, Walton, died in Geneva, Switzerland.

Walton's life had been an eventful one. After working with me through the early period of our resurrection of the old Warner Company, he had again struck out on his own. For a time he became an international pharmaceutical agent in London, but he found that a life in business was not as fulfilling to him as it had once been. He was an inherently intelligent person who made up for what he had missed during his athletic years in school by reading widely as an adult. Somehow, the subject of gerontology caught his interest, and he became deeply absorbed in organizing international support for studies of the aging process, an area that had been largely overlooked by medicine until that time. He successfully engaged in this work in England for some years, then shifted his base to Geneva, which was more of an international scientific center, and continued it there with great satisfaction. He wrote to me about his life and his work each week, and I replied to each letter as soon as I got it, but our lives kept us mostly apart. Dodo and I visited him whenever we went to Europe or the Middle East, and we were overjoyed when he blessed our marriage with his wholehearted approval. But our visits were brief — too brief — and we saw too little of one another. I suppose that a father always wishes that he had made more time to spend with his son and promises himself that he will remedy the shortcoming some day: I know that I did, and I still wish I had. But time ran out on a July night in 1964, when Walton suddenly and unexpectedly suffered a coronary arrest and died in his sleep.

Although Walton lived a full and rich, if sometimes tempestuous, life, he missed one of life's greatest joys: watching the growth of his grandchildren. Anne has two sons and one daughter, and Stephanie has one daughter. As I watch them at play I like to think that I can see in them not only a trace of such an ancient ancestor as myself, but the handsome, thoughtful features of their grandfather, my son, Walton.

● *Chapter Twenty-Seven*

● Bernard Baruch, who was a dear and close friend of mine until he died in 1965 at ninety-four, once told me a story about his aging friend, Winston Churchill, that reinforced my own feelings about old age. Like many old men, Bernie suffered from prostate trouble. In his anxiety to overcome this distressing fact of aging, he began visiting a famous, albeit scientifically misguided Swiss clinic. A dubious doctor there became rich on the fees of his anxious patients — heads of state, millionaires, and kings among them — by injecting macerated organs from the unborn fetuses of lambs to "preserve youth" and "cure" such ailments as Bernie's. The treatments did not do Bernie or anyone else a particle of good, but the psychological uplift made him feel so chipper that he thought the injections were miraculous. He became such a disciple of the Swiss doctor that he tried to convince his friends that they should go to him, too. One day, while he was visiting Churchill in England, the great statesman confided to Bernie that he, too, suffered from prostrate trouble.

"Sir Winston, I want you to go with me to Switzerland," Bernie urged him. "I go there every year and the doctor has done a tremendous amount of good for me. He's got secrets that no one else has developed."

"Tell me, Bernie, to what must one subject oneself during the two weeks of the treatments?" Sir Winston inquired.

"Well, Sir Winston, he doesn't allow you to drink any alcohol."

"What about smoking cigars?"

"He doesn't allow you to smoke, either," Bernie answered.

"Not going," Churchill growled.

"Why won't you go? It only lasts two weeks."

"The cost is too great!"

Like Churchill, I believe that the aging process is not one that an elderly person should become too absorbed in. It may be a fascinating subject for scientific inquiry, but too great a preoccupation with the frailties of age merely distracts a person from the precious remaining joys of life. I have never done anything particularly noteworthy to guarantee my own preservation except to follow common sense. I live a full and active life, in every respect. I eat and drink whatever appeals to me. I dance and sing at parties. I love to sit up late, talking with old friends. I golf every week. I go fishing. I travel when the mood suits me. I take bracing cold showers every morning. I spend a full day, almost every day, at work in my office. I love my wife, and I love my life, in that order.

The only precautions that I take are regular physical checkups and careful attention to the first signs of any unusual symptoms, such as the early hint of cancer that I detected in time for Dr. Ravdin to cure. At Morris Fishbein's eightieth birthday party, of which I was chairman, I asked Dr. Michael E. Debakey, the great cardiovascular surgeon, how we could account for our longevity and apparent good health. He answered in five words: "Thank your father and mother." My heredity is good. My attitude helps, too, I suppose, because I do not worry about my age.

Throughout my years I looked with great interest at the activities of older men who made great successes in business. For most, I noticed, success and age combined to slow them down, not only in business but in life at large. When they held on too tenaciously, as G.A. Pfeiffer had done, trouble resulted. Other influences, too, played a part in retarding them. Success, for one thing, begets a feeling that one can take more and more time away from his business. Wealth often leads to unhealthy and time-wasting extravagance. Although I believe that I have succeeded in avoiding most of the pitfalls, the knowledge that I could not go on for many more years as I had began to weigh rather heavily on my mind in 1967, when I was eighty-two years old. I still felt strong, vigorous, and open to new challenges, but I knew that I could not trade on these refreshing feelings forever, nor continue to bear on my own shoulders the futures of many people — stockholders, employees, and fellow executives — who depended upon me.

I had been far more fortunate than most men, not only in forestalling a premature retirement, but in creating a full second career, far more satisfying than the first, during what for others might have been superannuated years. As I look back upon it, I believe that I owe my extraordinary success in these later years entirely to Dodo. Without the youthful rejuvenation that marriage to her has meant to me, I doubt if I would have retained the same zest for life and business that I have enjoyed. Her love for me, her unusual intellectual depth, her energy, her beauty, and my love for her have somehow combined to create for me a figurative fountain of youth. The result was that the decade from my mid-seventies to my mid-eighties was the most productive and undoubtedly the happiest of my life. It also marked the years of my greatest advances in business.

Warner-Lambert had grown substantially through the decade and had become one of the world's largest and most successful companies. We had acquired through merger or purchase a number of growing firms, including the American Chicle Company, the Lactona Dental Supply Company, the Smith Brothers Cough Drop Company, the Texas *Pharmacial* Company, the American Optical Company, and several others in the U.S. and abroad. We also had introduced a number of new and successful pharmaceutical products. By 1967, our worldwide sales had grown to $656 million, and net earnings to $51 million. We were well on our way toward the billion-dollar mark that I had dreamed, of, but we still had a distance to go.

Although there was no doubt that our growth had been extraordinary, I certainly could not take credit for all of it myself. The success of any large organization never depends upon any single individual at the top, regardless of how knowledgeable, energetic, and imaginative he may be. But it does depend, to a large degree, upon the character and qualifications of the men whom the chief executive officer can attract to the company.

With the help of Governor Driscoll and Paul van Der Stricht, the president of our international company, I had gathered a highly effective and competent management which was responsible for the rapid growth of both the volume and profits of Warner-Lambert. In looking back, I was justifiably proud of our work. But upon returning from a trip to visit our facilities around the world in 1967, I took a sharp look forward and began to worry. There appeared to be a faltering in our projected earnings for that year, and to me it indicated a weakening in our management. It was not anything that presaged a doomed future, or even a loss, but a slackening in what I believed should be our growth process. I must admit that in all of my business life I have never been entirely satisfied with growth or profits, regardless of how good they have been. I was always happy when the figures showed fine gains, but I was never contented. Consequently, I have always driven harder for more than ordinary achievement, and I thought that it was time to do that now, before trouble began. I also began to think anew of my own role in Warner-Lambert. I could no longer duck the fact that more than eight decades of my life had gone by. Our business was huge, and many thousands of people depended upon us for employment, for the growth of their investments, and for the continued expansion of our dreams for the future.

With the concurrence of Governor Driscoll, who was now approaching sixty-five, we set out to find new blood. We found what we were looking for in the person of Stuart K. Hensley. I had known Stuart for some years, since he brought the Toni Home Permanent Company to the top of the hair beauty field. He did so well with that company that the Gillette Company bought it, and soon he rose to the presidency of the parent company, too. Most men who have met all of the challenges of one field are ripe for the challenge of another if the situation is right, and Stuart was no exception. He agreed to join us as president of Warner-Lambert. I resigned the chairmanship and became honorary chairman, so that Al Driscoll could succeed me. A year later, we completed the planned realignment of our senior executives with Al Driscoll's retirement. Stuart Hensley became chairman and chief executive officer, and we engaged E. Burke Giblin, executive vice president of General Foods Company, to serve at his right hand as president.

In a sense I suppose the recruitment of Hensley and Giblin was the fulfillment of what Ferd Eberstadt had told me long ago when he said, "The trouble with you, Elmer, is that you are looking for another Elmer Bobst." Stu Hensley fits that bill and Burke Giblin enhances it. Like myself, Stu sort of came up out of nowhere to become one of the outstanding marketing, advertising, and promotional men in American industry. He excels in analyzing and solving business problems, and he is a born innovator, which, I think, gives him an overall business capability very similar to my own. Burke Giblin came up the hard way, too. As a young public accountant, he struggled in his free time to complete courses at the Harvard Business School, then attended night classes in law at Boston University until he qualified for the bar. After eighteen years at General Foods, he rose to become the chief administrative officer with all divisions of the company reporting to him. C.W.W. "Tex" Cook, the chairman of General Foods, who is an old friend of mine and one of the most respected of American business leaders, came up to me after we lured Burke Giblin to Warner-Lambert and said, "Elmer, I would have been mighty sore at you for taking Giblin away from us if you hadn't made him president of your company." With Hensley and Giblin in position, we began to increase the strength of our second, third, and fourth echelons of younger executives. The result, I believe, is the best management team in the pharmaceutical industry, and the gratifying growth of Warner-Lambert since 1968 is proof of it. With both internal growth and further acquisitions, our sales reached $807 million and net income $73

Architect's drawing of the Elmer Holmes Bobst Library and Study Center of New York University. The 12-story building is one of the world's largest open-stack libraries, with study facilities for 4,000 persons.

million in 1969. Then in 1970 we announced two mergers that put us well over the magic billion-dollar mark. In May we acquired the wetshave business of Eversharp-Schick Company in an exchange of stock. And in November we announced a merger with a company that had been dear to my heart ever since I first called upon it as a salesman for Hoffmann-La Roche.

When I was a young man in the pharmaceutical business, the Parke, Davis Company of Detroit was known as the "Tiffany of the pharmaceutical industry." Its products were superb, its research was imaginative, and its business methods were among the best. As the representative of a young Swiss firm, I looked up to Parke, Davis the way Fiat must have looked up to General Motors. Over the years the firm never faltered, but its "Tiffany" reputation faded with the great growth of competing companies. When it became ripe for merger in 1970, we sought it out. I wanted to have a hand in restoring the "Tiffany" luster to this grand old firm, and that process is under way as I write this. Parke, Davis is a wholly owned part of Warner-Lambert but will continue to operate under its own illustrious name. Although the Federal Trade Commission has taken legal steps to contest the merger on anti-trust grounds, I am confident that there is no basis for the government's concern and that Parke, Davis and Warner-Lambert will continue to move forward, hand-in-hand, to an even more glowing future.

The Parke, Davis merger in 1970 made Warner-Lambert the world's largest manufacturer of health products, with assets of more than a billion dollars, including more than a hundred production facilities in forty-seven countries and twelve major research facilities in the U.S., Canada, Germany, Austria, and Italy. An investor who bought 1,000 shares of William R. Warner stock in 1951 would have paid about $19,000. If he held on to it through the years, his investment would be worth more than $470,000 today. Is it any wonder that I am proud of the dreams that I had nearly sixty odd years ago when, as a perhaps overconfident young man from Philadelphia, I foresaw revolutionary growth in the pharmaceutical industry?

The office of honorary chairman is usually thought of as

an emeritus pasture where organizations quietly slip their old
codgers to get them out of the way. I wasn't slipped into my
present post, but created it by my own design, and I have chosen
to make a full-time job of it. I do not engage in day-to-day executive decision-making, because that is the chief executive's job, and
the only way he can perform it well is on his own, without interference. But I do play an active role as chairman of the policy
committee and a member of the executive committee of Warner-
Lambert. In a company of our size, these are full-time responsibilities. Furthermore, as my colleagues will confirm, I play the role
faithfully. For another, I have more experience in the pharmaceutical business than anyone else. And for still another, I am
the only trained, registered pharmacist in the top management,
which remains an invaluable asset. When our scientists try to explain new compounds to the management, I know what they are
talking about, not merely what the marketing potential of their
product is.

I am honorary chairman of the American Cancer Society,
too, and although no longer as active as I used to be, I remain
involved and my involvement has had a measureable effect on
the national commitment against the disease. Because he knew
of my experience and knowledge, President Nixon called on me
to consult with him before he decided to commit his administration to a national program for the conquest of cancer, which
he subsequently announced in his 1970 State-of-the-Union message. It has long been my feeling, which the president shares,
that the cancer research programs funded by the society and by
the National Cancer Institute of NIH have been unfocused. Too
often, universities and research organizations have sought and
received large cancer grants which went to support institutional
budgets rather than pure research. I recall once witholding a
grant that the Cancer Society was preparing to give to Harvard.
Dr. James Conant, then president of the university, worriedly
called on me to try to talk me into releasing the money. "Not
until you have your people revise their proposal so that I know
the money is going to cancer research, not simply to the maintenance of an institution at Harvard," I told him. The program

was revised to a smaller figure that did not include extraneous overhead not connected with the research, and we gave them the money.

For four years I served on the panel of the National Cancer Institute and saw the same thing, magnified many times, happening to the money appropriated for cancer research grants there. Moreover, the many layers of bureaucracy in the National Institutes of Health and its parent, the Department of Health, Education, and Welfare, led to such a scattershot spread of research money that it was doing little good where it really counted: In laboratories working on the four or five most promising leads to the causes of cancer. I urged the president to support a proposal that would make the Cancer Institute autonomous, thus stripping away the bureaucratic layers on top of it, give it an annual appropriation without any definite limitations, subject it to a carefully considered program of *directed* research in the most promising areas, and have it report directly to the president. My ideas became the administration's Conquest of Cancer Act, which was amalgamated with Senator Edward Kennedy's cancer legislation in the Senate and passed by a vote seventy-nine to one in 1971. Unfortunately, a House-Senate conference committee watered down the legislation at the end of the year, but it met most of the objectives that President Nixon and I had sought. The directed research programs that result from the legislation will bring us much closer to conquering the disease many years sooner than if the old scattershot approach had been continued.

I have witnessed a near-miraculous number of medical advances in my lifetime, including the ends of most of the historic scourges of mankind. I doubt that I will live to see the end of the war on cancer. But it is coming. I know that it is coming. When it does, there literally will be an army of people to thank for the momentous achievement, but near the top of the list, if not leading it, will be the names of Dr. Charles Cameron, son of a Philadelphia druggist, Mrs. Mary Lasker, public-spirited widow of one of the great humanitarians of this century, Dr. Alton Ochsner, great and courageous surgeon, Dr. Frank Adair, Jim

Adams, Emerson Foote, a host of American Cancer Society
workers and, without modesty, Elmer Bobst, pharmacist.

*The author, at right, on the scene during construction of the New York
University library and study center that bears his name. He pledged
$11 million toward the project.*

● *Chapter Twenty-Eight*

● No matter who a man is or what his position in life, he cannot escape a feeling of awe when he enters the White House, where both the history and the power of the greatest nation on earth reside. And no matter how intimately a man knows the president before he takes residence in that grand old mansion, he will feel a thrill unlike any he has known before when he visits his friend there. I have felt the awesomeness of the White House many times, and it is as great when I visit there today as it was when I first entered it to talk with President Coolidge. But being a friend of its occupant, the man in whom the people of the United States have entrusted their power and their faith, inspires a feeling of exhilaration far greater than the elation common to most of us when we meet and become friendly with a public hero. It does not alter the character of the friendship, although the bonds may be drawn taut by the weight of the president's responsibility and the protocol of his office, but it does alter the easygoing camaraderie in which friendship usually thrives. There is no escaping that, for the demands on the time and energies of the president of the United States are incalculable, and no true friend would presume to encroach upon the little time that he can spare from duty. On the contrary, one is fortunate to catch him for even a few moments from time to time. I was enormously flattered, therefore, to be invited to spend the night at

343

the White House on December 16, 1969. It was my eighty-fifth birthday. President Nixon planned a birthday party, and I was to be the guest of honor.

It was supposed to be a surprise. Rosemary Woods quietly called Dodo on behalf of the president and Mrs. Nixon to tell her of the president's plans and to work out a guest list of 110 of my best friends. But one of the invitees inadvertently slipped in conversation with me one day, so that I began to suspect that the White House was preparing a surprise. As it happened, the party came as the climax of an exhilarating and exhausting series of events.

On the 15th of December I was honored to receive the Gold Heart Award of the International Cardiological Society in New York. The cardiologists flatteringly had billed the event as "Elmer Bobst's Eighty-fifth Birthday Party." I knew that I would be called upon to speak at the dinner, and meant to get a little rest before-hand and prepare a few notes for my address. But I had to spend the entire afternoon with my business colleagues in a complex discussion of the possible purchase of two dental companies, so there was time for neither rest nor preparation. Added to that, some of the events of the evening came as a complete surprise. Vice President Agnew appeared unannounced during the cocktail hour, and Rosemary Woods arrived for the dinner. She asked to say a few public words to me on behalf of the president. For a moment, I wondered whether this, perhaps, was the occasion that I had begun to suspect was to be my birthday surprise. "I represent the president," she announced with a smile. "I am in-structed to inform you that the reason he did not come to this dinner to present you with the award that you are to receive . . . " she paused, " . . . is that he is busy planning for your birthday dinner at the White House tomorrow." I went on then, quite happily, to make a twenty-eight-minute extemporaneous speech to the cardiologists. But the exhilaration of the evening so keyed me up that when I got home afterwards I could not sleep at all.

In the morning, Dodo and I hurried to prepare for the trip to Washington. After a sleepless night, I had several matters to take care of before we left, but finally we got away and arrived in Washington at three o'clock in the afternoon. We were driven to the West Gate and ushered directly to the Nixons' second-floor living quarters. The president and First Lady met us there. After chatting for a while in the sitting room at the end of the long, wide hall that bisects the second floor of the White House, I confessed that I was ready for a nap.

"Elmer, I haven't forgotten that your father served in the Civil War and saw Lincoln," the president said. "You're going to stay in the Lincoln Suite. You can rest there now. Dodo, you will stay in the Queens' Suite. Five queens have slept in that four-poster bed there, and you will be the sixth."

Although Lincoln never slept in the famous room to which I was assigned — it was his cabinet room in those days — I could almost feel his presence. The richly carved rosewood bed with its elaborate, eight-foot-high headboard dominates the bedroom, and beside it is the famous Lincoln portrait-in-profile by Douglas Volk, on loan to the White House from the National Gallery. On the mantelpiece of the marble fireplace is a plaque which reads, "In this room Abraham Lincoln signed the Emanicipation Proclamation of January 1, 1863, whereby four million slaves were given their freedom and slavery forever prohibited in these United States." The image of a gangly, top-hatted Lincoln, coat-tails flopping and legs too long for his saddle's stirrups, riding slowly past my father's platoon of infantry with Tad tagging along behind on his pony, passed through my mind.

I wanted to rest; in fact I knew that I must rest, because I was exhausted. But as I lay on the huge bed, so many images of the past flashed through my mind that I could not keep my eyes closed. I had met and had visited in this house with every president since Coolidge, save one. That was Harry Truman, whom I met and came to like only after he left the White House. During his administration, my friend and his treasury secretary, John Snyder, asked me to come to the White House, but I was still so upset by Truman's early association with the corrupt Pendergrast machine in Kansas City that I declined. But I had never

before had one of the historic suites of the White House to myself.
I was simply too excited to sleep away the afternoon.

I wandered into the treaty room next door, where Andrew
Johnson and a long list of his successors held their cabinet meetings. It was still in use when the treaty of peace with Spain was
signed on its massive pedestal table in 1902, at a time that I was
living in near-peonage as Dr. Bethel's apprentice. I returned to
the bedroom. There, beneath Lincoln's favorite portrait of Andrew Jackson, stood a small table and two chairs that once flanked
the Great Emancipator's cabinet table. Thinking of my father,
I rested a hand on one of the chairs and pictured the famous
men of the Civil War who sat in them and counseled their tower-
ing president through the agony of those years when my father
suffered. Near the table was Lincoln's own secretary-desk. I
walked to it and looked at the three sheets of his meticulous handwriting that were preserved there, enclosed in glass, on its surface. It was one of five copies that President Lincoln made from
his original draft of the Gettysburg Address, the only one that
he signed and dated, November 19, 1863. My eyesight has dimmed
with the years, so I took out my reading glass in order to read
it through slowly, three times. For a while, I was back in the
1860s.

At about seven o'clock, I slipped across the wide hall in my
robe to see Dodo. I had not wanted to bother her earlier, because
I thought she was napping. But, she, too, had found the associations with the history of the White House too great. She had
tried the huge, pink-canopied four-posted bed in the Queens'
bedroom, but she had not slept. As we thought of the illustrious
guests who had slept there before her, I was reminded of another
great honor Dodo had received a few years before. It was conferred on her by Francis Cardinal Spellman. The cardinal and
I had become close friends during the late 1940s, after meeting
at the first telethon on behalf of the American Cancer Society.
As chairman of the event, I had been dismayed when most of
the notables who were called upon to speak uttered tedious, boring addresses. When it came my turn, I ignored my prepared
speech and tried to enliven the show by ad-libbing. As I returned

to my seat, Cardinal Spellman congratulated me and asked for a copy of my speech. "You're welcome to it, your Eminence," I said, "But to tell you the truth, the words are all in my heart. I never looked at my prepared speech." We became fast friends after that, along with his close associates Monsignors Terence (now cardinal) Cooke and Patrick Ahearne, and we lunched and dined together often. After Dodo and I were married, the night before we sailed on our honeymoon, the cardinal gave a wedding dinner for us at his residence behind St. Patrick's Cathedral. He placed Dodo at his right hand, and every time we dined with him thereafter he accorded her the same honor. Then, at a small dinner one evening not long after Pope Paul visited America, he inexplicably placed Dodo all the way down at the other end of the table. Neither of us took it as a slight, but we were puzzled that he had not given her the place of honor she had occupied in the past. After dinner he came up to us and smilingly asked if we had noticed the change in seating arrangements.

"Of course we did," I said. "I'm hurt that you put Dodo so far away from you."

"But I gave her the most honored seat of all," said the cardinal. "That is where His Holiness sat when he ate at this table." Dodo, a Moslem, had occupied what for a brief time, at least, had been the temporary throne of St. Peter.

I left the Queens' Suite so that Dodo could dress and slipped back across the hall to the Lincoln room. There I found a uniformed member of the White House staff, holding my dress shirt in her hands. It was a black-tie affair, and those bow ties are a terrible nuisance to get on. "Mr. Bobst," she said, "I'm here to help you put on your shirt and your tie." I've never had such delightful service. I asked her how long she had been in the White House and she told me, "I came here at the same time the Roosevelts came." Since she appeared to be much younger than me, I did not ask her which Roosevelts.

One thing I knew about the White House from past experience is that presidents do not participate in a cocktail hour before White House dinner parties. The magic efficiency of White House service, however, saved me from drought. Manola Sanchez, the

The author and President Richard M. Nixon
in the White House, April 27, 1971.

president's personal valet, came into the room and fixed me a tall Chivas Regal and water. By the time I finished fortifying myself, it was time for Dodo and me to join the Nixons in the yellow oval library on the second floor. Mamie Eisenhower was there, along with Pat and Tricia. Julie was away. We exchanged greetings and talked of old times — other birthdays and Christmases that we had spent together — until it was time to go down. Here the president had to follow strict protocol. Normally we would escort our ladies to the dining room. But in the White House, the party must line up in careful order behind a formal military escort. The president went first down the curving red-carpeted stairway, flanked by Mamie Eisenhower and the First Lady, slightly behind him. Dodo and I came next. There was the sound of ruffles-and-flourishes and as soon as the president appeared, "Hail to the Chief," by the Marine band. But when Dodo and I appeared, the bandsmen shifted without the slightest pause to "Happy Birthday." I don't know if my tears were hidden by my glasses or magnified by them, but they were there.

The State Dining Room was beautifully arranged with flowers and Christmas decorations on formally-set tables for eight. Dodo sat beside the president, and I sat at the First Lady's table, between her and Tricia, with my friends the Italian ambassador Eligo Ortona, Mrs. Joan Payson, owner of the New York Mets, Arnold Palmer, the great golfer, Mrs. George Champion, wife of the chairman of the Chase Manhattan Bank, and Dr. Daniel Patrick Moynihan, then a special assistant to the president. The dinner was delicious, but the dessert was overwhelming. I looked up at the end of four courses to see a huge three-tiered birthday cake being carried in by the White House chef and three assistants. To my surprise, the famous White House efficiency manifested itself again: Without my knowledge, the decorative, flowered top of the cake was removed after I cut the first piece, carefully packed, and sent to New York the next day with our luggage.

The greatest delight of a formal eighty-fifth birthday, however, is the speech-making that comes with the birthday cake and champagne. One gets a chance to hear himself prematurely eulogized. The president started it with a warm recital of our seventeen-year friendship that had been and remains unmarred by any ill-feeling by either of us. Some of the things he said about me were so sentimental that I blushed. Next came my old colleague, Al Driscoll, then Congressman William Cahill of New Jersey, whom I helped the following year to gain the governorship, William Rogers, the secretary of state, George Champion, my old business friend, and Vice President Agnew. All spoke such glowing words about me that I had to pinch myself to see if I was still alive.

Finally, the president called on Dodo. She was so surprised that she forgot her diplomatic training in formal protocol and exclaimed, "Oh, Dick, please don't call on me! I can't do it!"

"I've heard you speak before," he chuckled reassuringly. "You're next."

Dodo talked about some of the many intimate moments that we have shared with the president and his family and spoke of me in such tender terms that I was moved to tears. I was so proud of her that I could hardly follow her words. In fact, all of the speeches were so adulatory that I promptly erased their words from my mind lest I come to believe them. But I remember my own words when I made the final speech, because I had something very special that I wanted to say about my dinner companion. I bowed to the host and began, "Mr. President . . ." Then turned to her . . . "and Mrs. First Lady . . . I want to say that I know it might not be protocol for me to address Mrs. Nixon in that way. But I have done it for a purpose. As far as I have been able to determine, in all I have read and heard about the histories of our First Ladies, each one up to now has come into this title simply by marriage to a man who became president. It is different with our First Lady . . . " I recounted stories of the many arduous chores she had undertaken during her husband's five campaigns, and her valiant courage as she supported him through the crises of his life. "I believe that Pat Nixon is the first person who has ever come into the White House bearing the title of First Lady because she *earned* it in her own right.

I went on, then, to talk about the president. I remember

beginning with the words, "On what a slender thread do great events oftentimes depend," after which I recounted the story of how General John A. Sutter, the Swiss soldier of fortune who is buried behind the Moravian church in Lititz, discovered gold in California. Had he not noticed bright yellow flecks of the precious metal in the paper that came from his crude pulp mill, the Gold Rush of 1849 might never have taken place. California probably would have developed differently, I said, and perhaps the Nixon family would never have migrated there. In that case, perhaps we would not all be in the White House on this particular evening.

I did not realize, as I spoke, how close to total exhaustion I really was, for the exhilaration of the occasion was keeping me going. I went on to recount some of my experiences with the president and to describe my friendship for him. Then I began to conclude my speech with the hope that his efforts toward peace and justice would soon be realized. As I neared the end of my talk, I remembered something that my father used to say when he lectured on his trying experiences as a Civil War soldier and prisoner of war. He always concluded, as I did that evening, with these words:

"But there is a better day a'coming. Nations will not quarrel then to see which is the stronger, nor murder men for glory's sake . . . wait a little longer."

As I sat down, the exhilaration ended and exhaustion overtook me. For a moment, I felt dizzy, then I blacked out. It was only a momentary spell, and few besides Pat Nixon, the president, and my own physician, Dr. Norman Wikler, noticed it. My head cleared and I stood to shake hands with well-wishers who crowded around me. But Dr. Wikler hurried to my side to take my pulse, and the president worriedly sent out for the White House physician. While the other guests enjoyed a cordial, he urged Dodo and me to come with him and Pat to the family quarters upstairs. I felt tired but perfectly well. The White House physician looked me over and confirmed that nothing was wrong. (Several months later, however, after suffering similar spells, I realized that my heartbeat was slowing on occasion to the danger level, a not unusual occurence in older people. If it drops below thirty to thirty-two beats a minute, the show is over. I decided, with my cardiologist, to have a newly-developed "demand" Pacemaker implanted in my chest. The device, a tiny metal object attached to a small nickle-cadmium battery, was developed by the American Optical Division of Warner-Lambert. When needed, its measured electrical impulses stimulate the heart to maintain normal rhythm. It does not go into action unless my heartbeat slows below seventy to seventy-two beats per minute, which rarely happens, but it is comforting to have it there.)

After the White House doctor had checked me over, the four of us relaxed together in the family sitting room, where the president and the First Lady became, again, Dick and Pat, to Elmer and Dodo. Gently, I admonished the president for his too-kind words about me, but he protested that he had never said a word about me that he did not mean from his heart. I was deeply moved and immeasurably flattered, for he had uttered similar sentiments once before in words that I still remember, when he spoke at the dedication of the Elmer Holmes Bobst Laboratory for Clinical Research at Hahnemann Medical College in 1967. "Elmer Bobst," he said then, "could have been successful as a doctor . . . as a minister . . . as a lawyer . . . as a politician. I can say to you that in all those fields he will give you advice, if you ask for it, and advice that will be very, very good . . . in the field of politics, I can only say that I have valued his judgement and his counsel through the years . . .

"Education, for this man, has been a passion. He wants it for others and he has been able to do what many of us have been unable to do — to contribute generously not only his money but his talent and his wisdom.

"Health, for him, is a passion, not simply because he has been in the field of business which is related to health, but because he sees the immense role that health can play in America and in the relations between countries . . .

"He is a man who will never be old. Play golf with him. Go fishing with him. Go boating with him. Go out on a party with him and I can assure you that here is one of those unusual men who stay young because he thinks young, because he likes young people, because he gets more out of helping young people than helping himself. When I think of him, one of my favorite quotations comes to mind.

"The poet Sophocles once wrote, 'One must wait until the evening to see how splendid the day has been.'

"Elmer Bobst, some would say, is in the evening of life, but he is a man who will never grow old. He can look back on a life which is rich . . . rich in achievement, rich in business triumphs, but primarily rich because he did not stop there, because he lived the complete life and did not paint on the narrow, limited canvas on which he could have painted."

After we had chatted for a while with the ease and comfort of old times, I thanked the president again for his words at the birthday dinner, and we retired. I was exhausted. But still, as I lay on the Great Emancipator's bed, I was like a small child on Christmas Eve.

Several times I arose to reread the Gettysburg Address in his own hand. Memories of visiting Ford's Theater in Washington with my father when I was five years old passed through my mind. I did not sleep a wink until I returned to New York the next day.

December 16, 1971

 *Epilogue*

Today, as I read over and revise these pages for the last time, is my eighty-seventh birthday. I would rather not pause to mark the occasion, for age no longer has any meaning to me. But my friends will not let me forget it. I have a fresh letter on my desk from the president. "In some lives a birthday marks the passing of another year," he writes, "but your birthday — as your friends and associates can testify — is the beginning of twelve more months of the great inspiration, strength and happiness you give to us." That is how I prefer to look at this day: as another beginning, like the uplifting aphorism, "Today is the first day of the rest of your life." If a birthday is anything to me, I suppose it is a day of thanksgiving, that my days remain as rich and full and comforting to me as my memory.

A memory as long as mine is filled with too many lasting impressions to recount more than a fraction of them. Some are mere fleeting images whose edges have dimmed: others remain as vivid as the day they were formed. The most enduring are the ones that have helped to form the structure of my beliefs. Often they have required but a moment of time to implant themselves indelibly in memory. One of the most lasting images in my mind is that of a picture which I saw many years ago in a small art gallery in Switzerland. It showed two simple figures against a rolling pastoral landscape. One of them was an aged farmer, bent from years of toil. He appeared to be saying something to a young boy, perhaps his grandson. Behind them the

morning sun was lifting over the landscape, and one sensed that
it was spring, for the farmer held a planting spade in his hand
and also a part of a potato. As I looked at the picture I could
almost literally hear the old man's voice: "To grow, potatoes, son,
you first have to plant them. To build a future, you must plant
for that future. I wish that I had bought the painting when I
saw it, for that image by an unknown artist remains more clear
in my mind than the dozens of canvases — great works by Renoir,
Chagall, Vlaminck, Utrillo, Monet, Bonnard, Pissarro, Sisley,
Constable, Copley, and other master artists — that I have acquired and love. The simple picture of the farmer and the boy
is a foundation stone beneath the structure of my personal faith,
an enduring illustration of the first lesson that my father and
mother taught to me.

Few of us ever are called upon to reduce our beliefs to
words, but we feel them deeply within and at many times in our
lives they find expression in some way. I once was asked by my
friend Ed Murrow to present my thoughts on his daily radio program, "This I believe." My address began with these words, "Man
is like a fruit tree, when a fruit tree ceases to bear fruit regardless
of how green its' leaves, it is really dying. It is also so with
men: When they cease to be productive in this life of ours, they,
too, regardless of age, are beginning to die." He later included
that brief summary of my faith in his book, *This I Believe*.
I had little time to reflect before we went on the air, but my
beliefs today are the same as I expressed them then.

I have certain strong and basic convictions about God and
prayer, although I can no longer fit my religious feelings into
the strict doctrinal mold of any particular theology or religious
sect. I believe with William James that God shows himself to us
in "the complexity of the moral life, and the mysteriousness of
the way in which facts and ideals are interwoven." I do not pretend to know more of this mystery than any other living man,
but I have faith that behind the mystery there is purpose, and
divinity. Whether my daily prayers are literally heard or not, I
have no idea and perhaps never will, but, again like James, I
know that they have "regenerative effects unattainable in other
ways," because I have felt those effects. Perhaps, as the poet

James Montgomery wrote in one of my father's verses:

Prayer is the soul's sincere desire,
Uttered or unexpressed,
The motion of a hidden fire
That trembles in the breast.

As I have grown away from the strict dogmas of the Lutheran faith in which I was born, I have seen a general escape from the confusions of sectarian orthodoxy, not only among Christians but among religious men everywhere. It has encouraged my growing conviction, and that of my godly father, that there will one day be a coming together of all religions into a single, open ecumenism. This will bring to an end what historically has been the greatest cause of anguish and death, religious animosity. The frictions between sects traceable to the whims of their founders already are disappearing, as is blind faith in symbolic objects. As my father counseled, "There is a better day a'-coming . . . wait a little longer." I used to joke with my friend Cardinal Spellman by asking him, "How close have I come to getting you to become a Lutheran?'" He always replied, "Elmer, how close are you to becoming a Catholic?" Both of us were closer, I think, than we knew.

On a more worldly level, I believe deeply in the purpose and the future of my country as a unifying force in the liberation of all mankind, to the end that all men everywhere will one day lead lives of health, hope, freedom, and opportunity. We have not always been a noble nation — our treatment of the Indians and the blacks are historic examples — and all that we are doing now is not noble. But I firmly believe that there is a spiritual nobility in the breast of the American people that will expand to fulfill our destiny.

I believe that the greatest individual happiness comes from achievement, whether it be a monumental accomplishment such as the discovery of a cure for cancer, or a private achievement of little public note, such as simply doing a job and living a life to the best of one's ability. Achievement is the goal, sufficient in itself, not power of wealth or celebrity. The latter are like the wake that follows behind a boat. If one concentrates alone upon gaining them, he will never steer a true or satisfying course.

The goal of achievement is standing on the bow of the boat and observing the power that drives the boat through the seas.

I believe that a man of ability in this nation can gain whatever he seeks if he is willing to work hard enough and patiently enough to earn it. I have seen hundreds of men who dreamed lofty dreams but did nothing to realize them, because they were too timid, or too weak, or too apathetic to act. A dream becomes real only through dedication and toil, not through the mere hopes of the dreamer. It helps, too, to be an innovator, for it is better to be first than second.

I believe that each of us owes a debt to his fellow man, and that the debt is magnified many times over for those who have gained wealth or power. Among the hardest of this world's accomplishments is acquiring wealth by honest effort and, having gained it, learning how to use it properly. Andrew Carnegie began his philanthropies like a good Presbyterian by giving away pipe organs to churches. They probably made more bad music than good and enriched the religious impulses of man hardly at all. His wealth did not begin to grow in benefit to mankind until it was sent into libraries which subsequently enriched millions, including me. I have been blessed with great good fortune during a lifetime of hard work and gratifying achievement, and after carefully studying the examples of others, I am trying repay the debt that I owe as well as I can. Through most of my life I have chosen health care, medicine, and education for my philanthropies. My own formal education stopped short in a small-town high school, but continued in libraries and, when I could afford to buy them, books of my own. This is why I presented a gift of $6-million worth of my Warner-Lambert stock to New York University in 1966, toward the construction of a sorely-needed library. Due to the growth of my company, by the time the stock was converted in 1971 it was worth almost double the original value. I am happy to state, as I write this, construction of the world's largest open-shelf library, a beautiful, twelve-story building designed by Philip Johnson and large enough to accommodate about 4,000 students in privacy among two-million volumes, is nearing completion. It will be called the Elmer Holmes Bobst General Library and Study Center of New York University.

But the name on the building is not what thrills me. William James said that the great purpose of life is to leave something behind that will outlive us. Longfellow spoke of leaving "footprints on the sands of time." For me, the partial payment that I have made on my debt to mankind by my gift to the library will live on long after the building crumbles, in the minds of those who will learn from the books it will contain and who will pass their learning on to future generations.

It is almost trite, certainly a commonplace, to repeat what so many have said in so many ways before, but the destiny of all future generations lies in the hands of the last one, those who were born after I reached three-score years. As I look at the members of that generation today, I am deeply troubled, not so much by appearances nor even by the rather bizarre behavior of many of them. I am troubled mostly by what their parents have done and are doing to them by confusing love with irresponsible permissiveness. I believe that young people want guidelines. They want to learn the challenging philosophy and rules of an orderly and peaceful society. They want to assume responsibility. They want to work. Parents who ignore these natural needs of childhood, who in the false name of love set no limits, inculcate no sense of personal responsibility and discourage honest and responsible labor by their children are, to my mind, the source of the despairing hysterics we have witnessed among some of the young in recent years. If men all over the world are to achieve their true capabilities and build a peaceful, healthy world that will be safe and beneficial for countless generations to come, those who are the parents of young people today or who will become parents tomorrow must become the inspiration of it. Inspiration begets aspiration, and aspiration will beget the perspiration essential to meet this greatest challenge that man has yet faced, his own continued civilized existence.

It has not been an easy thing for me to remain still for the many hours and days during the last two-and-a-half years that I have worked on this prescription of my life, for I am not by nature an introspective man. My memories are mostly good ones, and relivin some of them in these pages has at times been pleasurable, but like Longfellow, I believe, "Look not mournfully into the past. It comes not back again. Wisely improve the present. It is thine. Go forth to meet the shadowy future, without fear, and with a manly heart." In spite of my years, that is my attitude. My hope is that some one among the few who read this volume will make my effort in coping with its unnatural demands worthwhile by taking from it something of value that will improve his own life.

Some years ago, while visiting Bombay, I heard one of the many myths that man has devised to explain the creation of the world. The story goes that five Gods of those days joined together to produce a sphere, a world. Each day, the Gods performed some magnificent task, as our Judeo-Christian God is said to have done in Genesis. Then they created man and woman. All was well with the world until one of the Gods suddenly recalled that they had neglected to safeguard the most valuable creations of all, Faith, Hope, and Love. "We must protect these verities," said the God, "by hiding them in a place where they cannot be stolen or destroyed and no one will think to look. We will hide them in the heart of man." There in the heart they have remained through the eon, Faith, Hope, and Love.

In my mind, these verities still remain in our hearts, like glowing embers, dimming at times, even threatening to go out. But when times are most critical and all seems lost, they become like a burning fire again, and save man from himself. I believe that the embers of Faith, Hope, and Love are beginning to flare again today, and that I shall live to see them burst into a flame that will bring us peace and happiness. I hear in my mind's ear, the angelic choir singing, Glory to God on the Highest — Peace on Earth, Good will Toward Men.

I approach my life today, the beginning of my eighty-eighth year, as I have approached it always, eagerly embracing what each day brings to me, loving deeply those who are closest to me, and hoping for my fellow man, as my father did, that "there is a better day a'coming." I believe that there is, and I want to live to see it.

Elmer Holmes Bobst
New York, N.Y.